B-17 FLYING FORTRESS
RESTORATION

B-17 FLYING FORTRESS RESTORATION

The Story of a WWII Bomber's Return
to Glory in Honor of the Veterans of the
Mighty Eighth Air Force

Jerome J. McLaughlin

Dudley Court Press
Sonoita, Arizona

Also by Jerome J. McLaughlin

D-Day +60 Years

A Small Piece of History

Published in the United States of America by
Dudley Court Press, LLC
PO Box 102
Sonoita, AZ 85637

www.DudleyCourtPress.com
520-329-2729

ISBN: 978-1-940013-25-1

Cover photo: Matt Stephan
Back cover photo (top): *Savannah Morning News*
Back cover photo (bottom): CoS Archives
Design: M. Urgo

Quantity discounts are available.
Please contact the publisher at www.DudleyCourtPress.com

Connect with the author and learn more about *The City of Savannah* at
www.b17restoration.com or at **small history@aol.com**

Publisher's Cataloging-in-Publication Data

Names: McLaughlin, Jerome J., author.

Title: B-17 Flying Fortress restoration : the story of a WWII bomber's return to glory in honor of the veterans of the mightly Eighth Air Force / Jerome J. McLaughlin ; foreword by Lt. General E.G. Shuler, Jr.

Description: Sonoita, AZ : Dudley Court Press, [2016]

Identifiers: ISBN: 978-1-940013-25-1 (pbk.) | 978-1-940013-26-8 (hardcover) | 978-1-940013-27-5 (Kindle) | 978-1-940013-28-2 (ePub) | LCCN: 2016939437

Subjects: LCSH: B-17 bomber--Conservation and restoration--Personal narratives. | B-17 bomber--Maintenance and repair--Personal narratives. | B-17 bomber--History. | United States. Army Air Forces. Air Force, 8th--History. | World War, 1939-1945--Aerial operations American--Personal narratives. | LCGFT: Personal narratives.

Classification: LCC: UG1242.B6 M355 2016 | DDC: 623.74/63--dc23

DEDICATION

This book is dedicated to many people: all of the young Americans who served in the Eighth Air Force during WWII, especially those who did not come home or suffered for the remainder of their lives from the experience; and to the men and women who served as volunteers or museum staff with, or in support of, the *City of Savannah* restoration project between January 2009 and January 2015.

WELL DONE!

And especially to

Dr. Walter Brown
President and CEO of the National Museum
of the Mighty Eighth Air Force
2006–2009

Walter "Skip" Shelton
Pilot and Nose Artist, 488th Bombardment Group
1945

Arnold Kolb / Nathan Kolb
Father and Son—The final crew of 44-83814
1984

Rest in peace, my good friends.
I wish you had lived to see what we accomplished.

CONTENTS

FOREWORD

The reader is about to embark on a unique story in the annals of military aircraft restoration. The story is about a B-17G bomber, tail number 44-83814, produced at the close of WWII, which did not see combat, but never the less accrued an interesting history from the time it rolled off the assembly line until its restoration was completed by the talented and dedicated volunteers at the National Museum of the Mighty Eighth Air Force in Pooler, Georgia.

The museum, honoring the men and women who served in the Mighty Eighth in peace and war, opened its doors to the public on 14 May 1996. In relating the history and heritage of the Eighth, the museum always had as a key objective, the procurement of a B-17 bomber. As a matter of fact, during the museum's design phase, the Combat Gallery was sized to house a B-17 sitting on a "hard stand" as if it were ready to taxi and fly a combat mission. In retrospect, there should have been a bit more space allocated for the aircraft, which, as you will see in the narrative, would have made the restoration effort somewhat easier for the volunteers.

My association with the museum project began with a board meeting in Atlanta, Georgia, in April 1992. From June 1992 to May 2004, I served as chairman of the board and CEO as well as the construction monitor during the construction phase of the museum facility. My service on the board as well as the Eighth Air Force Foundation continues to this day. As a result, I am intimately familiar with this story and am honored to have been invited to pen this foreword.

The procurement and restoration of this B-17 would never have been possible without dedicated leadership, and on this project the museum enjoyed the confluence of some very talented individuals. Leadership comes from the top, and in this case the museum was extremely fortunate to have Dr. Walt Brown on the controls. Walt and I became colleagues when we both joined the then Board of Directors at the April board meeting in 1992 in Atlanta. At that time Walt and I were the only non-WWII veterans serving on the board. Although he was a trauma surgeon, his appetite for pressing forward with the creation of the museum was insatiable. As you will read in the narrative, he proved to be the pivotal person who oversaw the process of bringing this B-17 to the museum. Sadly, Walt made his final flight without seeing the completed product.

All successful leaders surround themselves with competent subordinates. Such was the case of two hardworking museum volunteers, Jerry McLaughlin and Jim Grismer, that Walt appointed to lead the B-17 restoration project. I first met these two multi-talented gentlemen, when as volunteers they were tasked to establish order in the archival division of the museum's library. As a team they spent hundreds of hours successfully accomplishing that task. They did such a marvelous job that I had the honor, in 2008, of presenting both of them with the Shuler Award for Museum Service, recognizing their significant contributions to the museum's archive. Jerry and Jim very willingly accepted the challenge of the B-17 restoration project, with Jerry acting as the overall project manager. If it had not been for them and their abilities to solve problems and lead the special restoration teams, this project would not have garnered the national recognition it so richly deserves.

I was privileged to follow all phases of the restoration as a result of Jerry's updates and briefings to the board of trustees and my periodic visits to the aircraft to observe the progress. I have seen other aircraft restorations, but none that equals the B-17 that now bears the name *City of Savannah*, representing the original B-17 by that name that passed through Savannah in December, 1944. I must say that I was truly awed by the entire effort and was privileged to be asked to participate in the ribbon cutting at the dedication ceremony. Enjoy the read.

E. G. "Buck" Shuler, Jr.
Lt. General, USAF, Retired
Former Commander Eighth Air Force

PREFACE

I began preparing to become the project manager for the *City of Savannah* (CoS) restoration when I was about 10 years old. I was an avid reader and developed a strong interest in military history, especially military aviation, with an emphasis on World War II. Perhaps the driving force in my interest was my uncle, Lt. Joseph J. Sullivan, a navigator in the Ninth Air Force who was KIA on D-Day. The mystery surrounding the circumstances of my uncle's death was a constant subject on family occasions as I was growing up. Further, it seemed like I was always listening to my father and his friends talk about "during the war" and their time in the military. I believe that most children my age had similar experiences with our Greatest Generation families during the 1950s.

Later in life I passed on a teacher's deferment and served in the military when many of my peers went out of their way to avoid service. I am very proud of that decision.

When my wife, Denise, and I retired, we joined our best man, Jim Grismer, in Savannah, Georgia. One of the first things Jim mentioned was that he and I needed to find out if we could get involved with the Eighth Air Force Museum. We went out to Pooler for an interview and were hired as volunteers to work in the archives. This WWII student and ex-history teacher had found a new home! My emotional connection to the museum's honoring the history of the Eighth Air Force and the veterans who served in that organization, particularly during WWII, was engrained within me from day one. I remember the first time I walked into the Combat Gallery. My reaction: "There should be a B-17 in here." Little did I know.

Jerry McLaughlin
Skidaway Island, Georgia

ACKNOWLEDGMENTS

It is not easy to write a book! I know. This is the second time I have done it. As one sits down when you are about to submit your work to the publisher, many, many thoughts are going through your mind, among them: "I had better remember to thank everyone who helped, and not omit a single name of anyone who deserves credit." The acknowledgments that follow are specifically related to the creation and publication of this book. Those who deserve so much credit for their work in the restoration of the B-17G, 44-83814, now known as the City of Savannah, will receive their due rewards later in the book.

My first literary effort, entitled, D-Day +60 Years, A Small Piece of History, was published in 2004 by a team known as "My Wife and Me, Two People from the Office, and Jim"—in addition to my wife, Denise, I had recruited an excellent editor and a graphic designer who had been colleagues when I actually worked for a living, and my good friend Jim Grismer. The book was well received, and we still get a minuscule check from the publisher every quarter. Having learned a bit from my first book, I decided to once again recruit some first-class help. The carry-overs from the first book team are my bride of thirty-three years, Denise Mary Catherine Broderick McLaughlin, and Jim. The others who joined the team are: Jack Devine, Dick Gorman, Jane Grismer, Ruth McMullin, Samantha Reid, Scott Whitcher, Jim Young, Mayela Cardenas, and Gail Woodard.

Denise is a veteran of 16 years of Catholic education during the 1950s and 1960s. With that credential, you know that she can identify a dangling participle or a run-on sentence. Further, I am sure that I am not the first author to state emphatically that it was his or her spouse that provided the push and spirit to make the work a success. I love you DMC!

As for the rest of the team, Jack Devine is a working member of the City of Savannah restoration team and a retired attorney. He spent a major portion of his professional career writing and editing documents so that others might more clearly understand the meaning of the written words. He provided the same service for us. Dick Gorman is another transplanted "Jerseyite." His professional skills in the public relations business, and his friendship, were both important elements in our effort. Jim Grismer and I have been best friends since the minute we met, sitting on adjoining bar stools in 1971. We were best man at each other's weddings and have been partners in various endeavors for 45 years. We can just look at each other and start laughing. Jim was not only my friend on the City of Savannah project, he was the invaluable project logistics officer, and even more important, chief advisor to the project manager for the restoration effort and to the author in this book. Jane is Jim's daughter, and like all of his children, an inheritor of the Grismer family sense of humor. Most important of all, Jane was born after 1960 and so she actually understands technology. Thank goodness for her presence, or this book would have been written in longhand, or on a typewriter.

Ruth McMullin is a friend, a neighbor, and a past member of the Board of Trustees of the National Museum of the Mighty Eighth Air Force. She is the current chairperson of the Mighty Eighth Foundation. Prior to retiring to Georgia with her husband Tom, Ruth had an amazing career, including working as an editor for both Doubleday and McGraw Hill publishers—a skill she has utilized for this book project. She is also an advisor extraordinaire when it comes to both publishing and people. Samantha Reid is a very talented graphic artist, a mom, a grad student, and an Eighth Air Force aficionado—a very busy lady. Scott Whitcher is a fellow intelligence community retiree. He serves on the *City of Savannah* team as one of our outstanding carpenters, and also includes IT advisor and picture librarian in his job description. Scott's technical skills, and ability to locate and edit pictures needed for the manuscript, have been of exceptional value to the project. Jim Young and Mayela Cardenas are a cousin and cousin-in-law who initiated our website: www.b17restoration.com. Gail, who lives in some place called Arizona, joined our merry band as our publisher through her friendship with Ruth at the Yale University School of Management. All in all, quite a crew.

Thank you everyone—it's a wonderful feeling when you are surrounded by competent professionals whom you can also call your friends. I doubt, despite all my best efforts, that this work has been completed without errors or omissions. If you should find either an error or an omission, or if you have any other thoughts regarding this work, please feel free to contact me at: smallhistory@ aol.com.

A NOTE TO THE READER

During World War II several iconic warplanes became the symbol of a portion of that war. The P-40 fighter with a snarling set of jaws painted on its nose will always indicate the famous Flying Tigers of the war in China. The appearance of a B-25 bomber on any occasion is referenced for its history with the 1942 Doolittle Raid on Tokyo. The most famous aircraft in the European Theater of the war will always be the Eighth Air Force's B-17! In addition to the B-17, the Eighth flew may other types of aircraft during WWII, including the Army Air Force's other heavy bomber, the B-24. The fighter protection for the big bombers included P-38, P-47, and P-51 fighters. It was the B-17, however, that dominated the Mighty Eighth's history. The media in wartime England made the B-17 the everlasting symbol of the Eighth Air Force in the skies over Western Europe. Stories describing the adventures of the "Flying Fortresses" and the men who flew in them appeared in newspapers and radio broadcasts on a daily basis. In addition, Hollywood presented the B-17 to the public in *Twelve O'Clock High*, *Command Decision*, *The War Lover*, and *Memphis Belle*.

Nearly 13,000 "F" and "G" model B-17s were produced by Boeing, Douglas, and Vega Corporations during the war years. While B-24 bombers eventually filled one-third of the bomber slots in the Eighth Air Force, the B-24 is more renowned for its success in the Pacific because of its ability to fly longer missions with a larger bomb load. The B-17 could fly higher and faster than any other allied bomber in Europe, a distinct advantage when battling the Luftwaffe's fighter force and highly accurate anti-aircraft flak batteries. Additionally, when the Eighth Air Force was formed in 1942, the B-17 was the most readily available bomber in the American arsenal.

While, hopefully, other aircraft flown by the Eighth during World War II will one day be displayed at the National Museum of the Mighty Eighth Air Force, the B-17—and particularly the G model—is the true symbol of the Eighth during that time.

Note the following diagram of the B-17G that marks the various portions of the airplane that are referenced in the manuscript. It is followed by descriptions of the combat assignments of the ten members of the crew of a B-17G.

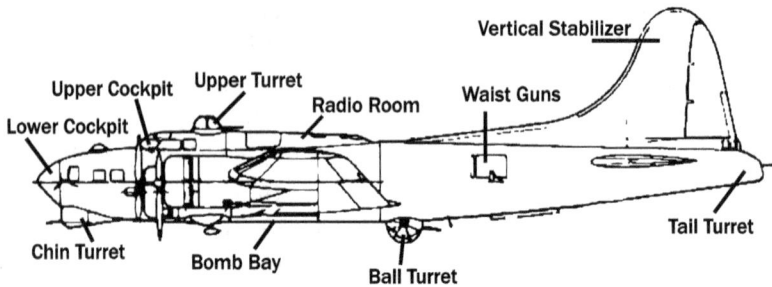

The Crew of a Flying Fortress

Almost all of the B-17s that saw service in the Eighth Air Force during WWII were "F" and "G" models. These airplanes carried a crew of ten. The pilot and co-pilot operated from what was known as the upper cockpit. The bombardier and navigator were stationed in the very forward compartment of the airplane, known as the lower cockpit. The senior noncommissioned officer, who was also the in-flight engineer, was stationed directly behind the pilots in the upper gun turret. The bomb bay separated the upper turret from the radio compartment. Early in the war the radio operator also fired a machine gun through the upper hatch at the rear of his compartment. This gun was later deemed ineffective and removed from the "G" model aircraft. Immediately aft of the radio compartment was the ball turret, which protected the airplane from attacks originating below the formations. Aft of the ball turret was an extended area known as the waist. Two gunners, left and right, were stationed in the waist, protecting the B-17 from attacks originating on either side of the airplane. The final crew member was the tail gunner, located in his turret beneath the tail of the airplane. (During the course of the war, tail gunners suffered the highest casualty rates of any crew position in the B-17 fleet.)

Pilot – The aircraft's commander, most often a First Lieutenant. Early in the war candidates for pilot training were required to have at least two years of college credits. This was dropped as the demand for pilots outgrew the number of college students in the pool of candidates. In 1944-45 many pilots were commanding aircrews before they were legally old enough to order a drink at the officer's club.

Co-pilot – Many co-pilots started their tours as second lieutenants. The co-pilot was the second in command of the aircraft, a fully qualified pilot who, for various reasons, was not awarded command of a crew prior to leaving the United States. Many co-pilots were promoted to pilot positions during their combat tour.

Navigator – A commissioned officer, usually a lieutenant. Lead crews often carried more than one navigator—a senior primary navigator used the standard methods of navigation, while the second navigator would be equipped with photos and other materials that enabled him to compare these materials with what he was seeing on the ground. This was called "pilotage" navigation. Late in the war some navigators were trained in the used of radar navigation which was used for bombing when the target was obscured with clouds.

Bombardier – A commissioned officer fully trained to operate the sophisticated Norden bombsight. When carpet bombing was adopted by the Eighth in 1945, the commissioned bombardier was often replaced with a sergeant/gunner officially designated a togglier. The togglier was trained to drop the aircraft bombs upon receiving a signal from a designated lead aircraft where a bombardier, using a Norden bombsight, located the target and released his bombs. The bombardier or togglier also operated the airplane's defensive chin turret.

Upper Turret Gunner – This gunner position was located directly behind the pilots in the upper cockpit. This position was usually manned by the senior noncommissioned officer in the crew, who also functioned as the flight engineer, responsible for keeping all of the airplane's systems functioning during the mission.

Radio Operator – This crewmember was kept very busy during missions, monitoring several radio frequencies for information and direction from the home base, mission, group, and squadron commanders. He would also broadcast a general message, when possible, if the crew was forced to abandon the aircraft.

Ball Turret Gunner – This gunner position was located in the turret that hung beneath the B-17 with the mission of protecting the bomber from attacks initiating from below. Cramped space within the turret required that ball turret gunners be small in stature and free of claustrophobic tendencies.

Waist Gunners – These gunner positions were on each side of the B-17 in the midsection of the airplane.

Tail Gunner – This gunner position operated from a stationary turret in the very last compartment at the rear of the airplane. He had a hatch that allowed him to enter or exit the airplane at the start or finish of a mission—or in the case of an emergency, exit the airplane with a parachute.

CHAPTER 1

Finding Our B-17

"When can you come and pick her up?"

Dr. Dik Daso, National Air and Space Museum

The National Museum of the Mighty Eighth Air Force (NMMEAF) opened its doors on May 14, 1996, in the city of Pooler, Georgia. The museum is located several miles from the birthplace of the Eighth Air Force, the National Guard Armory at 1108 Bull Street in downtown Savannah. Today, a historical plaque stands outside that building, which is now the home of American Legion Post 135, describing the founding of the Eighth Air Force at that location.

Since the museum's opening day, it had been the wish of the museum's leadership and Board of Trustees to present visitors with the display of a genuine WWII heavy bomber, a B-17 or B-24, the bombers that were the backbone of the Eighth in the air war against Germany from 1942 until 1945.

During the first decade of the museum's operation, there were many near misses and disappointments as various opportunities to obtain a bomber were unsuccessful. Finally, on December 16, 2008, an e-mail arrived at the museum from Dr. Dik Daso, curator, modern military aircraft at the National Air and Space Museum (NASM), addressed to the president and CEO of the Mighty Eighth Air Force Museum, Dr. Walter Brown. The e-mail said, "*It is my privilege to inform you that the de-accession and transfer of the Air and Space Museum's B-17G to the Mighty Eighth Air Force Museum has been approved by the Regents. Congratulations! When can you come and pick her up?*"

Our story begins with the receipt of that e-mail by Walt Brown. There is, of course, a long story leading up to the arrival of the good news that the B-17 (tail number 44-83814) had been gifted to the

Mighty Eighth, and then another story, lasting six years, depicting the restoration of the airplane.

Most of the activity leading up to the gifting of the B-17 to the Mighty Eighth occurred in 2008. There are several versions of the events. I have come to the conclusion that, while there are two separate descriptions among the museum staff and volunteers as to what occurred in Pooler, there is no one who can authenticate events that occurred in Washington, resulting in Dr. Daso's e-mail announcing the awarding of the B-17 to the Mighty Eighth. What follows has been gleaned from first-person descriptions of two events that occurred at the National Museum of the Mighty Eighth Air Force in 2008—one, or both, could have started our story.

The first account was developed from an interview of the then museum's chief of maintenance, Rick Ennis, by the *City of Savannah*'s first project historian, Doug Reed.

Doug Reed: *(Project historian [edited by the author]) During July of 2008, an event took place that (may have) changed the National Museum of the Mighty Eighth Air Force in a most extraordinary way. On display in the Museum's Combat Gallery was a German Messerschmitt 163B Komet, one of Hitler's so-called "secret weapons." Records indicate that approximately 300 Komets were manufactured. One of the rare survivors had been loaned to the Mighty Eighth by the*

The battered Messerschmitt 163B Komet that may have played a large role in bringing a B-17 to the Mighty Eighth Air Force Museum. (Scott Whitcher)

Smithsonian Institution. The loan agreement expired in 2007 and the Smithsonian, needing the Komet for a new exhibit, had dispatched personnel to the Mighty Eighth to retrieve the tiny aircraft. The process of crating and shipping the Komet took several days and involved concerted efforts of both Smithsonian and Mighty Eighth personnel. During one of the frequent conversations among these workers, one of the Smithsonian crew made the casual comment, "You need a B-17. The Smithsonian has one that I'll bet you could get with just a phone call—it's in moth balls in a hangar up in Virginia."

The Mighty Eighth's enthusiastic maintenance chief, Rick Ennis, pushed for details and immediately reported the conversation to Walt Brown. Subsequently, Walt made a phone call to Dr. Daso and began a serious campaign to obtain the mysterious B-17 mentioned by the Smithsonian technician.

Brenda Elmgren: (Museum staff member) *Dr. Daso told Walt Brown that it was true that the Smithsonian was looking for a home for their B-17G, a home where the airplane would be put to use for educational purposes, and with an organization that would give its word that the airplane would never be flown again. Walt Brown assured Dr. Daso that the Mighty Eighth met both of those requirements. Dr. Daso expressed a willingness to bring a request to the Smithsonian's Board of Regents urging release of the B-17G 44-83814 if the Mighty Eighth would agree to a series of terms.*

- The museum must document its educational mission.
- The airplane was to be stored within the museum, on a permanent basis.
- A signed agreement would state that the aircraft would never again fly.
- The Mighty Eighth was to pay the costs of transportation to move the airplane.
- If the Mighty Eighth should end its service as a museum, 44-83814 would revert to Smithsonian Institution ownership.

After a trip from Washington, DC, to Pooler to inspect the museum and assure himself that he was backing a worthy candidate, Dr. Daso told Walt Brown that he would petition the Smithsonian Board of

Regents at its meeting in August of 2008 to release B-17G 44-83814 to the Mighty Eighth. The requested document was immediately prepared and forwarded to Dr. Daso. The date of the August meeting came and went with no reply from the Smithsonian. Finally, word was received that the subject of gifting the B-17 to the Mighty Eighth had not been presented to the Board of Regents after all. Priority items had pushed the request from the board's agenda until the next meeting, which could be six months in the future. The reaction in Pooler was, of course, deep disappointment. Walt tried to make the most of the situation by telling everyone that surely the approval would happen at the next meeting. The disappointment for him, however, was especially devastating. He had been diagnosed with a rare type of melanoma, and feared his chances of ever seeing a B-17 arrive at the museum were now very slim indeed.

Meanwhile, wheels continued to turn. A senior member of the Mighty Eighth staff made a behind-the-scenes call to Dr. Daso and explained the situation to him, including the most recent news that Walt's disease was considered incurable and that he might only have several months to live, much less continue in his role as the president and CEO of the Mighty Eighth. Dr. Daso was very understanding and in several days contacted the museum staffer to say that he was going to personally walk the de-accessioning papers that would release the airplane through the Board of Regents. He would even take the unusual step of calling a special meeting solely to address this issue. Following this conversation, there was no contact from Dr. Daso for several weeks until the now famous December 16, 2008, e-mail asking, "When can you come and pick her up?"

The second story of how events got started for the Smithsonian B-17 to be gifted to the Mighty Eighth began not with a US government employee, but with the very top of the US government itself—the president of the United States.

Everyone who was involved with the Mighty Eighth in 2008 agrees that Walt Brown's goal when he became the president and CEO of the museum was to obtain a B-17 as the museum's central exhibit to honor the veterans of the WWII Eighth Air Force. During the summer of that year, the museum was contacted by the campaign committee of Congressman Saxby Chambliss, requesting space at the museum for a campaign rally at which it was hoped President George W. Bush would be the featured speaker. Arrangements were quickly completed.

The museum staff vividly remember that Walt immediately went into high gear with plans to somehow tell the president that a B-17 bomber should be sitting in the Combat Gallery of the museum.

Shortly before the president was due to arrive, Walt and staff member Brenda Elmgren met with the Secret Service agent in charge of the president's schedule. He told them that as the museum's president and CEO, Walt would have a very brief window of time to engage in a private conversation with the president. There is no doubt of what Walt would say, "I need a B-17."

Brenda Elmgren: *When the president did arrive, Walt met him, shook hands, and they were escorted to the Art Gallery, where the president's entourage was gathered. I watched as Walt talked with several members of the presidential staff, particularly one close aide with whom he chatted amicably. A Secret Service agent reminded Walt that he would have a brief window to chat with the president personally. Finally, Walt and I had our pictures taken with the president, who then turned and looked sincerely at Walt. "What can I do for you, young man?" the president asked. Walt did not hesitate, "You can get us a B-17," Walt responded. "Do you know where one is?" asked the president. "Yes," replied Walt. President Bush said, "We can do that," and turning to a young aide, he said, "Get this man a B-17." The aide wrote furiously in his notebook and just a few seconds later the president was whisked away by his handlers.*

Did the Smithsonian gift the B-17 to the Mighty Eighth at the direction of President Bush, or did they do so in response to the museum staffer's phone call regarding Walt Brown's illness—or was the gifting a result of both events? The accepted story inside the museum walls is that the Mighty Eighth was on a list of candidates competing for 44-83814, and that a word from the White House moved us to the top of the list. We'll never know for sure. What we do know is that Dr. Daso's e-mail started a wonderful story.

During the summer of 2008 while Jim Grismer and I were doing our chores signing in and documenting donations to the museum's archives, Walt Brown came to see us in the Mighty Eighth archives—something that was very unusual. He took the two of us aside and started asking us questions about our pre-retirement careers, particularly what kind of management roles we had held. He also asked us about our past histories in leadership positions that we had held in the volunteer fire service in New York and in Georgia. We talked for quite a while, and then he thanked us and left. We were perplexed about the conversation and did not realize until later that we had been undergoing a dual job interview for management of the soon-to-be-starting B-17 restoration process.

Anticipating that the Smithsonian would be approving the transfer of the B-17 to the Mighty Eighth, the museum had entered into a tentative agreement with a group of retired US Navy aircraft maintenance veterans and their company, All Coast Aircraft Recovery Inc., to move the B-17 from Chantilly, Virginia, to Pooler. Everyone was on standby, hoping that the okay would arrive from Washington.

__Jim Grismer:__ In late July, 2008, word came down that a B-17 bomber might be headed our way. The aircraft in question had been sequestered in an old hangar since 1984. The Mighty Eighth Museum had worked out an acquisition agreement to free up the plane for transfer to our ownership. At the time I had plans to visit family in New York. Walt Brown, the CEO of the museum, asked me if I could take a detour on my route north and do an inspection of the aircraft. There was concern about its condition after such a long period of storage. The possibility of corrosion and vandalism lingered in our minds. After all, we had no idea in what conditions it was stored, or what, if any, maintenance had been done on it. On my arrival at Dulles, I was met by Dr. Dik Daso and Lars McLamore. Despite the presence of these two museum officials, I had to undergo a detailed and tedious search of my vehicle and its contents. The security guards went through every compartment, the underside of my truck and the toolboxes on board. It was the same routine on the way out. Impressive security measures indeed! The level of security to gain access to the storage hangar was extreme, and it helped dispel any thought of past illegal access or vandalism to this historic airplane. I was escorted through the gate to the airport and then to the museum's storage hangar. The vintage hangar structure was a huge, drafty facility riddled with holes in the roof and walls. The openings provided easy access to the interior for pigeons and other nesting birds. The birds had found comfortable housing within the engines and interiors of most of the

B-17G, Tail Number 44-83814, as photographed in a Smithsonian hangar, located in Chantilly, Virginia, in July of 2008. (Jim Grismer)

several aircraft within the hangar. Apparently, they found the B-17 much to their liking.

My first image of the B-17 was of a partially stripped down aircraft. It was jammed among a multitude of historic aviation classics. It sat beside the Space Shuttle Enterprise in a gloomy setting. The exterior was covered with duct tape, a preservative sealant, dirt, grease, and bird droppings. A nasty sight! However, it appeared to be structurally sound. I saw the possibility that it could be successfully dismantled, transported to Pooler, and reconstructed on our turf (given four or five years and a few thousand man-hours). Those items were a challenge that my colleagues at the museum and I were ready to accept. The assessment I gave to Walt Brown when I returned to Pooler provided the green light for approving the acquisition of the B-17 from the perspective of the Mighty Eighth. In December, after several days of telephone negotiations involving the legal community, it was approved for representatives of the Mighty Eighth to travel to Dulles and take possession of the airplane on the behalf of our museum. That task was assigned to Jerry McLaughlin and Marshall Brooks. Both were eager to accept that honor. Knowing now what lay ahead of us, I'm not sure I envisioned the magnitude of the work or the thousands of man-hours in our long path to completion of the restoration. At the time, my only, and very huge, concern was, "How the hell are we going to squeeze this huge beast through the garage door at the rear of the museum?"

When the word finally came from Dr. Daso on December 16 that the airplane was ours, I was attending an Eighth Air Force Historical Society meeting. Everyone was asked to pay attention for an important announcement. Brenda Elmgren then read Dr. Daso's e-mail to the crowd. There was considerable cheering and clapping and, as I remember, the bar did a fairly brisk business for the next hour or so. Walt Brown also announced that he had been in touch with the All Coast Aircraft Recovery team and that they were ready to go when dates could be worked out with the Smithsonian staff. It was finally decided that the All Coast team would arrive in Chantilly, Virginia, on January 4, 2009, and begin work the next day. Jim and I were preparing to meet the team in Chantilly when Jim had a medical problem that prevented him from making the trip. Marshall Brooks, my neighbor, good friend, and fellow archive volunteer, stepped up in Jim's place and we left for Virginia on January 4.

The morning of January 5, Marshall and I arrived in the lobby of our hotel and met Chuck Mosely and the All Coast team. We departed in several vehicles to the Smithsonian's hangar where 44-83814 had spent the past several decades, and the adventure was officially underway. The first Smithsonian employees we met were, as expected, the facility security team. Our personal data had been forwarded to the museum and after routine certification of our bonafides, we were all passed through the gate and parked our

44-83814 as we first saw her in the early morning of January 5, 2009. (CoS Archives)

vehicles outside of the immense open doors of the hangar . . . and there she was!

Marshall Brooks takes over the narrative of our trip from Savannah to the Northern Virginia area where we coincidentally had both spent a significant portion of our lives before retiring to Savannah.

Marshall Brooks: *In December 2008, Dr. Walter Brown, the CEO and president of the NMMEAF, received word from the Smithsonian National Air and Space Museum that they were gifting our museum a coveted B-17 Flying Fortress.*

There was paperwork to be completed and red tape to be tended to, but the more impressive question, at least in my mind, was how to move a WWII bomber with a wing span of 103'9", length of 74'4" and height of 19'2" from a Dulles Airport hangar to the Combat Gallery of the National Museum of the Mighty Eighth Air Force in Pooler, Georgia? The answer was to hire a company which specializes in dismantling, transporting, and reassembling aircraft. Who knew? The museum hired the services of a well-established firm called All Coast Aircraft Recovery, Inc., headed by retired Navy Commander Chuck Mosely. Chuck Mosley hired seven men from his list of trusted experts, mostly ex-military, whom he considered best-suited for our project. He also hired a trucking company that specialized in transporting dismantled aircraft.

Jerry McLaughlin and I (I was standing in for Jim Grismer, who was unable to leave Savannah at that time) were designated as representatives of the Mighty Eighth to be on-site at Dulles as the plane was being dismantled, loaded piece by piece onto trucks, and transported to Pooler. On January 5, 2009, we attended a pre-dawn organizational meeting in Fairfax, Virginia, with the All Coast crew. We introduced ourselves and met our new colleagues and listened as Chuck gave out assignments and explained what he expected of his team on day one of this great adventure. Finally, we left in a convoy to the Smithsonian storage hangar.

The B-17 was in an oversized hangar together with other important aircraft, including the Space Shuttle Enterprise, *in a secure area of Dulles Airport. We were escorted to the hangar location by security officers after being cleared through a security gate.*

While we were catching our breath and walking around the aircraft, we suddenly saw two smiling faces headed our way, with a

Marshall Brooks signs the Deed of Gift for 44-83814 with Dr. Dik Daso, curator, modern military aircraft at the Smithsonian Institution, on January 5, 2009. (CoS Archives)

small group in tow; the Smithsonian team had arrived. The two lead-ers introduced themselves as the Dr. Daso whom we had been hear-ing about for all these months, and Lars McLamore, a supervisor for aircraft restoration. Dr. Daso was holding an envelope with the Deed of Gift for the airplane, and in just a few minutes, as the designated Mighty Eighth representative, I signed the papers transferring owner-ship of the B-17G 44-83814 from the Smithsonian Institution to the National Museum of the Mighty Eighth Air Force. I was thrilled to hold up the document and waved it to Jerry as I shook hands with Dr. Daso.

The Mosely team had never before taken apart and moved a B-17. Despite their vast experience with other types of aircraft, it proved to be a difficult task and required three or four more days than Chuck had anticipated. They carried on, and finally the airplane was dismantled to the extent possible and trucked to Pooler. The City of Savannah fuselage followed the rest of its many parts and sections and rolled home on a flatbed truck on January 15, 2009. It was brought to our Museum's exhibition space and reassembled by the Mosely team.

Because we were neighbors, the McLaughlins and the Brooks put on a festive farewell dinner for Chuck and his compatriots. It was a great celebration.

Intelligent minds may ask what Jerry and I contributed during the four working days that we were at Dulles. Well, we assisted in man-ual labor, packing and toting. We also took a lot of pictures, drank cof-fee, and asked questions. Jerry had clearly started the learning process

about the airplane, which led him to be designated the project man-
ager of the restoration when we returned to Pooler. As for me, after
signing the official papers, I spent most of my time standing around
and admiring the work of some very interesting aviation profession-
als. The hangar doors were fully open every day, there was no heat,
and the rain and sleet never seemed to stop. That did not keep those
four days from being, for me, a fascinating and not-to-be-forgotten
experience, one of those far removed from anything I had ever done
before, or could have imagined.

Marshall and I had seen the pictures that Jim took of 814 the previous July, and we knew that she wasn't as beautiful as she once was, and as we hoped she would be in the years to come, but we were not ready for the filthy pile of metal that was before our eyes in the very dimly lit hangar.

Two decades of storage had left the fuselage and wings covered with an enormous amount of grit, and there were generous amounts of what looked like packing plastic clinging all over the aircraft. The tail turret and nosepiece were missing, and she was sitting on boards both at the tail wheel and where the retracted main gear peeked out beneath the wings. She was not a pretty sight!

We were standing behind the starboard wing, near the waist door, and I asked Dr. Daso if it was OK if I entered the aircraft. He smiled, and answered, "Go ahead, you own it!" I climbed into the door and began to head for the cockpit. It had been my plan to call Walt from the pilot's seat to tell him that the airplane had been signed over to the Mighty Eighth. I quickly stopped and, once again, had to catch my breath. The interior of the airplane was filled with filthy material that I could not identify, and a bird's nest, really—a huge bird's nest! I took stock and decided that none of the mysterious material was a danger to my safety, and that my wish to call Walt from the cockpit was still an attainable goal. I walked through the waist area, carefully avoiding the partially covered hole that had once held the ball turret, and opened the plywood door to the radio room. Several more bird nests! Then a bigger test came. A narrow steel girder ran the length of the bomb bay, with sturdy support beams forming a *V* near the doorway into the cockpit. I somehow managed to get through the support beams with my no-longer-slim body and a large winter coat making it something of a challenge.

As the sun came up and more people arrived, our morale rose accordingly. (CoS Archives)

The entire crew pushing 814 to the center of the hangar. (CoS Archives)

Then I was in the cockpit. The windows were almost opaque with dirt and age. The instrument panel seemed to be totally intact. The complex throttle quadrant seemed complete and, thankfully, there was no debris on the pilot's seat. I sat down in that seat on the left hand side of the cockpit and began to call Walt, whom I knew was in his office awaiting news of what was happening. I paused and thought of the reaction that would occur when I called with the news that the airplane was ours. There would be bedlam. Then I thought of Walt's personal reaction. One of the issues that Marshall and I were facing while we were in Virginia was heartbreaking to both of us: Would Walt Brown, our leader and the man who had been the spirit of the search for a B-17, and in fact, the spirit of the museum itself, be able to witness the arrival of 814 at the museum? He would be leaving Pooler to consult with a group of fellow physicians in Pittsburgh regarding his cancer and then, hopefully, be returning to Pooler for our arrival. The effect of this call was going to be significant to everyone, but particularly on Walt. I placed the call and soon heard the familiar voice of the museum receptionist. I asked for Walt and was transferred to his private number.

From the description of staff members to whom I spoke after our return, Walt literally pounced on the phone as soon as it began to ring. "Walt," I said, "I'm sitting in the cockpit of your brand new B-17." I would like to report that he responded with some great quote, or an expletive, or silence. Truthfully, I can't remember. All I can remember is that when the conversation started to make sense, he told me that he would give anything to be sitting in the cockpit next to me, and that the board of trustees had voted to name 814 the *City of Savannah*, after a B-17G that had been given that name in 1944 at Hunter Field. I could feel the emotion in Walt's voice, even in the freezing cockpit of the B-17, six hundred miles north of

A very cold Mighty Eighth volunteer just moments after reporting to Walt Brown that the papers transferring ownership of 44-83814 to its new family in Pooler had been signed. (CoS Archives)

Pooler. He ended the conversation with an almost trembling voice. "Bring her home, Jerry," he told me. "We're all depending on you." It was the first, but not the last, time during the next six years that I would end a conversation with tears in my eyes.

During the days that followed, I was on the phone with Walt on a regular basis, discussing various aspects of the progress of the disassembly of the aircraft, and almost as frequently, with Brenda Elmgren, the museum's chief of administration, regarding Walt's commencing a specialized treatment regimen that was going to take place out of town. It was impossible to think that the airplane would arrive at the Mighty Eighth without Walt standing at the door to witness its arrival.

While we were juggling schedules and watching the *City of Savannah* slowly come apart (engines, trailing edges of wings, wings themselves), Marshall and I were prowling through the hangar with Lars McLamore and found several boxes of spare parts for the airplane, including brake pads and inner-wing air ducts.

Wednesday morning, January 7, began with the arrival of a box tractor-trailer at the entrance to the hangar. The All Coast team, plus a group of Smithsonian staffers who had joined us, began loading the truck with the spare parts we had located, as well as the wingtips and rudder.

After the departure of the truck, the next project was to bring the engines and the trailing edges of the wings out of the hangar

The first of four tractor-trailers that would transport 814 to its new home. (CoS Archives)

and place them in position to be loaded on a flatbed trailer, which would be arriving the following morning.

Thursday morning started off with a serious challenge to the All Coast crew. Prior to leaving for Virginia, they had prepared a cradle that they planned to mount beneath the nose of the airplane to support the weight of the fuselage during the raising of the landing gear, the removal of the wings, and the trip on the trailer to Pooler. The measurements supplied to All Coast had been inaccurate and they had a major problem, but a problem that they were up to solving. Standing in a circle, trying to stay warm in the freezing hangar, they decided that they would build a new cradle from scrap materials in the hangar. First, they took a large piece of Styrofoam and used it to form a template for the B-17's fuselage directly beneath the nose. Large scrap wood pieces from the outside dumpster were then brought in and matched to the Styrofoam. When the carpentry work on the cradle was finished, it was fitted, along with several wooden pallets, beneath the aircraft. When everyone was assured that the nose cradle and pallets that had been placed beneath the tail were firmly in place, Bill Mosely, Chuck's nephew, climbed into the bomb bay. After a signal from his uncle, Bill began to turn the crank that would manually lift the landing gear for the first time since 1984. Slowly the gear lifted and the wooden pallets and cradle beneath the fuselage began to bear the weight of the fuselage. The new cradle under the cockpit fit perfectly, and our B-17 was another step closer to leaving for her new home in Pooler.

While the All Coast crew had a stressful morning in Virginia, the folks in Pooler had been more than happy to welcome the arrival of the first shipment of parts that had left Virginia the previous day. Museum staff, visitors, and even local media were on hand as the truck pulled into the museum parking lot and backed into the workshop entrance to unload its cargo. After ten years of waiting, the spectators watched the first parts of 814, the wingtips, come out of the back of the truck. Rick Ennis, chief of museum facilities, demonstrated his considerable skill as a forklift operator as he carefully removed the wingtips and rudder from the truck and placed them inside the building, with the help of museum staff who had been drafted for the event.

The improvised cradle put together by the All Coast crew. (CoS Archives)

The cradle fits perfectly on its mount. (CoS Archives)

While the museum team was unloading the trailer, the All Coast team was doing just the opposite, loading the engines and trailing edges of the wings onto trailer #2, the first of three flatbeds that would bring most of the aircraft sections to Pooler. During the loading process, those of us of a certain age were quite impressed as a problem emerged regarding how the engines were being secured on the trailer. Rick called and asked questions as to how the engines were being secured and how he should lift them off the trailer when the truck arrived in Pooler. One of the All Coast crew, Jeff Gonzales, used his Blackberry to take pictures of how the crew was rigging the engines and immediately e-mailed the pictures to Rick in Pooler,

Mighty Eighth staff unload the City of Savannah's *rudder from the first trailer load of parts to arrive from Virginia.* (CoS Archives)

who was then able to talk to Jeff on the phone about unloading the engines while he was looking at the just-taken pictures on Walt's desktop computer. It was quite amazing to Walt and I, from a previous generation, as we listened to the two men discuss the technical issues of the pictures Jeff was sending to the computer screen that Walt and Rick were looking at! Jeff just shrugged. (Ironically, by 2015, we were all using this technology on a daily basis for project issues.) Several hours later, as the cold and rainy Thursday came to an end, the first flatbed left for Pooler with the engines and trailing edges. It had been another amazing day.

Friday morning, flatbeds #2 and #3 were waiting at the hangar when we arrived at 8:00 a.m. Another cold day, but the rain had stopped and the sun was finally shining. Immediately, Chuck and the team began to remove the wings from the fuselage. As with the previous morning, problems emerged. Marshall and I were surprised to learn that each of the wings was attached to the airplane by only four very large bolts. These bolts had apparently not moved in many decades and they were not going to make it easy for anyone who wanted to move them now. Finally, an improvised lug wrench with a very long handle and a very determined young man from Vermont with a sledgehammer prevailed over the bolts, and the wings were removed. They were immediately placed on flatbed #2. Mounting the fuselage on flatbed #3 would take the remainder of the day. When I called the museum to report the latest events to Walt, he said that he wanted Marshall and me to return to Pooler as soon as possible to help prepare for the "formal" arrival of our B-17, now officially being referred to as the *City of Savannah*, by both the museum staff and the expectant media.

There was now very little that Marshall and I could do to contribute to the work being done in the hangar. We were very glad to check out of the motel and head south where life was warmer and we could make more of a contribution to events. We talked over last-minute details with Chuck and were soon on I-95 headed to Savannah. The All Coast team spent the rest of the day lifting the fuselage onto flatbed #3 and securing it to the trailer.

Shortly after Marshall and I left Chantilly, flatbed #1 arrived at the Mighty Eighth with the engines and trailing edges on board. Thanks to Jeff Gonzales' Blackberry and Rick's expertise operating a crane, the engines were quickly lifted from the trailer and placed at the maintenance entrance to the museum. Chuck Mosely and Rick had had a long conversation on Thursday afternoon about the trailing edges' lack of structural stability when not attached to the wing. Once again, volunteers were selected from the museum staff

Dawn, January 9. Finally, there is sunshine in the morning. A good thing, as most of the day was spent working outdoors, loading the flatbeds. (CoS Archives)

All four engines on the flatbed. (CoS Archives)

and the trailing edges were very carefully removed from the trailer and placed delicately on tarps at the maintenance entrance.

Chuck had the fuselage mounted on flatbed #3 before darkness arrived on the cold tarmac in Chantilly. The team would leave in the morning, Saturday, as would flatbed #3. While the men would arrive in Pooler the next day, it would be several days before the arrival of the fuselage. The special load required a license to

The All Coast team in one of the few moments that they were standing still. (CoS Archives)

pass through every state on the way to Georgia and special licenses to divert off of I-95 on two occasions because of low bridge problems. On the morning of January 14, flatbed #2 arrived in Pooler and the All Coast team began unloading the wings from the trailer and moving them inside the museum prior to the arrival of the fuselage. January 15 was a beautiful day and, while not warm, a great deal warmer than the weather had been in Virginia. There was a large turnout of staff and associates in the museum's parking lot, including Walt Brown, the man who had worked so hard to make this happen, and who had just returned from a meeting with his cancer team in Pittsburgh. Around 10:00 a.m., a call was received from the Pooler Police Department saying that the convoy with the fuselage was almost at Exit 102 on I-95, where they would leave the interstate and arrive at the museum. Suddenly the intersection to Bourne Avenue in front of the museum was a mass of flashing blue lights. Sirens began to sound. These were the signals that the B-17G 44-83814, now known as the *City of Savannah*, was finally arriving at her new home. The driver of the tractor-trailer carrying the fuselage saw the large group of media trucks and individuals holding cameras at the entrance to the museum and, with a big smile, he stopped his rig so that four or five thousand pictures could be taken of the *City of Savannah* before he made his final turn into the museum parking lot.

Jim Grismer: *The emotional highlight of the day for me was my participation in the convoy escorting the B-17 to the museum. Because of my role in the local volunteer fire department, my truck was equipped with flashing lights, a siren, and an air horn. I don't mind saying that it was an unforgettable hoot to actually ride down I-95, five abreast with other emergency vehicles, as the convoy arrived in Pooler, exited the interstate, and then arrived at the museum with everyone's sirens and horns blaring. A wonderful moment that will never occur again!*

Finally, the driver made a very wide turn and, amid the sirens and flashing lights, brought the *City of Savannah* into the parking lot where, once again, he stopped so an adoring crowd of onlookers could gather around the fuselage and gaze in awe. I saw many moist eyes from the folks who had been involved with the museum for many years.

The next hour was taken up with media interviews and a great deal of picture taking, until it was time to move the airplane around the museum to the maintenance entrance. Here, it would be lifted off the trailer and placed on a specially built dolly, where she would remain overnight. The following morning she would be rolled through the maintenance shop and into the Combat Gallery.

On the morning of January 15, 2009, Mac McCormick, who later became a stalwart member of our radio team, published the following on his blog:

The City of Savannah *pauses on Bourne Avenue so that the welcoming crowd can get pictures and cheer.* (CoS Archives)

The City of Savannah *arriving at the NMMEAF on the morning of January 15, 2009.* (CoS Archives)

41

Mac McCormick: *When I read the* Savannah Morning News *at lunch, I noticed a story about a B-17G fuselage being delivered to the NMMEAF at noon today. After lunch, I grabbed my cameras, the BC-396, and the FT-50 and headed out to the museum. I arrived as the arrival ceremony was ending and hung around to watch them remove the fuselage and some of the parts from the flatbed. All Coast Aircraft Recovery and Les Chapman Transport moved the B-17. All Coast Aircraft Recovery will also be doing the reassembly of the aircraft.*

Watching the movement was fascinating. To remove the fuselage from the flatbed, they used a crane from Tim's Cranes and Rigging to lift the fuselage up in the air. They then drove the truck out from underneath and set it down on wheels that were affixed to the fuselage. The tail rested on a 4×4 underneath the tail wheel assembly. A forklift was being used to move the wing sections around. During the first wing section move, they had to move some fencing around one of the museum's HVAC units. Apparently one of the fence posts caught an underground water line as it came out and caused a leak. This put a delay in the works and they were trying to stop the leak when I left. I can't wait to see the aircraft assembled and put on display inside. It will be wonderful to have a restored B-17 in Savannah! Mac McCormick III, KF4LMT

I arrived at the museum at 8:00 a.m. on the morning of January 16 to find Chuck and the All Coast crew moving the fuselage

Mac's picture clearly illustrates how low the fuselage was to the ground on the custom dolly when it was rolled into the museum's Combat Gallery. (Mac McCormick)

through the museum maintenance door. They had started operating as soon as it was light and had already moved the wings inside the museum.

As seemed to happen every morning, shortly after my arrival, a problem arose. Despite the top of the museum's maintenance entrance having been removed, the vertical stabilizer of the *City of Savannah* was nearly a foot higher than the enlarged entrance. The team, as usual, had an answer: they were removing the top eighteen inches of the stabilizer at what is called a "builder's seam." Chuck explained that removing the top of the stabilizer at that point would not impinge on the structural integrity of the stabilizer and the removed portion could readily be reinstalled. Bill Mosely was given the assignment to remove the top of the stabilizer.

Jim Argo: My boss at Gulfstream Corporation in 2009, Brian Leftwich, asked me if I had heard that the Eighth Air Force Museum was getting a "new" B-17 the next day. He knew that I had experience working on radial engines that were used to power the Flying Fortresses and thought I might be interested. I certainly was. I worked a four-day shift at Gulfstream from Friday–Monday and I was free the day the airplane arrived. I was in the parking lot when the sirens sounded and the beat-up fuselage turned into the museum parking lot. There were a lot of media people around, and I eventually learned that nothing would happen until early the following morning, when the wings and fuselage would be moved into the museum.

The inner-wing sections were the first components to enter the museum. (CoS Archives)

I was there bright and early and jumped in to help wherever I could. (Years later Jerry McLaughlin told me that the airplane moving crew thought I worked for the museum, and the museum crew thought I worked for the airplane people.) It took quite a while to get the wings unloaded and moved inside, and even longer to get the fuselage moved off of the flatbed trailer and onto its custom carriage. I worked with the museum team that was preparing the building. First, we realized that the fence next to the service entrance would have to be removed. I was setting the chain on the fence posts as they were lifted out of the ground by a crane. The first popped out easily, as did the second. The third was almost blown out of the ground by surging water, which became a real gusher. That was followed by a LOT of confusion. The flooding had to be stopped, but there was reluctance to shut down the museum water supply or possibly the water to the adjacent motel. The local water company was called. They arrived, announced that it was not one of their water mains, and left! After about an hour the shut-off for the line was found on the opposite side of the museum. The deluge stopped, but nothing inside the museum was affected, nor was the motel. To my knowledge, they never figured out why.

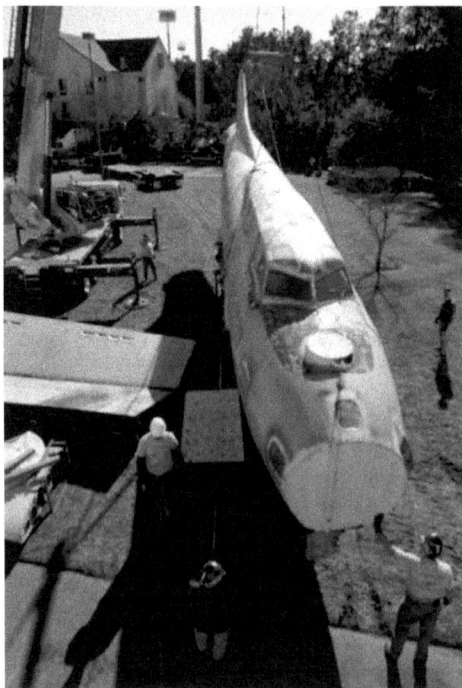

Lowering the fuselage on the dolly. (CoS Archives)

Next, I attached myself to the crew that cut the top off the garage door entrance to the museum, with a notch in the middle so that the tail would fit into the entrance. Another mess! We measured what we figured would be the height of the tail from the ground after the aircraft was lowered onto its dolly and then cut a BIG hole in the area above the entranceway. The airplane was lowered onto the dolly, lifted by a forklift, and they began moving it into the service entrance. As the tail

It was right about here when someone said, "Whoa, is the stabilizer going to fit under the top of the door?" Yet another surprise. (CoS Archives)

Bill Mosely, solving the problem of the stabilizer height. (CoS Archives)

got closer to the door, it was obvious that it was still too high to fit into the building. The decision was made that no more cuts would be made to the building: THEY WOULD CUT OFF THE TOP OF THE TAIL! That was more than I could take. I left to pick up my kids at school. I couldn't watch.

While Bill Mosely was removing the upper section of the vertical stabilizer, I walked the length of the fuselage. I carefully noted that the forward section of the fuselage was resting just several inches off the ground on a custom-made dolly, produced on-site by Chuck's welder, the same team member who had put together the unique wrench that loosened the wing nuts from the fuselage. The custom-built dolly would enable the *City* to roll smoothly, only several inches above the ground, on wheels that had been built for use on a handcart. As soon as Bill had cut the 18 inches off the stabilizer, Chuck had a brief meeting with his team, moved his forklift behind the B-17, and very gently lifted the tail several inches off the ground. Then, with everyone holding their breath, he slowly moved the forklift forward and the airplane responded correctly, smoothly inching into the maintenance shop.

As the airplane moved slowly through the door we were all holding our breath—yes!—the cut-down vertical stabilizer fit beneath the top of the door. Slowly, the fuselage moved toward the door from the shop into the Combat Gallery.

Jim Grismer: *While Jerry and Marshall were up in Virginia, we had been working on how the airplane would best fit into the Combat Gallery. We found an original blueprint in the museum records and measured the size of the gallery with the known measurements of the airplane. We also made a scale drawing of the airplane and began moving it into various positions over the blueprint. Walt and I finally agreed on what seemed to be the most appropriate location, at least temporarily, to position the B-17 within the gallery.*

Once again, word had spread throughout the museum and every visitor and staff member seemed to be present as the *City of Savannah*

The City of Savannah *enters her final home, the National Museum of the Mighty Eighth Air Force.* (CoS Archives)

Dr. Walt Brown (right) talks with Bill Mosely as the City of Savannah *rolls into the Combat Gallery. Note the custom-made dolly beneath the wing root.* (CoS Archives)

entered the gallery. Cheers and applause greeted the aircraft on its second significant arrival in as many days. The aircraft moved slowly across the floor and stopped, exactly where an *X* of tape had been placed on the floor to ensure that there was enough space to the left and right of the airplane so that the wings would fit between the walls.

After ten years of effort, a WWII B-17 bomber had finally arrived in the Combat Gallery of the National Museum of the Mighty Eighth Air Force!

Over the next two days, the process of reassembling the aircraft continued at a steady pace. On the night of January 20, the All Coast crew was welcomed as honored guests at the monthly meeting of the Birthplace Chapter of the Mighty Eighth Air Force Historical Society. It had been only one month earlier, at the December meeting of the society, that Brenda Elmgren had announced that the Smithsonian Regents had agreed to gift the airplane to the Mighty Eighth—and what a month it had been!

47

CHAPTER 2

The First 90 Days

JANUARY–MARCH 2009

"We don't know what we don't know!"

Jim Grismer

After the All Coast crew left for home on the morning of January 21, 2009, Jim Grismer and I sat at a table in a local restaurant and looked at each other saying, "Now what do we do?" Jim summed up our concerns with what would become our mantra, "We don't know what we don't know." We were facing an enormous challenge with our assignment from Walt Brown to restore the treasured B-17 that was now sitting in the Combat Gallery of the NMMEAF. As if the airplane restoration itself was not enough to overwhelm us, we were very worried about our good friend Walt. The entire time I had been in Virginia with Marshall and the All Coast team, Jim and Brenda Elmgren had been keeping me abreast of the latest events regarding his declining health situation.

We had made several adjustments to the schedule before returning to Pooler with the B-17 to ensure that Walt would be in town for the arrival of the airplane in between treatments he was undergoing in Pittsburgh.

Dr. Walter Brown, president and CEO of the NMMEAF 2006–2009. (CoS Archives)

When we arrived back in Pooler, the news was not good. One of the museum staff told us that Walt would be leaving his position as president and CEO of the museum because of his illness, and that it had not yet been decided if he would continue, in any manner, to be directly involved with the museum and the restoration.

After discussing the concerns for our friend, we began to address the many administrative and logistical issues facing us with the airplane. We began writing a list of chores we had to undertake. Jim is a retired senior executive with the Port Authority of New York and New Jersey. He retired as general manager of Operations, Safety, and Security at the New York World Trade Center. He knows how to put an organization together, manage that organization, and provide for its logistical support. He also has more than fifty years of service as a volunteer firefighter, so managing volunteers is another of his many skills. I had also been a manager in a previous life, with an emphasis on project management and human resources, and as with my partner, nearly two decades of volunteer experience in the fire service. We knew that we could form a volunteer restoration team and keep it operating.

The third member of the "Three Amigos," as we had been known when we were working in the archives at the Mighty Eighth, was my "Road Warrior" partner in Virginia, Marshall Brooks. Because Jim, Marshall, and I had worked together at the museum prior to the B-17 project, we were familiar with the museum, its operations, and the staff. Most of all, our previous experience impressed upon us the emotional and physical significance of what we were about to undertake to both the museum and the many living veterans of the Eighth Air Force who visited "their" museum. We discussed how we would begin recruiting volunteers to work on the project, and it was agreed that Marshall would be our Human Resources contact and would do a light screening of applicants. Jim would be the hands-on supervisor of all work on the airplane as the new volunteers came on board, and I would assume the role of coordinating all of the actions taking place with the museum. We were not sure what our job descriptions should say. We were not even sure to whom we reported in museum management. Fortunately, several wonderful museum staffers stepped up from within the confusion and provided guidance and support during those hectic first days in January. Brenda Elmgren and Sheila Saxon, Walt's administrative assistant, deserve medals for their help as we got started.

Within a week of the arrival of the airplane, and the news that we were losing Walt, events happened that would impact the restoration project for many years to come. The biggest event was the appointment by the executive committee of the museum's board of trustees of Henry Skipper as Walt's replacement. Meeting the new boss, as you are still figuring out what your job involves, makes for a dicey situation. None of us, not Henry Skipper, Jim, Marshall, nor I, knew what was expected from us as the Three Amigos moved from the archives to the Combat Gallery; and of course, Henry had no standard to measure us against in our new jobs.

Several days after Henry assumed the leadership role at the museum, we had worked out reasonable expectations for managing the project. My role and title, in Henry's eyes, were something of a shock to me, but one I welcomed. Walt had made it clear that he would personally direct the restoration and I would be his on-site "coordinator." Henry had a different idea. I would be the project manager for the entire restoration and report directly to him on all aspects of the project. I had, without asking for it, been promoted from first sergeant to company commander.

Regardless of what rank we would be holding, the Three Amigos were looking for help from somewhere so that we could get started. It didn't take very long for that help to arrive.

The media coverage of the arrival of the airplane was fantastic. All the Georgia and South Carolina TV stations and newspapers gave us excellent time and space. During that coverage, we mentioned that we were looking for volunteers. We didn't mention requirements. We were, at that point, looking for bodies who would show up. One of the first to contact the museum was retired physics professor, Milt Stombler, from Sun City, South Carolina.

Milt Stombler: *I first heard about the* City of Savannah *project on the TV news. I phoned the museum and asked how I could volunteer to be part of the restoration. They sent me an application, and after some delay, I was finally called and asked to come to the museum on a Wednesday morning. There were a small group of volunteers already working. They seemed like "can do" people and were all nice* *guys. I have been part of the organization ever since that day. The* City of Savannah *has been the most exciting part of my retirement.*

We also picked up two first-class retired military aircraft maintenance professionals: Rocky Rodriguez and Bill Liening. Both Rocky and Bill had moved to Savannah after their military careers to become instructors at the Flight Safety International School that supports Savannah's largest employer, Gulfstream Corporation. Bill is retired from the US Navy and Rocky from the USAF. Almost immediately we noticed the leadership and technical skills that these career NCOs exhibited. They both became (shift) crew chiefs and have been major contributors to the success of the project ever since.

Bill Liening: *I'm not quite sure how I found out that the museum had acquired a B-17 and was looking for volunteers (I think it was a newspaper article), but as soon as I did I went to the museum and dropped off my card. This was sometime in late January or early February, 2009. When I got to the museum, I asked if I could have a look at the aircraft. The lady at the front desk kindly allowed me into the Combat Gallery to have a look. As far as I knew, the aircraft had not been touched since it had been reassembled inside the museum. My first impression of the aircraft was "WOW, this thing needs a lot of work!" Instead of having second thoughts about volunteering, I couldn't wait to get started. I was soon contacted by Marshall Brooks. He e-mailed me the volunteer application and invited me to the museum for a talk. He was very interested in the fact that my father was a B-17 waist gunner/radio operator during WWII. It was Marshall who recommended that I be a crew chief (to this day everyone wonders why he did that). I started working on Saturdays cleaning (and cleaning and cleaning) the aircraft until we had a few more volunteers, at which point we started more shifts and I took over the Wednesday night crew.*

Rocky Rodriguez: *I first heard about the B-17* City of Savannah *from an article in the Savannah Morning News in January, 2009. There was no doubt that I was going to volunteer to restore this aircraft as I knew my thirty-seven-plus years of aircraft maintenance experience would be helpful. For many years I had worked in an USAF overhaul facility, rewiring and restoring damaged aircraft. I completed* *a volunteer form in February of 2009 and began volunteering with the Saturday crew. We were responsible for cleaning and polishing the aircraft exterior. Subsequently, as electrical systems and avionics are my specialty, I was asked to assume responsibility for restoring all the airplane's electrical systems to operable condition. I became the Saturday crew chief in early 2010, and my crew became the electrical crew.*

Rocky and Bill were not the only volunteers to immediately surface from the local aviation community; LMI Aerospace Corporation was well represented by one of their engineering managers, David Pinegar.

David Pinegar: *I was watching WTOC one morning when they had a story about a B-17 that was going to arrive at the Mighty Eighth that day to be restored, and that the museum was looking for volunteers to work on the restoration. The airplane was to be named the City of Savannah. The Company that I work for, LMI Aerospace Corporation, is only several miles away from the museum. LMI is very big on community involvement. I knew that we supported a local food bank and several other programs. I thought to myself that getting connected with the B-17 project would be an easy sell to both my plant manager and the corporate CEO, as it was a community volunteer project and aviation oriented. I talked to a fellow manager, John Calvert, and we planned to attend the arrival of the airplane later in the day.*

One of the first sub-projects in our unofficial overall plan to get started with the project was initiated by David. He talked with us about the poor condition of the fabric on the flight control areas of the airplane. He explained that he competes on a national level with remote control flying model aircraft and much of his model building involves the use of fabric construction. We were convinced that he knew what he was talking about. In retrospect, it was a major decision to let David take the ailerons, rudder, and horizontal stabilizers out of the museum so that he could set them up at the LMI facility and completely recover them with new fabric. It was also the beginning of a very important corporate relationship between LMI and the National Museum of the Mighty Eighth Air Force that would mature and grow over the years with David's initiative and direction. That decision paid off with significant positive results.

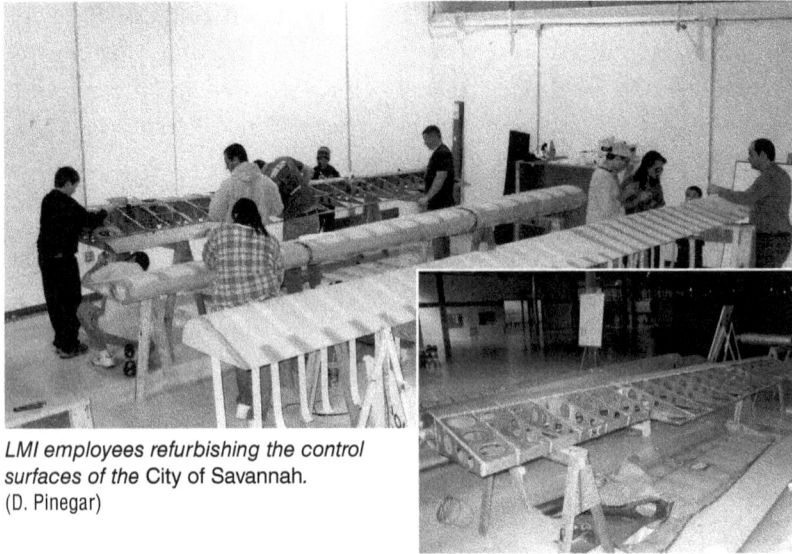

LMI employees refurbishing the control surfaces of the City of Savannah.
(D. Pinegar)

From the very beginning there has been a hard-core group of retired noncommissioned officers from the local Air National Guard's 165th Airlift wing involved in the project. The first to join our ranks was Bill Burkel.

Bill Burkel: *I started on the B-17 at the very beginning of the restoration. I saw on the news that the aircraft had arrived at the museum, and knew I had to be a part of its restoration. I had been working on the aircraft for a while when I went to one of the Wednesday morning SAFANG (Savannah Association of Flying Air National Guardsmen) quarterly breakfast meetings before coming to the museum and ran into Danny Harden. He asked me about the* City of Savannah *shirt I was wearing and I told him about the project and he asked if he could follow me to the museum after breakfast. He then became one of our valued restoration members. Joe Pritchard was at one of the breakfast meetings a few quarters later and asked the same question. He followed me to the museum and also joined the team.*

The volunteers began to assemble and an organization started taking shape. Our first official communication was sent out to the early volunteers on February 27, 2009, in the form of an e-mail written by Sheila Saxon, asking for everyone involved in the project to recruit friends with skills in carpentry, research, and writing. She explained that Marshall was organizing the various contacts that he had received and that we would be bringing everyone on board as soon as possible. She also included some history behind the project. With Sheila's letter, we began to feel as if we were becoming a real organization.

Sheila Saxon: *If you are receiving this e-mail you have volunteered to assist in the restoration of the B-17G* City of Savannah *here at the Mighty Eighth Air Force Museum. Our project is just getting started and we are contacting each of you to let you know how much we appreciate your interest in the project, and to explain our plans and expectations for the weeks and months to come.*

Many of you are probably asking, "When do I get to do my part?" The answer is to stand by. We have been overwhelmed with requests to help with the project, and we are contacting <u>everyone</u> *with a phone call to let you know that we have received your paperwork.*

This is a good time to explain how our project is organized: three senior volunteers head up the project team. Jerry McLaughlin is the overall Project Manager. Jerry reports to the museum CEO, Henry Skipper, and has full oversight on the project. Marshall Brooks has been tasked with managing all of the project's Human Resources matters. Marshall will make initial contact with you and then determine where your knowledge, skills, and abilities most closely fit the needs of the project. Airplane related skills such as working with sheet metal or electronics are not the only skills Marshall is looking for from our volunteers. He would like to hear from those of you who would be interested in doing research on our B-17, and others who might be interested in preparing literature related to the aircraft and the project. If any of you have woodworking skills we are planning some serious carpentry projects for exhibits that will surround the plane. Please let Marshall know if you have a special skill that we can apply to the project. The third member of the management team is Jim Grismer. Jim has the most important job in the entire project. He is the aircraft's Crew Chief. Nobody touches the aircraft without Jim's OK! He will be supervising all volunteer and contract work on the aircraft.

Thus far the project is still in the organization phase, with interior and exterior cleaning of the aircraft dominating the chores. A great deal of protective storage materials on the outside of the plane need to be removed before the surface can be buffed back to its original sheen. Some of you are already involved, and are doing a great job. If you have not heard from us yet, stand by, there is a lot of work to do, and we are going to do our best to get all of you involved.

Finally, a little history on our B-17: it rolled off of the assembly line in Long Beach, California, on May 20, 1945, as B-17G 44-83814. This was two weeks after the German surrender in Europe. The aircraft was immediately flown to a storage facility in Syracuse, New York. It eventually was moved to Arizona, where it stayed in storage until 1947, when it was given as a gift to a school district in North Dakota. It was purchased by an aircraft broker in 1951 and then began an active operational life in 1953 when it was sold to the Kenting Aviation Corporation of Toronto, Canada. Kenting used the aircraft mostly for aerial survey work. The next change in the aircraft's work life occurred in 1971, when it was sold by Kenting to Black Hills Aviation of Spearfish, South Dakota. Black Hills was a fire bomber operation and the aircraft spent the next ten years fighting fires throughout the western United States. Black Hills traded our B-17 to the National Air and Space Museum in 1981 for two surplus Navy P-2 Neptune patrol bombers. The aircraft was on display at the Air and Space facility at Davis-Monthan Air Force Base until 1984, when it was flown to Dulles Airport in Chantilly, Virginia, and placed in permanent storage. The word "permanent" was erased on January 5th of this year (2009) when our team arrived at the Dulles facility and signed a document transferring ownership to the Mighty Eighth. Now the aircraft is in our Combat Gallery, and we are glad to welcome you to the team that will restore the City of Savannah to its original combat configuration.

More to follow.

In many ways, Sheila's words officially got the restoration of the *City of Savannah* underway. Along with the LMI fabric replacement project, we began to identify other specific tasks that needed to be accomplished and the individuals to carry out those tasks. One very important volunteer trio was Ron Gunnells, Mort Glick, and Chuck Brisbin. Ron and his team began removing everything from within the airplane's fuselage that was not welded to the frame. They put together a book naming each part, with a matching number which was placed on the part itself with white tape. A room was set aside on the second floor of the museum so that the parts could be secured.

While Ron and company were working inside the aircraft, a large group of volunteers was working on the crud-covered exterior. In addition to the dirt and bird droppings that encrusted the airplane, we discovered some type of plastic protective material similar to today's bubble wrap. During the 25 years in the Virginia hangar, this material had adhered to the airplane and was very difficult to remove.

The exterior cleaning got started with a great deal of enthusiasm; and, as you would expect, the enthusiasm lasted for only several shifts until the cleaning became drudgery. Eventually, it was finished to the point that the initial layer of filth was gone and it was obvious that some serious cleaning techniques would be necessary in order to return the airplane to its natural gleaming aluminum shine. There was, however, a side benefit from the initial cleaning exercise: the volunteers began to bond as a group. At this point most of the volunteers did not realize that Rocky Rodriquez was a skilled aviation electrician or that Mort Glick was an aerospace engineer who had worked on the X-15. It was just a bunch of new friends taking the very first steps on restoring a WWII aircraft from our fathers' and grandfathers' generation of WWII veterans.

March also saw the very first organizational structure appear within the project. Two formal teams were organized for various

Joe DeNapoli cleaning the nose in the early weeks of the restoration. (CoS Archives)

JEB Harper and Scott Whitcher (on wing) work with fellow plank owner Bill Burkel, cleaning "Virginia Crud" from the fuselage. (CoS Archives)

cleaning details. Jim Argo from Gulfstream Corporation and Bill Liening from Flight Safety Corporation were appointed as crew chiefs. Both crews worked on Wednesday, with Jim leading the day team and Bill reporting in the late afternoon to supervise the evening crew. Jim Grismer remained as the overall chief of all the cleaning operations.

Jack Nilsen: *Starting out with a project of this magnitude can certainly be daunting. The overwhelming filth on the airplane goes a long way to explain the high turnover rate we experienced in the beginning. People came and went, but the Wednesday night crew began to come together, with the same guys showing up every week. The one thing we had in common was that we all came from the aviation industry. The removal of the silicon sealant on the top of the wings will always remain an unpleasant memory in my mind. That type of drudgery brought flashbacks to when I was restoring cars, so I was well aware of what had to be gone through before the fun part would begin. During the cleanup phase, we found some structural damage to the fuselage, which may have happened during shipment and required the replacement of two pieces of skin. We also removed the ice shields from both sides of the fuselage. I'll have to admit the metal work was a welcome respite from cleaning.*

Near the end of March, there was a phone call from a woman who introduced herself as Maurita Autry. Maurita's dad had been the last owner of our B-17 before it was traded to the Smithsonian in 1984.

Maurita Kolb-Autry: *I was visiting my parents in Alamogordo, NM, when my dad (Arnold Kolb) showed me the newspaper article about the B-17 en route to the Mighty Eighth, driven by a man who used to be a mechanic for us at Black Hills Aviation. When I read the article, I turned and said: "Dad, I wonder if the museum would like a copy of the video of the last flight you and Nathan took when you gave the aircraft to the Smithsonian, and the ceremony at Dulles?" Like the businessman he was all during his career, with me as his employee, he said, "Why don't you give them a call?" I immediately called the Mighty Eighth after locating the number on their website and Sheila Saxon answered the phone, asking what she could do for me. I told her that I thought I could do something for the Mighty Eighth, said I had just read the article about the acquisition from the Smithsonian, and wondered if the museum would like a video of the last flight and the ceremonial flyover before landing at Dulles, and speeches by dignitaries at the dedication. Sheila connected me with Jerry McLaughlin, and we eventually sent the Mighty Eighth a great deal of material about that B-17.*

So, there you have it. The first 90 days of the project ended on March 31, 2009. It had been quite a start to what would become more than six years of hard work with every kind of emotion that goes with a passionate undertaking. And this was just the beginning! We still didn't know what we didn't know; but we were learning. And, as we would learn to say on a regular basis . . . there was more to come.

CHAPTER 3

Taking It Apart

APRIL 2009 – DECEMBER 2010

"Tommy and I knew this was going to be a winning project. . . .
I have never regretted for a moment getting involved."

Dr. Harry Friedman

Jim Grismer arrived at the museum at 8:30 a.m. on April 15 with an industrial power washer in the back of his truck. He was met by a very excited crew of volunteers, and, by 9:00, the machine was attacking the gunk on our B-17—without a lot of success! While there was some progress, multiple volunteers worked the high-pressure water up and down on the landing gear and right wing until 8:00 p.m., but nobody was happy with the results. Years and years of crud on our "new" airplane was not going to depart without a fight.

Jim Grismer: The phrase "cleaning the airplane" implies an act akin to a car wash. The cleaning that we undertook in April of 2009 was something far more colossal. It took forty people a full year of very hard labor. We enlisted all nature of skills and devices to blast, grind, peel, scrape, brush, and flush away 64 years of foreign matter off of and out of the aircraft. A good deal of power washing and steam cleaning was successful in removing the material that had adhered to the airplane over the years, but much of the more difficult portions of crud under the wings had to be removed by hand.

After the failure of the power washer and discussion with Bruce Johnson, the museum's chief of maintenance, it was decided that the answer to our cleaning needs was not a power washer, but a more powerful machine, a steam cleaner, which could also be utilized by the museum in future cleaning chores. As our budget at this point was almost nonexistent, the museum purchased the machine, and we anxiously awaited its arrival.

Bill Liening: *I remember the volunteer turnover rate during this time was very high. Guys would come in once or twice and we would never see them again. I had to keep telling my crew to keep in mind the end product, a beautiful, shiny B-17. After a while, the hard-core guys that stuck it out would just tell me to shut up.*

While we were waiting for the steam machine that we believed would be the answer to our prayers, we received good news for both the museum and the *City of Savannah* team. Henry Skipper informed us that the museum was getting visitors at a record rate, a fact that the museum staff attributed to spring vacationers stopping by to see the museum's newest exhibit. The increased amount of visitors, however, created some awkwardness with regard to how the volunteers dealt with the public: the inquisitive visitors were constantly engaging the work crews in dialogue and cutting back on the amount of cleaning work that we were doing on the airplane.

In order to address the issue of providing goodwill discussions with visitors and also getting the job of cleaning the airplane done, a special recruitment request went out with Sheila Saxon's update to the volunteers on April 24.

Sheila Saxon: *Would you enjoy talking to the public about the "City" for three hours every Wednesday? We have immediate need for several volunteers from our pool of applicants to answer questions from the public as the Wednesday crew works on the aircraft. . . . The visitor population is increasing and many of them are asking questions of the volunteers, which, in turn, is delaying work on the aircraft.*

There was only one response to Sheila's plea for help; that came from yet another New Yorker, Dave Talleur. Dave was retired from a career in which he was both a corporate pilot and an aircraft maintenance supervisor—he knew a lot about airplanes! He was also the poster boy for extroverts. Dave was the perfect man for the job. He began his new job on April 30, 2009, and soon formalized his presence to the public by ditching his *City of Savannah* T-shirt and adding a set of mechanic's coveralls and patches from the Eighth Air

Dave Talleur interviewing a WWII veteran while wearing his "BS Guy" uniform. (CoS Archives)

Force and the museum. He was quickly dubbed "the BS guy" and took over the job of conversing with the public, leaving his comrades to devote their time to working on the airplane.

Attempting to clean the airplane during the month of April brought about concern from several of the volunteer aviation professionals that we needed to have a thorough corrosion inspection of the entire aircraft. Jim Argo was asked to conduct the inspection and let us know what work might be needed.

Jim Argo: *I was asked by Jim Grismer to go over the airplane from nose to tail and put together a report on what I thought were corrosion conditions that would have to be addressed early in the restoration. The first thing that I noted was several areas around the cockpit that would have to be worked on right away. There was more corrosion in the fuselage as I worked my way to the tail. I was worried that even though the airplane is indoors, the corrosion would get worse if it was not treated correctly. It was especially important for the final display of the aircraft, if the restoration was to be at the very high level that we were talking about. I inspected the fuselage through all 72 ribs and noted if they were clear or in need of work. Later I found more corrosion in the wings. We jumped on it with ACF-50—powerful stuff—and the immediate corrosion problem was under control.*

Early in April we received a request from the Eighth Air Force Historical Society's Birthplace Chapter to give its members an update on the plane's first 100 days under the museum's roof. We were more than happy to accommodate their request. Jim Grismer, Marshall Brooks, and I attended the society's April meeting to give a report on our adventures since we first heard about the gifting of the airplane to the Mighty Eighth at the December meeting only four months earlier. Jim spoke to the group first, explaining the plans for the restoration. Next, Marshall spoke about our adventures up in Virginia and about bringing the aircraft home to Pooler. Finally, we asked the group to adjourn to the Combat Gallery, next to the airplane, and I told them all that we knew about the history of our "new" airplane. There were many questions from the group and obvious excitement and pride that, after more than a decade of existence, the museum now had a B-17, the airplane that will always be associated with the Eighth Air Force in World War II, inside of the building.

Before the end of the month, the much-anticipated steam cleaner arrived. The first areas attacked with our new tool were the landing gear and the underside of the wings, areas that had seen little improvement with just hand cleaning or with the power washer. The big problem with the steam cleaner was how to deal with all the water it generated, which could easily flood the Combat Gallery. A very unique and strange-looking piece of equipment was invented by Jim and the Wednesday (Day) crew. It consisted of several commercial plastic covers, a half oil drum, and a dolly that was found in the museum shop. The contraption was moved around under the wings, engines, and fuselage as the steam cleaner attacked the grime on the airplane. Periodically, when the drum was near full, the steam cleaner would be shut down and the drum would be run outside the visitor's door of the gallery to be dumped in the garden's sewer system. Yes, a very strange operation, but it worked, and the underside of the aircraft and the landing gear began to look a lot better.

Jim Grismer: Eventually, our beloved contraption became more sophisticated with the addition of a submersible pump, which sped up the operation significantly. Several hundred feet of garden hose stretched from the pump to the museum's garden saved us countless hours.

"The contraption"—somehow it got the job done. (CoS Archives)

At the end of April, an event that started as a simple conversation with a parts dealer in Oregon became an iconic moment for the project. While reading a copy of *Air Classics* magazine, I had noticed an advertisement for a dealer who specialized in World War II military aircraft parts. I contacted the dealer, Don Keller, of Beaverton, Oregon, and introduced myself as the new project manager for the *City of Savannah* restoration. It wasn't long before I realized that I had made a very worthwhile call. Don was quite knowledgeable about the B-17 community and had me writing notes for almost 45 minutes. The most important part of our conversation was when Don told me it was imperative that I contact a man by the name of Harry Friedman in Memphis, Tennessee. Harry, Don told me, was the head of an informal group of B-17-related organizations throughout the United States and, in fact, had been the leader of the group that had rescued the most famous B-17 of them all, the *Memphis Belle.* Don gave me Dr. Friedman's e-mail address, and I immediately sent an e-mail:

Sent: Tuesday, April 28, 2009, 7:32 AM

Subject: Mighty Eighth Museum B-17

Dr. Friedman - my name is Jerry McLaughlin and I am the Project Manager for the restoration of the B-17 City of Savannah *at the Eighth Air Force Museum here in Pooler, Georgia.*

I was given your name and e-mail address by Don Keller. Don told me that you are involved with an association of owners/ restorers of B-17s, and that it might be to our benefit here at the museum to make contact with your association. We obtained our B-17G from the National Air and Space Museum three months ago, and are still in the very early stages of our restoration project. As the new guys on the block we are in the process of contacting as many B-17 related organizations as possible. Hoping to hear from you.

Jerry

Only several hours later, I received a reply from Dr. Friedman:

Hello Jerry. It's great to hear from you. I had been trying to find a point of contact for your restoration. We would welcome you and your group into the B-17 Co-Op. At present, I am planning the fall meeting. We are a group of B-17 owners, restorers, and current pilots and crew of the B-17. We have no dues or officers and have no official standing. We get together once a year to tour and discuss items of mutual interest both to the restoration and to the flying community. Re your a/c, we saw it several years ago at one of our meetings held at NASM. It was in pretty rough shape then so I can imagine what a job that you have on your hands at present. I'm getting ready to go into surgery but when I finish later today, I'll give you a call.

Regards,
Harry
Harry Friedman, M.D.
Memphis Belle Memorial Association, Inc.
Memphis, Tennessee

Harry was not kidding about contacting me, and called the same night. We talked for a very long time, and after our conversation, I began to see just a small crack in what I "didn't know" about my new job. The next morning I replied:

Harry - I can't thank you enough for your quick response to my e-mail and our great conversation last night. It was a relief to talk to someone who clearly appreciated my situation here on our project. Your multiple offers of assistance made my day. We are firmly committed to creating a first class restoration and look forward to seeing what the other B-17 groups in the country are doing with their projects. I anticipate more conversations and sharing of information in the months (years?) to come. Again, thanks for the quick response and the offers of assistance. I have informed the museum CEO that the Mighty Eighth is now an official member of an un-official organization of B-17 groups.

I will definitely be in touch. Jerry

If there was one event, one friend gained, that could be rated as the biggest event in the *City of Savannah* project, contacting Harry Friedman was that one event. I am sure that we would have connected eventually, but Don Keller's suggestion got things going sooner, rather than later, and, as you will see on the following pages, the good Dr. Friedman and his band of brothers began to play a major role in our work.

The month of April had been quite a leap forward for our still very young project.

The beginning of May, the fifth month of our efforts, saw cleaning chores expand from scraping the fuselage to cleaning years of petroleum-based debris from the airplane's engines. We took the cowlings off of the #1 and #2 engines and began using the newly

Jim Argo, JEB Harper, and Jim Grismer, discussing cleaning the engines and underside of the wings. (CoS Archives)

arrived museum steam cleaner on the exposed power plants. The work area was tented and as the power of the steam hit the engines, years of debris fell into Jim Grismer's catch-all "contraption." The #3 and #4 engines now had to undergo the same procedures. The second set of engines was cleaned at a much more rapid pace. At this point, Jim declared victory and announced that the engines were as clean as they were ever going to be on his watch, and the engine cleaning project was officially declared as completed!

Bill Burkel: *I remember looking at the aircraft with all the tape, Spraylat, Cosmoline, fire retardant, and other gunk that was on it and thinking this was going to be quite a job. We had a big learning curve as to what we had to use to get all the crud off the plane. But with cleaners, paint strippers, steam cleaning, wire brushes, and other methods, we finally got down to the aluminum skin of the aircraft. It seemed like we spent as much time mopping up our mess on the floor as we did cleaning on the B-17.*

It was about this time when we realized that we were accumulating some very interesting pictures and aircraft-related pieces that might be of interest to the museum visitors. As the organization we were creating always seemed to step up to any challenge, in this case it was Scott Whitcher, a multi-talented volunteer who happened to have strong carpentry skills on his résumé. Scott built two exhibit cases mounted on wheels. We dedicated one exhibit case to materials from the original *City of Savannah* and crew and the second to our airplane, and filled them with pictures and artifacts. While the pictures and artifacts have changed over the years, the exhibit cases remain next to the aircraft, and will be for the foreseeable future.

Scott Whitcher: *Jerry McLaughlin, the restoration's project manager came to me with a request to build a couple of display cases which would be used to hold articles relating to the project. He had seen a case at a display in Delaware and provided a photo to use as an example for our cases. I was able to come up with a design that was approved and built two display cases that resembled shipping cases that may have been used during the war period. Museum-quality acrylic tops were manufactured by Walter Sheridan of Sheridan Design, Charleston S.C., and attached to the top of the cases.*

Our next big event was the arrival of some serious polishing professionals who came to the museum to take over from the amateurs and make the *City of Savannah* look like she had just come off the assembly line. Steve Ward, who had visited the museum previously and asked how he could get involved, was employed at the time as a supervisor at International Aerospace Services, a company that just happens to polish airplanes as its main line of business. When Steve saw what we were doing on the *City of Savannah* he told us to "get the crud off of it and then I'll bring in my guys."

As the museum opened on May 27, Steve's crew arrived with the necessary polishing equipment in hand. Steve had arranged for a local tool rental company, NES rentals, to supply three air compressors to run his equipment. Something can be said for the hard work that our volunteers had done working on the airplane, but nothing was going to match Steve's crew with their compressor-driven equipment. The International Aerospace Services team was at the museum for two days, and when they left, you can be sure that 44-83814 had not looked better in 70 years! WTOC-TV came out on the second day to video the final result, and JEB Harper and Jim Argo got interviewed for the evening news. Our first media darlings!

Steve Ward (third from right) with the International Aerospace Services professionals who were finally able to clean the aircraft surface to its 1945 shine. (CoS Archives)

Symposium artists gathered around the nose of the City of Savannah. (CoS Archives)

Steve soon joined us as a full-time volunteer and worked with us for over a year until transferring out of Savannah for a new job, after a very "bright" tenure with the project.

June was a big month for the airplane on the public relations front. The first of two events was a gathering of the American Society of Aviation Artists at the Mighty Eighth, sponsored by Gulfstream Corporation. The two prominent leaders of the symposium were the internationally renowned artists Keith Ferris and Gil Cohen. The artists spent two three-hour shifts sitting around the *City of Savannah* while the volunteers worked cleaning the fuselage and became, as they were referring to themselves, "models" for the artists participating in the symposium.

Some of the artists were working with pencils, others charcoal; still others were painting. When the symposium was completed, several of the artists presented their work

Artist Priscilla Patterson presented Jim Grismer with her pencil drawing of Jim cleaning debris from the side of the aircraft. (Jim Grismer)

to the volunteers they had used as subjects, but alas, not a single modeling contract was offered.

It was during the visit of the artists to the museum that we first began to think about how we would paint the nose of the airplane to match the nose of the original *City of Savannah*. We discussed using a local artist, or art students, and finally decided that we would do some research and find someone with appropriate aviation credentials to do our work. Frankly, we never had any idea how lucky we would be in achieving this goal; more on this story further down the road.

The second national event involving the *City of Savannah* project in June of 2009 was the publication of an article in the magazine *Warbirds International*. I have been a subscriber to Challenge Publications' warbird magazine, *Air Classics*, since 1972 and thought I would take a shot at sending them an article about our early adventures with 44-83814. I took my e-mails and notes, along with a few pictures, and put together a story about moving the airplane from Virginia to Georgia. I sent the package off to California with little hope that there would be any result, and only a week later I was notified that my article would be published in Challenge Publications' *other* magazine, *Warbirds International*. Who knew? The article was our first national exposure and brought several inquiries via telephone and e-mail. The effort had paid off.

June also saw us starting to realize that while everyone had ideas about what we should do to organize our project, it was necessary to formulate an official plan that could be submitted to museum management who could, in turn, bring the document to the board

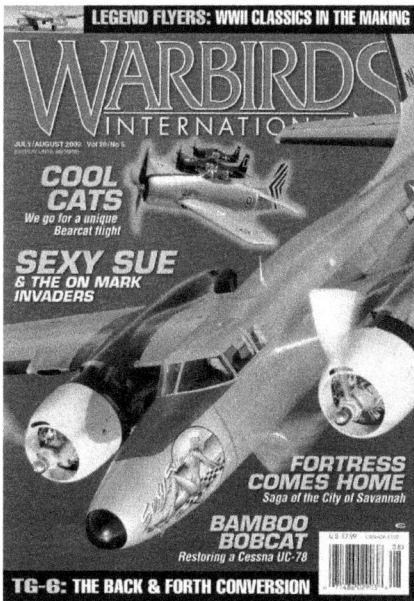

Cover of the July/August 2009 edition of Warbirds International. City of Savannah's *first national media coverage.* (Challenge Publications)

of trustees for comment and approval. All of the volunteers were asked to contribute. Despite a good amount of executive experience in previous lives by several of the volunteers, not one had any experience in preparing a plan for restoring an airplane. Examples of plans were checked on the Internet, and finally a document, which we billed as our Strategic Plan, began to come together. After several weeks of writing, rewriting, and asking both volunteers and friends with business experience to review our work, Jim Grismer and I submitted the plan to Henry Skipper on July 15. In retrospect, I believe that the plan was more of a *tactical* than a *strategic* plan, but it worked! Henry approved the plan and we began to organize teams with specific assignments to multiple sub-projects.

Thus, at the end of the first six months of work on the *City of Savannah* project, we had assembled a group of good people and we had a plan. We were on our way!

The assignments that evolved from the Strategic Plan had various degrees of difficulty. The four teams of volunteers were led by Bill Burkel, Wednesday (Day), Bill Liening, Wednesday (Night), Ron Gunnells (Friday) and JEB Harper (Saturday). The volunteers on the four crews all agreed that the very worst assignment during this period was removing the accumulated crud that built up over

First City of Savannah *Annual Group Photo (July 24, 2009).*
Front Row: *Bob Brunn, Tyson Morrison, Bill Burkel, Danny Harden, Dave Talleur*
Row 2: *Ben Ridgdill, Jack Nilsen, Tonnie and Mort Glick, Author, Scott Whitcher, JEB Harper, Henry Skipper.* **Row 3:** *Dave Pinegar, Jim Grismer, Bill Liening, Ken Rombouts, Joe DeNapoli, Bruce Johnson, Steve Ward* (CoS Archives)

the years on the underside of both wings, mostly between the engines. All four crews were involved and nobody was happy.

Paul Abare: I can say it was a lot of work upside down on the underside of the wings stripping the crud and other material one layer at a time. The chemicals were very strong, but not as strong as the crud. It took many days to get it all off.

Milt Stombler: Who can forget the thrill of paint stripper running down your arm as we worked on the bottom of the wings? As we labored on the wings, I remember that our motto was "do no harm to the airplane" as we tried one method after another to get the crud off. We slowly became more aggressive as we learned more about what we were dealing with and the proper tools and chemicals that we needed. Near the end we used wire brushes and Scotch-Brite abrasive pads that mounted on power drills. We had to keep ordering the pads by the case.

Joel Hedgpeth: I came on board when the main chore was cleaning the underside of the wing around #3 and #4 engines. What a mess. All that Jasco paint stripper burned my skin but had minimal effect on the wing. I think it must have taken two months just to get that one piece of wing cleaned.

Early in August, we received our first official visitor from the national B-17 community. Thanks to the efforts of Dr. Harry

Joe Pritchard, Mike Callahan, and Danny Harden working on the right wingtip.
(CoS Archives)

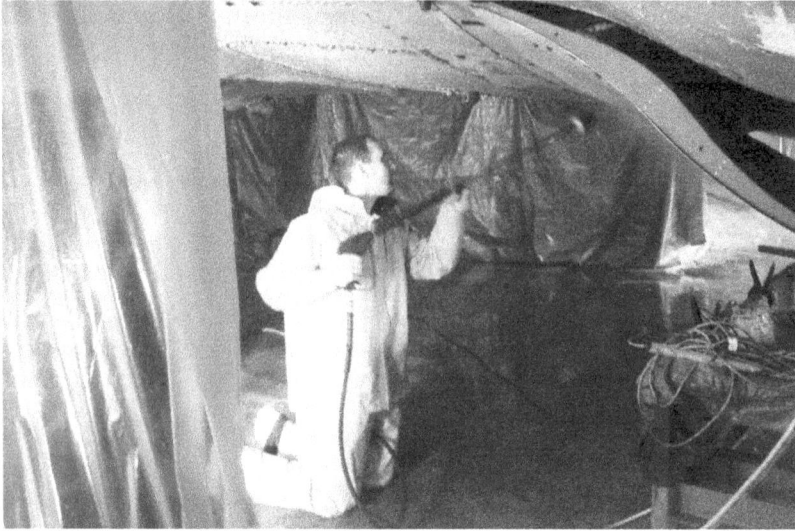

Greg Braselton mounts a crud attack. (CoS Archives)

Friedman, our visitor arriving from New Smyrna Beach, Florida, was Gary Norville, owner of a company by the name of American Aero Services (AAS). Gary is one of the premier B-17 maintenance managers in the United States. His company works with the Collings Foundation and does annual maintenance work on the Foundation's several flying WWII aircraft, including the B-17 *909*.

Gary met with the management team to learn where we were—not very far—and then climbed into the airplane and did a nose to tail inspection of both the interior and exterior of the *City of Savannah*. When he was finished with his inspection and we sat down with him again, he had suggestions for work on each interior compartment and for the repair of some exterior damage that had occurred during the trip from Virginia. His most important comments regarded corrosion issues throughout the aircraft. He also suggested we remove the bomb bay doors for a special cleaning due to the amount of residue accumulated during the aircraft's time as a fire fighting bomber in the 1970s. The several hours spent with Gary were very important to us in that he was generally impressed with the condition of the aircraft, a comparison that we were not qualified to determine, and his professional advice would guide us as we continued to prepare our B-17 for its restoration.

Jack Nilsen, Bill Burkel, Gary Norville, Mort Glick, Bill Liening and JEB Harper during Gary's inspection of the airplane. (CoS Archives)

Shortly after Gary's visit, Henry Skipper told me that he had been invited to speak to the Eighth Air Force Historical Society at their annual meeting in Cincinnati, Ohio, in late August, and that he would like me to attend the meeting with him and address the society on the early progress of our project. I could hardly say no! As a bonus the two of us would take a day trip and visit the National Museum of the Air Force at Wright-Patterson Air Force Base in Dayton.

The presentation to the Historical Society was well received. Walt Brown was able to attend and I spoke with him—for the last time. The next morning Henry and I left for Wright-Patterson where we met with General Charles Metcalf, the director of the Museum of the United States Air Force, and Roger Deere, the curator of restoration. Roger was a wonderful host, and we were given the grand tour of the museum's superb restoration shop and spent a great deal of time watching the museum team working on the most famous B-17 of them all, the *Memphis Belle.*

Little did I know that inspecting the work on the *Belle* would lead to a very embarrassing episode for me when we returned to Pooler. I noticed that one of the workers was using an amazing spray cleaning device that when run over the very old metal of the airplane gave the old metal a bright, new-looking sheen. When the worker stopped to look over his progress, I got his attention and

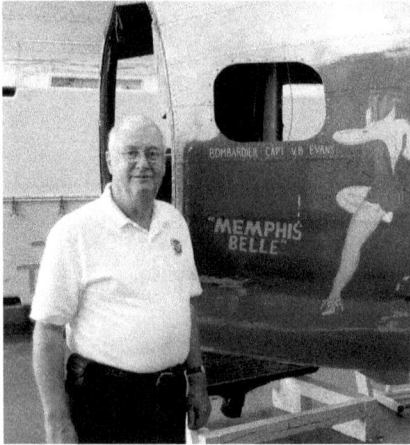

Visiting the Memphis Belle *at the National Museum of the United States Air Force.* (Author photo)

asked what the machine was called and how it worked. He was more than happy to praise the Cold Jet dry ice cleaner and explained to me that the machine had been rented from the manufacturer and was amazing in its ability to bring metal back to its original newly manufactured sheen. I was, unfortunately, very impressed. More to come on the now infamous Cold Jet technology later in our story.

Shortly after our return from Ohio, we had some important out-of-town visitors arrive to check out what we were doing on the project and offer help and advice for the future. The first visitor was Dr. Harry Friedman, the aforementioned leader of the National B-17 Co-Op. Harry served in various leadership positions for many years with the Memphis Belle Memorial Association in Memphis before the *Belle* was turned over to the National Museum of the United States Air Force for its final restoration. His traveling partner for this trip was Doug Birkey, the Co-Op's Washington Connection. Doug is on the staff of the Air Force Association in Washington, DC, having joined that body after serving for several years as a Congressional staffer. Prior to his white-collar positions he had earned his B-17 credentials flying as a crew member on the Collings Foundation's B-17, *909*. We were in pretty fast company when these two gentlemen showed up.

Harry Friedman: In 2008, rumors circulated that the Kolb B-17 that we had last seen in the Smithsonian hangar in 1986 might go to the National Museum of the Mighty Eighth Air Force in Pooler, Georgia. Several of us, including Tommy Garcia and Buck Rigg of the Barksdale Air Force Base Museum, wondered how the Mighty Eighth would be able to take on the challenge of restoring the aircraft. Tommy and I were wondering whether or not we should offer to inject ourselves into the project, when on 28 April 2009, I received an e-mail from

Dr. Harry Friedman. (CoS Archives)

Jerry McLaughlin, the Mighty Eighth's designated project manager for the restoration. Jerry told me he was looking for help and asked if the B-17 Co-Op would provide guidance on the restoration. He had learned about us through an aircraft parts vendor in Oregon. I responded that I would be more than happy to do so and called him that day to discuss the project further. This resulted in a visit by Doug Birkey and me to Pooler at which time we forged a personal commitment to helping out in this project. Tommy had planned on making the trip with us but had to cancel at the last minute. What impressed me was the intensity of purpose and enthusiasm of Jerry and his group. What they lacked in technical knowledge was quickly overcome by teamwork. It almost became an obsession with them to learn and perform. I told Tommy I knew this was going to be a winning project and that we were going to have fun helping the museum and preserving history. From the very first day I have enjoyed working with the City of Savannah *team.*

The visit from Harry and Doug was a giant step for us in that when they left, Jim, Marshall, and I finally felt as if we had, as Jim put it, "adult supervision." These were people who actually had done what we were just starting to learn. They were friendly while remaining professional, and they obviously were very interested in helping us in any way that they could, without telling us to do it their way. We would have been even more impressed with the visiting group had the third member of the trio, Tommy Garcia, not had to cancel his trip at the last minute. When Tommy heard from Harry and Doug that we were open to outside help (and needed plenty of it), he called and made arrangements for a visit to Pooler to see for himself what was going on at the Mighty Eighth.

Tommy is the hands-on guy of the Friedman, Birkey, Garcia trio, and in the years to come, he would spend many hours literally crawling around our airplane helping to instruct and solve problems. He would visit us in week-long working marathons, often bringing Karen, his wonderful wife, who, thank goodness, took a strong liking to the actual city of Savannah, not the airplane! When Tommy came into town it was called "Garcia Week" and everyone who could make time to participate spent as much of that week at the museum as possible.

Tommy Garcia: I first heard about the Smithsonian's B-17, 44-83814, going to the National Museum of the Mighty Eighth Air Force in Georgia from my longtime friend, and fellow B-17 Co-Op partner, Dr. Harry Friedman. Harry called me and said that the airplane had been awarded to the Mighty Eighth and would be moved there in January of 2009. We had no idea who might be in charge of the operation. Doc said he would do some research and find out what he could. I wondered how the museum planned on conducting the restoration, with staff or volunteers, or both? Most restoration projects begin with high expectations, but lose their staying power because of a lack of commitment. Would the museum team have that commitment? Personally, I was wondering if they would be open to talking with some of us that had experience in this field? Many new restoration projects do not accept offers of assistance because they feel that accepting such help is a sign of weakness on their part. I hoped that between Harry and me we could connect with the Savannah team and that they would be open to having us work with them.

Tommy Garcia. (CoS Archives)

I knew that the Savannah area had to have a good pool of aviation professionals available because of the presence of Gulfstream Corporation and military aviation, and I couldn't help but hope that the restoration team came from this group of people and that they had some type of organized plan for how they would conduct the restoration. The most important question on my mind would take a while to answer: Did the group have staying power – a strong level of commitment?

I also wondered if, despite what Harry had said, they would accept me to work with the project the way that I would like—getting my hands dirty—and if they would listen if I offered my opinions? My hope was that I could steer them in directions that I knew had been successful in the past, and away from what I knew to be bad practices with a start-up restoration.

Tommy had his concerns about what he would find when he visited the Mighty Eighth, but those concerns were put out of the way almost from the moment of his arrival. I was out of town when Tommy made his first visit, but Jim Grismer and Marshall Brooks could not have been better hosts. The three of us had a meeting before Tommy's visit and discussed that all we knew about this new visitor was what Harry and Doug had told us: "He knows more about B-17s than anybody we know." Now that's a strong recommendation! While Tommy was wondering if we would accept him, we were plotting to kidnap him, if necessary, to make him as involved in our project as humanly possible. He later told us that many new organizations are reluctant to accept outside help. We laughed and told him about our first motto: "We don't know what we don't know!" We were more than ready to bring in outside expertise; and based on our very positive opinion of our first visitors, Harry and Doug, and their recommendation for Tommy, he was in the club before he ever arrived in Pooler.

Tommy Garcia: *Returning home from my first visit to Georgia, I evaluated my visit and decided that this was a team of people I could work with, and even more important, that they were very open to help from those of us who had been restoring B-17s for many years. My fear that they would not be willing to accept outside help was never an issue. They were very interested in what I had to say, and their unexpected offer to pay my expenses on any return trips meant that I would be part of their project in the future. I did have several questions in my mind: Will my relationship with this new team allow me to leave a part of my spirit with this aircraft? How can I make them understand that part of what they are about to undertake is adding a soul to the machine? (Many, many of the men I met early on in* *my B-17 restoration days told me that if you cannot add a soul to the machine you have not done your job right.) Savannah has a very strong aviation community, the center of which is a local Gulfstream manufacturing facility. Thinking about the people I had met, I realized that the new restoration team had a good core of people with aviation backgrounds. The question was, will the rest of the group listen to the aviation professionals and can the professionals lead the rest of the group? My most important feeling was that they appeared to be serious about making their B-17 a real showpiece, honoring the Eighth Air Force.*

I was also glad to see that they were legally obligated to create a static display that would remain in the museum forever. The B-17 community, in my opinion, needs more static displays that put major effort into restoring the interior of the aircraft—effort that is not possible when all the cash and effort has to be expended in assuring airworthiness.

Now it is time to come back to the Cold Jet dry ice blaster story. As you remember, I was much impressed with the results I saw of the machine rejuvenating the metal of the fuselage of the *Memphis Belle*, and I was quick to point out that performance to Henry before we left the Air Force restoration facility. On the trip home we discussed at length the possibility of renting one of the Cold Jet machines for use on the *City of Savannah* in areas that still had crud problems, such as the underside of the wings and the bomb bay. The endeavor would be costly. In addition to the rental fee for the machine, there was the cost of the dry ice that the machine used to do the cleaning and, additionally, the machine required a large compressor to supply the force needed to spray the ice pellets. Henry listened to my plea and finally agreed that the possibilities of what the machine might accomplish on the airplane were worth the investment.

Contact with Cold Jet corporate management brought some unexpected good news. The company would provide a machine at no charge if they could use their involvement with our program for marketing purposes. Things were really looking up. The machine arrived with a company representative to instruct us how to operate the machine and, after several hours of instruction, the volunteers began to attack the *City of Savannah* gunk and sludge with a vengeance. The results were not what we expected! The *Memphis Belle* metal I had watched shine from the ice pellets had not been covered with the gunk that was everywhere on the *City of Savannah*. Then the final catastrophe came! After a frustrating day trying to clean the area beneath the wings and the interior of the aircraft, several of the volunteers decided to enhance the power of the system by disconnecting the governor on the compressor. "Now," they reasoned, "we'll really get some cleaning done." They attacked the gunk with the ungoverned Cold Jet machine and were very pleased with the results. Very pleased! They commented to each other as to what an amazing job the machine was finally doing cleaning the filth from the airplane! Their happiness was short lived. Museum staff came running into the Combat Gallery screaming for them to shut down the machine. The gunk that the dry ice was blasting off the airplane was leaving the airplane looking like new, but the flying gunk was entering the museum's air conditioning system. By the time the shouting staff members arrived in the Combat Gallery, there was not a flat space in the building that was not covered with a very slight, but rising, layer of black gunk that originated from our airplane. The Cold Jet dry ice machine, renamed "McLaughlin's Folly," was never seen again.

As the year came to a close, I was working on an end-of-year progress report for museum management when Marshall Brooks brought me some news that would have a great deal of influence upon the project—we would be meeting in several days with a gentleman by the name of Bob Mikesh. Bob literally wrote the book on how to restore airplanes (*Restoring Museum Aircraft*, Airlife, 1997) when he was the senior curator for Aeronautics at the National Air and Space Museum. Several unique circumstances brought Bob to the NMMEAF. First, he was a boyhood friend of Marshall's, and second, he had actually negotiated the trade for 44-83814 between the NASM and Arnold Kolb that had brought our B-17 from Arizona to the freezing cold hangar in Chantilly, Virginia.

Bob was very interested in what was happening to the B-17 he had worked so hard to obtain for the NASM. He stopped in Pooler on his way to Florida at Marshall's request. Saying that Bob's visit had a major effect on how we would conduct our restoration would be an understatement. Over dinner at a restaurant near the museum, Bob shared with Marshall and me a two-hour synopsis of his book, and a great deal of personal advice regarding conducting an aircraft restoration. I took several pages of notes, which boiled down into the four factors that Bob said determine if an aircraft restoration project succeeds or fails:

1. The airplane should be indoors. Volunteers do not show up when the weather is hot, cold, raining, and so forth.

2. A system of stable and firm management needs to be established from the very beginning of the project. A chain of command, hopefully a short chain, must be established and filled with individuals who have the respect of the participants.

3. There must be a process to raise money. Unless the project leaders are immensely wealthy, and willing to part with their fortune, an income flow, through donations or gifts, must be established; and

4. Local resources need to be available and recruited. These resources must have the requisite knowledge, skills and abilities to perform the technical requirements in support of the restoration.

The dinner with Bob was an evening I will never forget. It is not often that you get to sit down with an acknowledged world-class expert in an area in which you are just learning the ropes. Further, Bob is a fine gentleman to share a meal with, and he very much wished that his boyhood friend, Marshall, and the other volunteers working on the *City of Savannah* project, would be successful in the restoration of the B-17 that was part of his past with the Smithsonian. It was quite an evening.

As I drove home that evening I thought about how we matched up against Bob's make or break factors for a successful restoration:

1. The *City of Savannah* was indoors.

2. The management chain of command seemed to meet his requirement for being "stable."

3. The museum's fund-raising system was established and had been working successfully for years; and

4. The Savannah community is blessed with an abundance of aviation community organizations, ranging from Gulfstream Corporation and its many subcontractors to multiple military aviation units.

I felt very good about what Bob had stated and what I knew about how we matched up to his four principles for success. We were starting to graduate from "We don't know what we don't know," to learning how to function within a system we were developing and that we hoped would lead us to a successful restoration of the *City of Savannah*. Not a bad report card for our first year on the job!

2010

When we came back to work in January, we got some sad news when Sheila Saxon announced she was leaving the museum for a job closer to home. Her last assignment with us was to organize a dinner for all the volunteers on the 15th of January, celebrating the first anniversary of the arrival of the airplane.

Henry Skipper was the master of ceremonies at the dinner and thanked the volunteers for all their work and their families for all the time they spent away from home working on the airplane. He announced that the group had volunteered 3,391 hours during the first year of the project and that ten of the volunteers had contributed over 100 hours. At the end of the dinner, I asked Sheila to come to the front of the room where I thanked her for everything she had done for us and presented her with a bouquet of flowers, and the group gave her a major round of applause.

Following the dinner, it was time to start the second year of operation on our airplane. LMI Corporation started off the year with yet another contribution; this time their donation was not time and expertise, but hardware. Surplus workbenches were delivered to the museum, and the *City of Savannah*'s designated shop area, adjacent to the Combat Gallery where the airplane stood, began to look like a legitimate working shop. We also began to form something of an organizational structure with the appointment of Dave Talleur as the deputy project manager. As the technical nature of the actual restoration work was becoming more apparent, it was essential that a decision maker with aviation expertise become part

The Three Amigos and their first girlfriend, Sheila Saxon. (CoS Archives)

of the management team. Dave's background as both a pilot and a maintenance manager was the correct résumé. We let his new job evolve as the restoration developed, and his interaction with our contractors would later have significant impact upon our success.

It was also in January that Harry Friedman passed on another small gem of an idea that would have a large impact on the project. When I told him that the museum archives had a large amount of WWII radio equipment, but that we could not find anyone who had knowledge of what the equipment was, he suggested I contact the local HAM operator club and ask for some help. I did make the contact, and as Harry had predicted, big-time help arrived almost immediately! I was first contacted by Guy McDonald, a USAF veteran, an electrical engineer by trade, and most important to us, the president of the Coastal Amateur Radio Society (CARS). Guy and Mac McCormick, another CARS member, came out to the museum and met with us to discuss the equipment from the museum archives and, we hoped, to become involved with the restoration of the radio room. We were not disappointed! Guy arranged for the CARS' March meeting to be held at the museum, and I was asked to speak to the group about our project. After the meeting the group visited the Combat Gallery where Bill Liening had prepared the airplane for a tour by using ladders that would allow the visitors to actually view the radio room. Before the evening was over, the CARS members were on board with the *City of Savannah* project and have been ever since. A group of CARS members officially filled out project application forms and became our radio team, with Guy as their chief.

Guy McDonald: (*E-mail to his colleagues in the Coastal Area Radio Society*) *We have a very unique opportunity to contribute to the restoration of a piece of American history. We were contacted about our interest in helping restore the radio compartment of the B-17 that is currently undergoing a thorough restoration at the National Museum of the Mighty Eighth Air Force here in Savannah. Wow, of course we are interested. On January 20th Mac-KF4LMT and Guy-K4GTM went over to the museum and met with Jerry McLaughlin who is the Project Manager of the restoration. Jerry and Marshall Brooks took us into the aircraft, where we had a good look at the radio compartment. Afterwards we went into the artifacts room to check out all of the radio equipment and associated gear. What a treasure! We then spent some time with Jerry and Marshall discussing how we might be able to contribute to this effort. Some of the next steps will be to research what exactly should be in the compartment, determine the feasibility of making some of the radio gear operational, helping the museum to acquire any missing equipment, and, of course, installing the equipment in the radio room. Whew, lots to do. This should be an extremely rewarding project. Stay tuned for more information.*

While the volunteer work crews continued to work on the challenges of restoring the airplane, there were several events taking place that would significantly enhance the future of the restoration. The first was the arrival of Jane Grismer (Jim's daughter) as Sheila Saxon's replacement. Jane jumped into her new job with the enthusiasm you would expect from one of the Grismer clan, and almost immediately came up with an idea that would become institutionalized and bring considerable financial support to the project and the museum itself over the years to come: the annual Flying Fortress 5K Run and Walk. More to follow on this subject.

It was at this point in the project that we brought on board a most unexpected volunteer, Brigadier General Jeffrey Phillips, from the 3rd Infantry Division at nearby Fort Stewart. "General Jeff," as he became known, was a lifelong fan of B-17 bombers and the son of a WWII C-47 pilot. Jeff would work with us, getting dirty and

Our own "General Jeff" Phillips. (Jeff Phillips)

enjoying the camaraderie of the group, for almost a year, until his assignment at Ft. Stewart ended. After leaving, he stayed in touch, visited on several occasions, and turned out in uniform, sporting his second star, when the airplane was dedicated in 2015.

June of 2010 was also the first time that I was asked to address the board of trustees with regard to the project. I had made similar presentations to management groups back in the days when I worked for a living, but never on a subject in which I could still be considered a trainee. My philosophy was that while I was still learning, nobody in the room knew more than I did. The presentation went well and I breathed a sigh of relief as the board members gave strong support and congratulations on what had been accomplished in the first 18 months of the project.

The most significant issue we were facing in the summer of 2010 was what to do with the interior of the airplane. We realized that we would not be able to restore the fuselage interior to the bare metal look that we had been able to achieve on the exterior. It was finally decided that we would paint the interior of the aircraft in good old Army olive drab. We also knew that before we could begin the interior painting, there were two major chores that needed to be accomplished: a strong attack on the bomb bay, which contained enormous amounts of crud left over from the days when fire-fighting slurry was released from that compartment; and addressing many corrosion issues within almost every area of the aircraft. We thought we had solved the corrosion issue in 2009, but we were wrong. Gary Norville returned for a second visit to discuss our corrosion plans and helped a great deal with technical issues we were facing. Once again, we had a plan.

Cleaning the bomb bay was easier said than done. The crud, however, was not as bad as under the wings, and with the help of the steam cleaner and Jim's water-catching contraption, the Wednesday crew was able to finish the project in only several shifts.

Jim Grismer: Much has been said about the crud, the nature of which called for serious action to implement its removal, namely steam cleaning. In short order we realized that these methods created an ocean of water that we had to contain. Thus, we always had an army of squeegee men and wet-vac operators attempting to stay ahead of the tide of water. We designed a 300-gallon mobile trough to sit beneath the bomb bay doors and catch the bulk of the mess that flowed out during the cleaning. Most of us threw away the clothing we wore during this task.

Joel Hedgpeth: During the steam cleaning of the interior of the airplane, particularly the bomb bay, we had to wear rain gear, and there was a bucket brigade draining the crazy big blue drain pan in the museum storm drains. Later, I spent many, many shifts curled up in the area aft of the tail wheel trying to get the crud out of that small space.

The corrosion issue was a much more profound and sophisticated operation than the crud in the bomb bay. It was formally attacked, after a great deal of preparation, on the last day of June with what was advertised as a "maximum effort," an often-utilized expression with the Eighth Air Force in WWII. The all-day affair to apply an anti-corrosion agent, known as Cortec VpCI-427, throughout the interior of the aircraft began at 9:00 a.m. and was not completed until 7:00 p.m. that evening.

The group that showed up at 9:00 consisted of members of all four crews. Jim gave an in-depth briefing on the VpCI-427, addressing how it needed to be applied, and the safety measures that all involved would need to carefully observe. It was finally determined that two crews could, in fact, work at the same time in separate compartments within the airplane. A third team was stationed beneath the aircraft to catch the run-off after the 427 was applied. After application it was wiped from the metal interior which was then washed to remove any remaining chemicals. This method worked

Morning crew before attacking the interior of the aircraft with anti-corrosion material.
(CoS Archives)

well through the morning. Lunch was provided by the museum and refreshments were available all day for the volunteers. Mid-afternoon, more volunteers arrived to relieve the morning crew, and when a dinner break was declared, the evening crew ate a museum-supplied pizza dinner. Following dinner, the area surrounding the tail wheel was cleaned, and the day was declared a victory. It was truly a total day of dedication by the entire volunteer crew.

Even though we had made the decision that we would paint the inside of the airplane and had done so much preparatory work, we had not as yet determined just how we would do the painting. We came up against many issues. Our first concern was the memory of our environmental trauma over the Cold Jet machine. How could we use the appropriate spray method of painting the interior and not have the paint enter the museum air conditioning? How could we seal the airplane for the painting and not inhale all the paint ourselves? Could we do the painting with spray cans? Could we do the painting with plastic brushes? There was a great deal of hand wringing and no good answers. And then, as would seem to occur whenever we faced major problems, one of our original volunteers, Jim Argo, a Gulfstream Corporation employee, came up with a mind-blowing solution.

Jim met with several senior managers at Gulfstream and explained our problem. As a result of Jim's efforts, Henry Skipper and

I were invited to visit the Gulfstream aircraft repair facility, which is located near the museum. Jim met us at the gate and escorted us inside the facility where he explained how the company used state of the art equipment to paint aircraft interiors with total environmental safety while inside a building. Henry and I were shown the equipment that was placed outside the sealed aircraft to move the filtered overspray safely outside the building. He also introduced us to one of the painters, Tony Hall, who was preparing to paint the cockpit of the aircraft we had been observing in the paint shop. Tony explained to us how the aircraft was sealed and that the painters were equipped with completely secured suits with an outside air supply as they did the painting. It was an amazing set up. Then, once again, a stroke of luck hit. Tony asked why we were interested in the system. Jim explained that Gulfstream senior management had approved that he and several other *City of Savannah* volunteers would be trained to use the Gulfstream equipment and would paint the interior of the B-17. Tony broke out in a big smile. "You don't have to go through all that; I'll paint the airplane for you. It will be a privilege." Another major problem addressed.

It would take a while to make arrangements for the painting to be scheduled, and while those details, mostly logistical, were being taken care of, the first of what would become many working visits to Pooler by Tommy Garcia occurred in early September. Tommy arrived bearing gifts, many gifts! Over the years he had accumulated many B-17 parts that appeared on our ever-developing wish list. We were about to benefit significantly from Tommy's generosity.

Tommy was so anxious to get started that he showed up early, but luckily found Rocky Rodriquez and his Saturday crew on the job and ready to help him unload his truck full of presents. We were actually able to field a Sunday crew for this occasion. They were at the museum at 9:00 a.m. to get started with Tommy, as all of his gifts were lined up in the hall to be photographed and entered into the museum's archive storage list. Foremost among Tommy's gifts was a complete radio transmission set that he repurchased from a friend in nearby Charleston. Two volunteers from the radio team, Steve Jonas and Bill DeLoach, volunteered to drive to Charleston and bring the equipment to Pooler.

Monday of the first Garcia Week was to this observer the most exciting day of the project since the arrival of the airplane.

Material that Tommy Garcia brought with him to donate to our restoration, including radio transmission equipment that he purchased from a dealer in Charleston, SC. (CoS Archives)

Jim Grismer had seven carpenters and an equal number of helpers working with plywood that he had purchased the previous week. They were using the plans that Tommy had obtained from a Hollywood contact on the *Memphis Belle* movie that showed, in detail, all of the woodwork that was needed for completing the interior restoration of the airplane. Watching the woodworking team, one would have thought that this group had been working together for years. Not so! Some of the volunteers, because they normally worked different shifts, had not even met each other until that morning. Tommy was in the middle of the project, often interpreting instructions he had written on the plans and templates twenty years earlier when he had been hired by the Hollywood team to put them together.

We sent the carpenters home in the mid-afternoon, just prior to the arrival of Jack Nilsen, from the night crew metalworkers. Tommy and Jack introduced themselves and then began a nose to tail tour of the *City of Savannah* that lasted until the rest of the night crew arrived.

Tuesday, Wednesday, and Thursday became a blur as the carpenters began building the more complex wooden pieces for the

Tommy Garcia, in hat, explains B-17 plywood floor drawings he made many years earlier for the Memphis Belle *movie project to the carpentry team.* (CoS Archives)

airplane, including the floors and the tables for the navigator's station and radio room. Sixty-five years and thousands of flying hours had, as Tommy had anticipated, changed the shape of our airplane's fuselage from the exact dimensions it had when it left the factory in 1945. The carpenters spent hours adjusting the material they had built to fit the current shape of the airplane.

Everyone associated with the restoration had need for Tommy's expertise and he was very generous in sharing his time. On Wednesday evening a staff meeting was held, at which time the management team gathered with Tommy in the museum conference room and everyone was given the opportunity to discuss the issues that they were facing with regard to their distinct portion of the restoration. As always, Tommy had answers. When the meeting ended, he took the team through the airplane, discussing problems and offering suggestions for issues that he believed would challenge us. When the tour of the airplane was finished, the team sat in the shop and talked and talked and talked, until the museum maintenance man told us that we better leave because he was locking the doors.

The final event of Garcia Week I was the gathering of all of the volunteers who could make it to the museum on Friday to have lunch in the restaurant. Henry Skipper and I both heaped praise upon our Texas hero, and presented him with a copy of Donald Miller's ultimate history of the Eighth Air Force in WWII, *Masters of the Air*, which had been signed by all the volunteers, and a Thank

Tommy Garcia with the certificate presented to him at the end of Garcia Week I. (CoS Archives)

You certificate that included a 1-inch square of fabric from the *City of Savannah*'s original rudder. Tommy assured us that there would be more to come . . . and he was right.

Events were happening so fast at this point in the restoration that it was hard to keep up with all of the incoming great news. As soon as we were finished with Garcia Week, Jim Argo notified us that we needed to prepare for the arrival of the painting team and their equipment from Gulfstream Corporation.

The painting did not go unnoticed outside of the building. Thanks to a heads-up from the museum staff, a reporter from our local newspaper, *Savannah Morning News*, learned about Gulf-stream's upcoming gift to the project in the form of the painting equipment and professional team of painters. When we picked up the newspaper the next morning, there was a picture of our latest media darling, Jim Argo, on page one, with an accompanying story about how he had gone to his senior management to find a solution to our painting problem, and how the managers, as well as the painting team, became the solution.

The day of the big event, a large crew of volunteers turned out. They would mainly be observers after they helped to seal the air-plane, but they didn't care. This was going to be a very exciting day for the project. The day before, a very large Gulfstream truck had delivered the painting equipment (paint, hoses, etc, etc, etc) that was required for the painting to be conducted in an indoor facility that was not classified as a Gulfstream factory floor.

Jim Argo was, naturally, the crew supervisor for our volunteers. He had been carefully briefed beforehand by Tony Hall on how to prepare the airplane for the painting team. Under Jim's supervision all of the preparations were completed to the final details. There was no room for error with this system for indoor painting.

The most convenient surprise for the Gulfstream team was the fact that we did not have a tail turret on the aircraft. Although the empty hole at the back of the aircraft was an embarrassment for us (the original tail turret is on display at the American History Museum in Washington, DC), it offered a wonderful open port for the large orange hoses that would take the filtered air outside of the museum.

The entire aircraft was sealed to strict airtight requirements from nose to tail, under Jim's direction. A large plastic tent covered the tail area and five exhaust tubes led to a refrigerator-sized filter that rendered the overspray of paint from inside the airplane to an environmentally safe level as it was sucked out of the fuselage and forced out the door of the building. Another group of hoses entered the museum from a compressor parked outside, which powered the entire operation.

This was Jim Argo's page one macho shot. (Savannah Morning News)

After completing a full day of work at Gulfstream, Tony Hall arrived at the museum shop area with his painting partner, Frank Quirk. Tony and Frank inspected the work the volunteers had done sealing the aircraft, and then it was time for them to begin. The first night's work, Tony told us, would start from the tail and go through the radio room in the first of two phases they would use to paint the airplane. The bomb bay and upper and lower cockpits would be completed in the second phase. Tony also recommended that a primer coat of paint be applied to ensure the longevity of the interior paint. This would extend the length of the painting time required and the work of the painters, but Tony felt it was appropriate and it would not cause any additional expense to the project's limited coffers. Tony's recommendation was approved by Henry Skipper, and the painting

The amazing exhaust system required by the Gulfstream painting team. (CoS Archives)

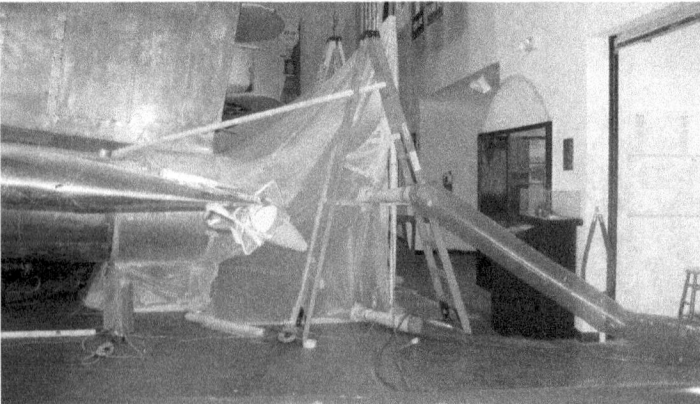

These pictures give a good look at how carefully the airplane was sealed. (CoS Archives)

began. Tony and Frank worked well into the evening hours before they called it a day, changed out of their painting gear, and headed for home. It had been a very long day for them, and we appreciated it.

The painters returned the following morning and applied their second coat of paint for Phase I of the painting project. When they

Left: Gulfstream painting team, Tony Hall and Frank Quirk. (CoS Archives)

were finished, they quickly departed for their real jobs at Gulfstream, and the volunteers, again under Jim Argo's supervision, packed up all the painting and environmental gear and loaded the equipment onto a Gulfstream truck to be returned to the factory. Phase I of the painting was complete and looked terrific—so much for spray cans or plastic brushes—the professionals had done a great job.

It seemed like the month of September 2010 would never end. The weekend after we finished Phase I of the painting, we had another visit from the American Aero Services (AAS) folks from New Smyrna Beach. This visit would mark the final movement of the *City of Savannah* before she was placed on stanchions that AAS had built for us. The stanchions would support the airplane's weight and take the tension off of the rubber tires. It was *essential* that the final location of the airplane be determined beforehand and that all parties concerned agreed on the best location. The final decision, of course, would be made by Henry Skipper. Henry and I met several times to determine what we considered the most appropriate location for the future presentation of the airplane to the public. We decided that guessing beforehand the best final location of the airplane was not a good idea. We would make the decision on the day it was moved.

The first chore after the arrival of the AAS team was to unload from their truck the jacks that would lift the airplane. For this chore we used a forklift loaned to us by our good neighbors, JCB Corporation. When the jacks were in place, the airplane was lifted off the ground and dollies were placed under all three wheels. At this point

Henry and I, along with the AAS supervisor, Whitney Coyle, held a discussion as to what would be the ideal location and direction for the airplane's final disposition as an exhibit in the Gallery. When we had made our decision, Whitney placed observers at each wing-tip and the tail of the airplane. He then arranged our volunteers in position to provide the muscle to have the airplane make its final move. Everyone was tense with what would happen when Whitney called out, "1-2-3, push." When everyone signaled that they were ready, he gave the command—and nothing happened! Then he had everyone stand down and gave some additional calming instructions. He went through his starting ritual again, and sure enough, the airplane moved several feet forward until he ordered everyone to stop pushing. Using this short movement method, which he was obviously familiar with, he got the crew to move the airplane to exactly where we had marked the floor for the port side main landing gear tire. The next chore was to change the airplane's direction. Again, observers were placed at the wingtips and, utilizing the dolly under the tail wheel, the *City of Savannah* made its final move, as it was pointed at the angle we had selected for its future display as the museum's premier exhibit.

American Aero Services team and City of Savannah *volunteers after moving the airplane for the final time.* (CoS Archives)

The final assignment of the AAS crew was to place the airplane on the steel stanchions that they had been contracted to construct for us. This was accomplished by once again using the jacks they had brought with them. Everyone gave a great sigh of relief as the jacks were lowered and the *City of Savannah* was placed in her final position. Yet another important step in preparation for the restoration had been completed, with the help of our ever-growing group of friends in the B-17 community.

The back-to-back major workweeks on the airplane during September were taking a toll on our volunteers; luckily, we got a two-week break as we entered October. Then the pace picked up when the Gulfstream truck pulled up, once again, at the door to the shop with the painting equipment. This time the volunteers knew what was involved and the airplane was prepared for the Phase II painting in short order, awaiting Tony Hall's return.

This time Tony had a surprise for us, a new partner. Frank Quirk, his original painting partner was not available, so he brought another expert painter, his son Terry. The Hall family checked out the preparations that the volunteers had made for them, gave a thumbs-up signal and then set to work. Again they worked into the evening. When Tony stepped out of the airplane at approximately 7:00 p.m., his face was beaming and he told us that the job was completed. Another major accomplishment moving us down the road

The cockpit of the City of Savannah, *sealed and awaiting the arrival of the painting team.* (CoS Archives)

Tony and Terry Hall dressed for the start of Phase II painting. (CoS Archives)

was now checked off the list, thanks to the initiative of Jim Argo and the cooperation of senior management of Gulfstream Corporation.

November 2010 brought a new event to our project that would have a long history of success, achievement, and income for our restoration! The event was the idea of Jane Grismer from the museum staff. Jane was involved in the road-racing community in Savannah and put together the idea of a 5K Run and Walk fundraiser for the *City of Savannah* project in coordination with some corporate friends and the museum's next door neighbor, JCB Corporation. Working on her own time and without a budget, Jane was able to work with JCB to have a portion of the race pass through their Pooler property at no charge to the museum. When the race was finally mapped out, the vast majority of the 3.1-mile course was run on the JCB campus. Jane also partnered with the Savannah Striders running club and Fleet

Runners standing by for the start of the first Flying Fortress 5K. (CoS Archives)

Milt "Crazy Legs" Stombler, surrounded by his adoring fans after his Flying Fortress 5K victory. (CoS Archives)

Feet Sports, a local company that provides management and timing services for Savannah-area running events. Museum staff members, particularly Maintenance Manager Bruce Johnson and the *City of Savannah* volunteers, helped Jane to meet the enormous logistical and administrative challenges involved with putting a race program together for the first time. Finally, with everyone hoping that the weather would be good, that the advertising had worked, and that many last-minute entrants would show up on race day, it all came together. A total of 346 entrants ran the race, which turned out to be a major financial success and finally allowed the restoration of the B-17 to have a working budget.

During the planning for the race, there was a strong effort put forth by all of those involved with the project, and the museum, to bring out as many runners as possible to participate. What we did not expect was that we would have a champion amongst our own. It was obvious that the race would be a financial success from the early morning arrival of the participants, and many of the volunteers gathered together when the race was over to talk to the runners who had participated. Then Mike Manhatton, the official race emcee, from local television station WTOC, started to announce the race winners according to their various age groups. Suddenly, our group was overjoyed to hear that Milt Stombler, our own retired physics professor and ace aluminum polisher, had won his age group. Milt quickly ran forward with us cheering behind him as he picked up his first-place medal. From that day on, whenever the race was discussed, Milt would always be addressed by his new nickname, "Crazy Legs." Another *City of Savannah* legend had been born.

The Flying Fortress 5K became an annual event and continues to provide income for museum projects that include the *City of Savannah*.

It would seem that the year 2010 had certainly been filled with enough events to keep those involved with the project busy and excited with future possibilities. But, as we would say many times, there was more to come.

The week after the race, we hosted a special new friend of the project by the name of Skip Shelton. In October our Saturday Crew Chief, Rocky Rodriguez, had come upon Skip standing near the tail of the B-17 talking to other visitors about details of the bomber. Rocky was intrigued that the speaker was obviously well informed and a terrific conversationalist. When the visitor group began to move on, Rocky stepped forward and introduced himself to Skip, who, it turns out, had been a 19-year-old B-24 pilot in the 448th Bomb Group in 1945. During their conversation, Rocky learned that Skip was an artist with a working business in South Carolina and that he had been interested in art his entire life. In fact, he told Rocky, he had painted the nose art on his airplane and many other airplanes in the 448th. Rocky knew that part of our plan for the future was to replicate the nose and fuselage "art" that had been on the original airplane. We had yet to determine who would do the painting. Rocky didn't waste any time and asked Skip if he would be interested in working with us. Of course the answer was "yes"!

Rocky called me to let me know about meeting Skip and to provide me with his telephone number. I called Skip right away and we began to make arrangements for him to return and do the painting. He asked for detailed pictures of the original markings, which we provided. We also prepared the logistical support he requested and notified the local media outlets that we would have a history-making event at the museum.

Skip and his wife, Shirley, also prepared well for their arrival. Utilizing the pictures that we forwarded, Shirley had created graphite forms of the lettering on the original airplane by matching the size of the written letters against the rivets on the airplane's fuselage! An *amazing* display of skill on the part of both Skip and Shirley.

We had a full team assembled in the Combat Gallery to prepare for Skip's arrival and the painting of the *City of Savannah* name on our B-17. The Wednesday Day Crew, museum staff, visitors, and the media were all assembling around the nose of the B-17 late on the morning of November 10 as Skip climbed the scaffold around the nose of the airplane with two of our volunteers, Allen Lewonski and Tom Van Tilson, to begin his work. Allen and Tom assisted Skip by using Shirley's graphite forms to mark the fuselage with outlines of the individual letters in the words "City of Savannah" in the exact format as they had appeared on the original airplane.

At one point during this very busy day, as things were getting a bit harried, Jim Grismer leaned toward me and, pointing to the nose of the airplane, he said, "Doesn't *Savannah* have two *n*'s in it?" I nearly fainted! Just the thought that I would have to correct the master at his work in front of this audience was overwhelming.

Skip Shelton replicating the nose art of the original City of Savannah. (CoS Archives)

However, it was just Jim trying to divert my mind with humor from what was going on. I still haven't forgiven him.

Skip worked through the day with only two breaks, one for lunch and one to hold a series of interviews with the several media representatives who were present. When the former Eighth Air Force pilot finished his work for the day, most of us who had been there when he arrived had departed for home, and it was the Wednesday Night Crew that escorted Skip and Shirley back to their hotel.

Thursday morning, appropriately Veterans Day, saw Skip and Shirley return to the museum to repeat the painting preparation process all over again, this time on the left waist area of the airplane. Again, there were ample volunteers to assist Skip and a new group of visitors to watch his work, as well as additional media as the day progressed. Working from the floor instead of a scaffold speeded the work up considerably, and on this day Skip finished his work during the mid-afternoon. I sat next to him as he was interviewed by a magazine reporter and learned more details of his very interesting life. Skip told the reporter that manpower requirements had forced the Army Air Corps to cut the two years of college standard to qualify for pilot training, and he had entered flight training right

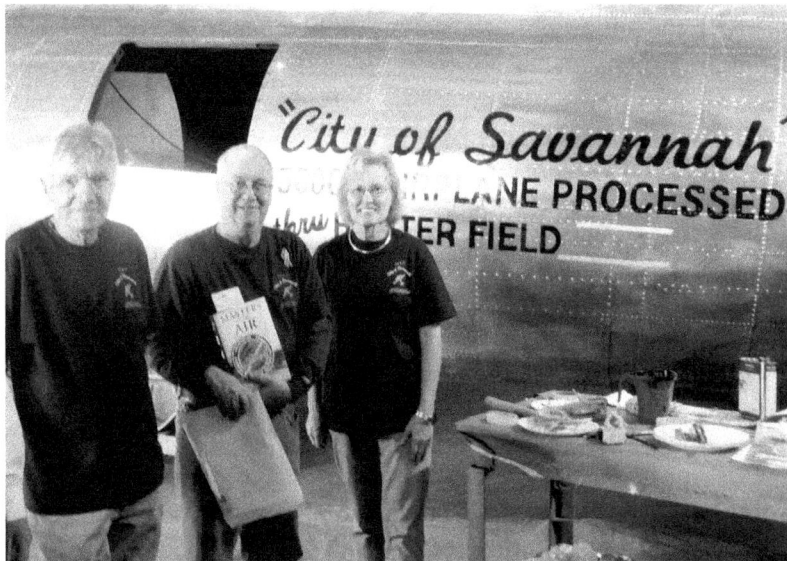

Skip Shelton, author, and Shirley Shelton next to the B-17 as Skip finished work on Veterans Day, November 11, 2010. (CoS Archives)

103

after completing high school in 1943. He graduated and received his wings in November of 1944 at the age of 19. He left shortly thereafter for England, where he was assigned as a copilot to the 713th Squadron of the 448th Bomb Group. His Group commander noted that the new lieutenant had a flare for art, complimenting Skip on the nose art on his B-24, *Frisky Frisco*, named after a night the crew spent partying in that California city. Thereafter, Skip was appointed to paint nose art on all newly arriving aircraft. At the commander's insistence, Skip was even removed from several missions to get the artwork done, something that Skip appreciated. As he told the reporter, "I was never shot at while painting an airplane."

After the war Skip had a career as a corporate pilot, starting with war surplus DC-3s and eventually retiring from the cockpit of Savannah-built Gulfstream jets. After retirement he went back to artwork on a full-time basis, opening a studio in South Carolina.

Skip remained a member of our family, attending our annual dinner every year with Shirley. He passed away, after a short illness, in 2014, a very good friend whom we treasured, but lost along the way.

After all the hard work in 2010, we deserved a high-note event to finish the year, and we got it. The story started in October when I was contacted by a woman named Margaret Watkins, who told me that her father had been the navigator of the original *City of Savannah* with the tail number 43-39049 that had departed Hunter Field in December of 1944. I was, to say the least, taken aback by her call. She explained to me, making a long story short, that a family member had noted a newspaper picture in the *Savannah Morning News* of the crew of the original *City of Savannah* that had been recently published in an article about the B-17 restoration at the Mighty Eighth. Her cousin, Jim Jones, had enlarged the picture and had brought it to family members, who agreed that the man kneeling in the front row in the crew photo beneath the nose of the original airplane was in fact Lt. John E. Watkins, father or uncle to all the senior family members. Margaret and I discussed some details of what she and I both had heard about the crew and their adventures, and we finished the conversation with an agreement that the family would come to Pooler to meet the restoration team.

The Watkins family arrived at the museum very near to the 66th anniversary of the day that Lt. Jack Watkins and the rest of

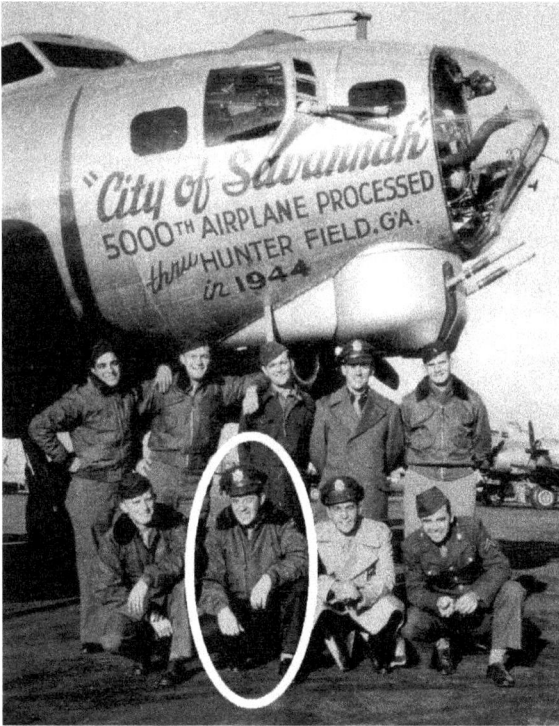

(Left) The original City of Savannah *crew just minutes before their departure from Hunter Field in December 1944. Navigator Lt. John Watkins is circled.* (Watkins family)

(Below) The Watkins family visit—(L-R) Beth Kennan (friend of family), Margaret Watkins (Jack Watkins's daughter), Katherine Watkins (Jack's wife), Robert Watkins (Jack's son), Taylor Jones (great-niece), Jim Jones (nephew)—66 years, to the month, after Lt. Jack Watkins and the Kittle crew departed Savannah for England. (CoS Archives)

the *City of Savannah* crew departed from Hunter Field. They met the Saturday crew, who went out of their way to show the family around the airplane and explain how the restoration was progressing. It was a great event for both the family and the volunteers— and would not be the last time that we would meet the great folks from the Watkins clan.

It was great to end a year with so much success on such a high note—actually meeting the family of a crew member of the original airplane. We were all excited about what 2011 would bring to us.

CHAPTER 4

Putting It Back Together

JANUARY 2011 – DECEMBER 2012

*"Experience is a hard teacher because she gives you
the experience first and the lesson afterwards."*

Vernon Law

We began the year 2011 with the airplane clean, painted on the inside and polished on the outside. We even had a bank account! Now it was time to get started with the reason that the B-17G with the tail number 44-83814, now known as the *City of Savannah*, had been brought to the Mighty Eighth.

Let the restoration begin!

Morale was high in January as we began to actually restore our airplane. Jim Grismer started off the year by taking a team to Tampa, Florida, for the first of several visits to the famous Jay Wisler stockpile of WWII warbird parts.

Jim Grismer: *This vintage aircraft parts bone yard has to be seen to be believed. Jay has a unique filing system that defies analysis. Only he can locate the items you request from within the piles of "stuff" stored in four warehouses.*

The crew returned with many basic interior parts for the airplane that would get us started. The Wednesday crew installed floors in the cockpit so that work could get underway in that portion of the airplane. The Saturday crew held an "off-site" workday on the first Saturday of the year at the LMI Corporation facility to help volunteers from LMI complete work on our fabric control surfaces.

The middle of the month saw a return to our normal frantic state as Tommy Garcia arrived for Garcia Week II. Tommy arrived on Monday morning and immediately began working with the three crews on their specific assignments. The Wednesday (day) crew, led by Danny Harden, was deep into their woodwork for the floors. Bill Liening and his Wednesday (night) crew had metalwork throughout the airplane, working especially hard to prepare the radio room for the CARS radio team to begin their installation project. Finally, Rocky Rodriquez's Saturday crew, our electricians, were working to bring power to the airplane with an emphasis on having the radio room ready for the CARS team. Each crew had many questions and Tommy had the knowledge to answer them. Other tasks that were underway included tracing and cleaning the airplane's flight and engine controls, installing the radio room desk and installing the working parts for the bomb bay doors.

One surprise for everyone was that on a tour of the museum's archives, Tommy noticed an obscure and undocumented box that held an auxiliary power generator appropriate for our airplane!

Another issue came about as we realized that for the majority of the time the museum was open to the public there was no representative from our project to explain to museum visitors what was happening. It was decided to build a video display next to the airplane that would run during museum operating hours with a regularly updated script and pictures depicting the current status of the project. Dave Talleur, Richard Moscatiello, and Mike Callahan put together a set of slides and wrote a script that told our story.

Homemade video display case at waist doorway of B-17. (CoS Archives)

We purchased a 37-inch flat screen TV and DVD player, which we mounted in a discarded museum display case that was painted and re-manufactured by Danny Harden and Paul Abare to become a stand-alone display. This display stands next to the airplane to this day, informing visitors of the status of the restoration in a recycling description of the history of the project as well as recent events.

The following weekend our second annual volunteer dinner was held on January 15, the second anniversary of the arrival of the airplane. Doctor Harry Friedman, from the National B-17 Co-Op, arrived on the day before the dinner, along with a van full of parts and equipment he donated to our cause, saving our very limited budget thousands of dollars. Other honored guests at the dinner included Tommy, Skip and Shirley Shelton, and the Gulfstream painting team of Tony and Terry Hall, Frank Quirk, and their spouses.

During February 2011, I was asked to speak to the board of trustees again. I was proud to explain that I believed the secret to our success thus far was attributed to the priorities that we had learned from Bob Mikesh:

1. The airplane was indoors.

2. We had created a stable and organized management team.

3. The museum had been able to successfully raise money for us through the Flying Fortress 5K and private donations; and

4. We had the expertise of our local volunteers with aviation experience from Gulfstream and LMI Corporations as well as the 165th Airlift Wing of the Georgia Air National Guard.

I added that the one major contribution to our success, which Bob had not mentioned, was help from the national B-17 community, particularly Tommy Garcia and Harry Friedman.

Soon after I spoke to the board, we were notified by David Pinegar of LMI Corporation that the rudder and control surfaces were nearing the completion of their restoration and would soon require the application of several coats of fabric-friendly paint. A painter from our ranks was requested, and John Finch stepped up to the challenge and began painting our flight controls after finishing his daily shift at Gulfstream.

Early March of 2011 brought us some very bad news. Dr. Walter Brown, the man who had put together the program to bring 44-83814 from the Smithsonian to the Mighty Eighth, had lost his battle with cancer. Walt had died in his family home in Tennessee and was returned to Savannah to be buried in a family plot at

Dr. Walter Brown standing next to 44-83814 on January 15, 2009. (CoS Archives)

David Pinegar with some of the LMI volunteers who worked on the City of Savannah *flight controls.* (CoS Archives)

Jim Argo supervises from the top; Milt Stombler makes adjustments at mid-level; the author, Danny Harden, and Paul Abare guide on the bottom, as the rudder is remounted. (CoS Archives)

Bonaventure Cemetery. I was extremely honored to be asked to speak at his funeral on behalf of all his friends, staff, and volunteers at the museum.

The installation of the first fully restored part to be exhibited to the public took place in mid-March when Dave Pinegar and John Finch completed the restoration of the flight control fabric project. The newly re-canvassed and painted control surfaces arrived at the museum in an LMI Corporation truck and were carefully carried into the shop. We decided that the ailerons and horizontal stabilizers would be temporarily stored for safety reasons, but that the rudder would be mounted for all to see. The rudder was brought into the Combat Gallery and remounted with several museum visitors applauding the success. Very special thanks went out to LMI Corporation as well as to Dave Pinegar and John Finch. Another great accomplishment!

Late in March of 2011 we finally solved a mystery that we had been working on since early in the project. We did not know, for sure, the tail number of the airplane that the Kittle crew had flown out of Hunter Field in 1944. We finally got confirmation with a letter from Ralph "Kit" Kittle Jr., including a picture of a flying B-17 with the tail number 43-39049. On the back of the original picture were notes from his father stating that this is the airplane that he flew out of Hunter Field—the original *City of Savannah*. The heroine of the task of locating Kit Kittle Jr. was museum staffer Brenda Elmgren. She located Kit at his home in Connecticut and initiated a friendship between the Kittle family and the *City of Savannah* project that continues to this day.

The original City of Savannah *(The first "3" indicates the aircraft was built under a 1943 contract.)* (Savannah Morning News)

Historical documentation of our airplane's history seemed to be taking over the month of March. Bill Burkel was utilizing his Internet search skills during this period of the restoration and, in addition to finding us some very rare parts on eBay, he also found several pictures of our airplane during its 30-year operational career. Here are two historical pictures: the first almost dates itself with the 1955 Plymouth parked in front of the #2 engine; the second was probably taken around the same period, as the airplane has the Kenting Aviation paint scheme and is obviously working in a northern climate.

Bill Burkel's Internet search revealed two pictures of 44-83814 during its career with Kenting Aviation. (Bill Burkel)

Rocky and His Friends celebrating the lighting of the City of Savannah's *navigation lights for the first time in twenty-seven years. (L–R) Peter Balsom, Ben Hedgpeth, Rocky Rodriquez, Mort Glick, Joel Hedgpeth.* (CoS Archives)

The month of March closed out with a very big day for Rocky Rodriguez and his Saturday electricians. For the first time in approximately 27 years, our B-17 had a functional electrical system operating within its fuselage. "Rocky and His Friends" had been running wire through the airplane for several weeks. Finally, they connected the airplane to house power from the museum and a

The official 2010 picture of the City of Savannah *volunteers.* (CoS Archives)

great cheer resounded throughout the Combat Gallery as the airplane's navigation lights burst into bright colors.

While the wiring team was cheering, the rest of the electricians were getting dirty as they manually lowered the airplane's flaps and removed the motors. The radio team had volunteered to check out the flap motors, and if necessary, repair them in order to ensure that the flaps would become a vital part of the planned public demonstration of the aircraft's components.

The month of April was a very rare, and welcome, period of calm for the project. The highlight was a second road trip to Florida by an intrepid foursome of volunteers to purchase parts from the Jay Wisler stockpile. Bill Burkel was the wheelman for the travelers with Jim Grismer in command and Danny Harden and Paul Abare riding in the backseat as the laborers who would drag the purchases into Bill's truck. Once again generous donations and the Flying Fortress 5K had provided us with much needed financial support.

The month of May began with more sad news of a loss from our *City of Savannah* family when we learned that Arnold Kolb, the last owner and pilot of 44-83814, had passed away. Arnold had owned the airplane from 1971 until he traded it to the Smithsonian in 1984, and flew as copilot with his son Nathan in the pilot

Nathan and Arnold Kolb, the father and son final pilot team of the City of Savannah. *Photo taken at Dulles airport in 1984 with the delivery of 44-83814 to the Smithsonian.* (Maurita Kolb-Autry)

seat, on the airplane's last flight from Arizona to Dulles Airport in Virginia.

During the period beginning in January of 2009, when we brought 44-83814 home from Virginia, until his death, I spoke with Arnold on several occasions. An outgoing man with significant business acumen, he took interest in everything that surrounded him in life. He was very interested in how we would conduct the restoration. Our final conversation included his request "to have a good seat" at the airplane's dedication. Unfortunately, he could not be present at that event in 2015, but we went out of our way to ensure that his daughter, Maurita Kolb-Autry, and her husband were very involved in the dedication, four years after Arnold's passing.

Late May saw a special effort to make the *City of Savannah* look her best for the museum's 15th Anniversary Legacy Ball, as many donors and guests from the community would be standing next to the airplane during the cocktail hour. The Wednesday (day) crew buffed the outside of the airplane to restore the bright polished look that the International Aerospace Services team had returned to the airplane the previous year and the Wednesday (night) crew removed the work scaffolding and wires that seemed to come out of every opening in the airplane. They also swept the entire floor of the Combat Gallery. Nothing was too much to make our airplane look good! The Saturday crew did a final dusting and sweeping and then the museum's events staff set up the bar beneath the right waist gun window. Finally, the newly built video display was placed next to the bar so that those on line would view the latest photos and comments on the restoration project. The Legacy Ball was a major success, and we were proud that the *City of Savannah* could make a good impression at its first formal affair.

Garcia Week III took place in June. As is Tommy's tradition, he arrived bearing gifts. The back of his pickup was filled with a B-17 tail turret that had been lifted out of the Alaskan tundra several years before, after spending 40 years as part of the wreckage of a B-17 fire bomber that had gone down in the 1970s. Working with another good friend of our project, Bruce Orriss, Tommy had been part of a group that had negotiated to have the wreckage lifted out of the Alaskan crash site and brought to California. Now the turret would become the template for our first class metal team as they began, yet again, to work in cooperation with LMI and Gulfstream Corporation professionals, to build an entirely new turret that would be mounted on the *City of Savannah*.

Our "Alaska turret" before it was salvaged. (Tommy Garcia)

Our tail turret problem was simple: we didn't have one. Several years prior to our first contact with the Smithsonian, the original Cheyenne model turret had been removed from the airplane by the Smithsonian, and incorporated into a WWII "Rosie the Riveter" exhibit at the Smithsonian's American History Museum in Washington, DC.

44-83814's original turret at its current location in the Smithsonian honoring the "Rosie the Riveters" of WWII. (Doug Birkey)

The first requirement for the newly arrived turret was to make sure that it matched up to our airplane. It was carried directly from Tommy's truck into the Combat Gallery to be matched up against the big hole that had been at the back of our airplane since its arrival. The match was perfect; Tommy had been in town for five minutes and had immediately renewed his hero status!

Next, the turret was placed on a workbench by the various volunteers who would be taking it apart and building an entirely new turret. The Alaska turret would be supplying templates for all of the major components of the turret structure, which, for the most part, was in such poor condition that restoration was not possible.

Wednesday (night) crew chief Bill Liening had previously brought up the very important point that his crew would require access to virtually all of the turret's exterior and interior surfaces, and that it would be very beneficial if we could determine a way to have some type of work-stand on which the Alaska turret, as well as the new turret could revolve, providing complete access to the metalworking team. Over several days, one of our more talented and imaginative carpenters, Gil Patrick, came up with an idea to address Bill's wish. Gil found a long piece of pipe in the back of the shop that he would use as a central arm for a revolving stand that the turrets (old and new) could be mounted upon. With the arrival of the turret, Gil began taking measurements of the interior, and in

Genius can come in strange packages—as when Gil Patrick was able to solve our turret access problem. (CoS Archives)

twenty minutes, he had assembled his now famous "rotisserie" that would see considerable service in the weeks and months to come.

Joel Hedgpeth: *Over the years we were faced with many difficult problems. It seemed that the skill of the volunteers always stepped up to the challenge. The rotisserie for the tail turret may have been one of the more clever solutions found.*

Bill Liening: *What I will remember most fondly about the years working on this project are the challenges that we overcame. It happened all the time. We would come up against some task and say, "How the hell are we gonna do that?" and someone would always come up with a solution. The tail turret rotisserie comes to mind.*

The plan for building a completely new tail turret for the *City of Savannah* was perhaps our most challenging task yet. However, we had learned that setting high goals was something the *CoS* volunteers accepted. In this case, the success would be extraordinary! The highly skilled artisans Jack Nilsen and Bob MacDonald led the way with their plan to use original drawings and templates from the Alaska turret to construct a new turret totally from scratch.

As our planning for the turret began, we received an unexpected out-of-town offer of assistance when we were visited by Chris Henry from the Grissom Air Museum, at Grissom AFB in Peru, Indiana.

Chris Henry: *I was visiting Savannah and stopped to see Jerry McLaughlin and his City of Savannah team after meeting them at the annual B-17 Co-Op meeting in 2010. They showed me their Alaska turret and told me how that turret was missing many important internal parts. I told them that we had a complete Cheyenne tail turret that needed some corrosion repairs and that maybe we could work something out where both groups could benefit. Eventually that is what happened. They came and picked up our turret, brought it to Pooler and took it apart to use as templates for their inner turret metalwork. While the turret was disassembled, they treated all the pieces with corrosion preventative, gave it a paint job, and reassembled it. Both projects got a good deal.*

Mid-June saw our status in the B-17 restoration community move up another notch. Henry Skipper notified me that after

The "Alaska turret" mounted on Gil Patrick's rotisserie pole (protruding out of the picture). (L–R) Dave Talleur, Darrell Schwartz, author, Jeff Hoopes, Jim Grismer, Tommy Garcia, Scott Whitcher. (CoS Archives)

discussion with senior staff at the Barksdale AFB museum, they had agreed to have our carpentry team visit the Barksdale facility and draw up plans for us to provide them with a complete woodwork package for their B-17. Gil Patrick and John Finch traveled to Louisiana and spent a day inside of the Barksdale B-17, *Miss Liberty*, bringing home measurements and pictures of the unique interior that the airplane had developed over the years.

An agreement was made between the two museums to cover expenses for travel, lodging, labor, and a small profit for the CoS program in exchange for a CoS team traveling to Louisiana and installing the woodwork in the *Miss Liberty*. Work began immediately to replicate the woodwork done for the *City of Savannah* so that, for the first time, we could export our expertise to another restoration. The fact that the word was out regarding the quality of our work was a strong statement of how far our team had come in just over two years.

While part of the team was making plans for working on the wooden interior of a B-17 in Louisiana, there was a large wooden package being delivered to the Mighty Eighth back in Pooler. Scott Whitcher had been tasked with constructing the ammunition boxes for the nose and waist positions of both the *City of Savannah*, and later, the *Miss Liberty*. Scott estimated that each of the six boxes had required an average of six hours of work in his home shop. Looking at the boxes, we all believed that six hours might be a low estimate. Each box held the classic nine-yard-long sleeve of .50 caliber rounds and included a finely tooled roller that allowed the ammunition to smoothly leave the box and enter the firing chamber of its gun. This was precision work.

Scott Whitcher: *In September 2010 Tommy Garcia arrived with a full set of plans and templates needed to prepare the woodwork for the interior of the aircraft. The museum had purchased these items with the help of Tommy from the movie production company that produced the 1979 movie* Memphis Belle. *The woodworking team went to work producing the needed floors, desks, and ammo boxes. My concentration was the ammo boxes. Upon completion, the boxes did not meet my standards for accurate representations of the boxes used on the WWII aircraft. Original blueprints were acquired and I made an additional set which accurately matched the WWII drawings.*

One of the historically accurate ammunition boxes built by Scott Whitcher that would be mounted in the City of Savannah and Miss Liberty. The hard-to-build roller is at the bottom right of the picture. (CoS Archives)

More Road Warrior action was called for when the wonderful friends we had made at the Experimental Aircraft Association (EAA) in Oshkosh, Wisconsin, worked out a trade with us that reserved one of our internal oil tanks for their use at some time in the future in exchange for a plastic ball turret cap that had been cut off a full ball turret for use in a movie. The purpose of cutting the cap off of the actual turret was that the cap could be mounted on our airplane, appearing to be a full turret, with considerable saving of weight. In our case it would appear that we had a ball turret, and that was what we would settle for on a temporary basis because that was what we could afford. Bill Burkel and Jeff Hoopes made the trip to Oshkosh. They must have appeared so pitiful to our EAA benefactors that they returned with not only the ball turret cap, but with a bonus: a weather-beaten, cracked, but usable upper turret plastic bubble. Thus, we had two faux turrets for presentation to the public.

Bill Burkel: *Jeff Hoopes and I traveled to Oshkosh, Wisconsin, in July of 2011, to pick up a half-shell of a ball turret to be used as a temporary display on the* City of Savannah. *The shell was part of a trade between us and the Experimental Aircraft Association (EAA). We got to Milwaukee, rented a truck, and drove to Oshkosh, where the EAA people gave us a great tour of the hangar and all the planes inside. We even got to see them running up their Ford Trimotor.*

The final note on the ball turret cap story involves one of the truly wonderful people at the National Museum of the Mighty Eighth Air Force. Bud Porter is a senior member of the museum's board of trustees, and a combat veteran of the Eighth Air Force in WWII, who flew his missions as a ball turret gunner. When Bud saw the turret frame mounted to the airplane, he was so happy he went directly to Henry Skipper's office and wrote a check for the expenses we had incurred to bring the frame back to Pooler from Wisconsin. Needless to say, we were very grateful for Bud's check, but even happier to have paid him the honor of replicating the dangerous home he had once inhabited beneath a B-17 in the sky over Europe.

July 13 saw a major milestone in the *City of Savannah's* history: the first broadcast from our radio room. The museum marketing department had contacted the local media and there were

Bud Porter smiling as he sits next to his B-17 crew position. (CoS Archives)

several TV video cameras poking into the two side windows of the compartment as the head of our radio team, Guy McDonald, sat at the radio operator's table as this historic event began. We had equipped Guy with plenty of WWII era gear, so he would look good for the media.

The radio team had done a great deal of coordinating for their first broadcast, with both Bruce Johnson, the chief of building operations at the Mighty Eighth, and with amateur radio counterparts in Shreveport, Louisiana, who operate with our good friends at the Barksdale AFB museum and the *Miss Liberty* project. Bruce had worked with the radio operators to rig their antenna from the left wingtip of the *City of Savannah*, through the wall of the building, and finally, between two light poles in the museum's Memorial Garden. In Louisiana, the Shreveport Amateur Radio Association (SARA) had jumped at the opportunity to participate in this first broadcast and had their operation set up in a tent beneath the nose of *Miss Liberty* awaiting Guy's first call from our radio room. (The 100-degree temperature in Shreveport that day prevented the SARA team from operating in the furnace of the *Miss Liberty* radio room. We are blessed being able to operate in a climate-controlled environment.)

As I sat on the floor next to Guy's desk and out of sight of the two TV station video cameras filming though the tiny radio room windows, he told me that he had just received a text message from his counterpart in Louisiana saying that they were ready to receive

Guy McDonald, Peter Levesque, Mac McCormack, and Steve Jonas hold a radio team meeting in the shop in preparation for installation of the fully operational City of Savannah *radio room.* (CoS Archives)

Guy McDonald, in appropriate attire, as he prepared for the first broadcast from the City of Savannah *radio room on July 13, 2011.* (CoS Archives)

a radio message from the *City of Savannah*, and that he was texting them back to stand by. I had to laugh, and told him I wanted to hear words like "Roger, Wilco" or "Over and Out"—words from the old WWII movies! The idea of a text message to get events started seemed very out of place for the surroundings of a 1945 B-17 radio room.

Guy began our first transmission at 4:05 p.m. on July 13, 2011, using our FCC-approved call sign, WW2COS, by asking several HAM operators who were monitoring this special event to terminate their transmissions so that he could reach the *Miss Liberty* team. He was then immediately able to make contact and the two stations exchanged congratulations as the historical link between our radio room and another B-17 was established, utilizing a complete set of restored 1940's equipment in the *City of Savannah* radio room.

One of the WWII-era pieces of equipment that was used in the broadcast was a BC-348 receiver that was rebuilt for us by one of the radio team volunteers, Carroll Baker. An electrical engineer by trade, Carroll purchased the receiver on eBay, using his own funds, and spent an entire year restoring the 65-year-old radio for use in our radio room. Talk about DEDICATION!

Carroll Baker with the radio receiver that he restored and donated to the City of Savannah's *radio room restoration effort*. (CoS Archives)

The month of August brought some earnest thinking about how we would spend our limited budget when it came to major advances in the restoration. We made what turned out to be a very good decision in many ways when we purchased a working chin turret for our airplane from a local Georgia contractor by the name of Fred Bieser. There is a reason that Fred is known nationally as "Fred the Turret Guy." It is hard to imagine that anyone in the country knows more about WWII bomber turrets than Fred. He even has a side business in which he takes turrets to children's parties and helps the kids spend hours riding in the turrets and squealing with delight.

We had learned of Fred's business and, because he was relatively close to Pooler, we gave him a call to talk about the turret requirements of our airplane. That conversation resulted in a visit with several turrets that he demonstrated for us. No group of kids had more fun than the *City of Savannah* volunteers did as we rode his turrets around in circles making the same high-pitched sounds that you expect from child party-goers. We were particularly interested in his B-17G chin turret, which he had told us was available for sale. Over the next several months, technical issues and costs were discussed between Fred and museum management, and finally, on July 27, an agreement was reached. Fred arrived at the museum three days later to deliver our first major purchase, the *City of Savannah*'s front showpiece to the world, our new chin turret.

The summer of 2011 turned out to be one of the few periods in the *City of Savannah* restoration program in which events actually slowed down to an almost normal state. After the arrival of the chin turret, there was not another major event until mid-August when we were honored to have a visit from the President-CEO of LMI Aerospace Corporation, Mr. Ron Saks. LMI was then, and continues to be, one of the project's major corporate supporters, led by one of our first volunteers, David Pinegar. Ron visited the facility with some of his senior staff from Savannah and a nearby South Carolina facility. I took Ron and the other LMI visitors on a walk around the *City of Savannah* so that they could see firsthand all of the contributions that their corporation had made to the project, especially

Our first major purchase. The fully operational chin turret, here mounted on a stand built by Fred Bieser for display purposes. (CoS Archives)

David Pinegar, author, Ron Saks (LMI CEO), Henry Skipper. (CoS Archives)

the fabric-covered control surfaces. After the tour, Henry Skipper presented Ron with a framed copy of the Mighty Eighth logo, the famous painting entitled *The Crewman*, signed by the artist, Gil Cohen. After the presentation of the print, all of the guests and the museum staff and volunteers who were involved in the event sat down to a wonderful dinner hosted by Mr. Saks.

While things had calmed down in the summer, the fall season brought more busy times to the project. One of the first events occurred in September, and was not exactly good news. John Finch had spent many, many hours in front of a computer screen looking at original Boeing drawings of the nose of the 1945 B-17G group to which our airplane, 44-83814, belonged. He came to the conclusion that during the twenty years that our airplane was in service with Kenting Aviation, the lower portion of the nose had been reconfigured from having to support a gun turret and a Nordon bomb site to accommodating very large packages of camera equipment. John asked for a management meeting and carefully explained to us that it was going to be necessary to rebuild a great deal of the lower nose area so that it could once again support our newly purchased chin turret and the bomb site that had been sitting in the archives for almost twenty years. John and the Wednesday (night) crew chief, Bill Liening, would be leading the work to rebuild the nose and would be assisted by a team from Gulfstream Corporation. This was a setback with regard to timing, but once again, our talented team of volunteers and the local aviation community would team up to get the job done.

Late October saw two big events going on in Pooler that affected both the museum and the *City of Savannah* project. A long-planned reunion of the WWII veterans of both the 486th and 487th

Bomb Groups was scheduled at the museum, and we began preparing to host the 2011 B-17 Co-Op Annual Meeting, our coming-out party to the B-17 community.

As part of the bomb groups' reunion, the organizers of the event had arranged for two flying B-17s, the *Yankee Lady* and *909*, as well as the last flying B-24, *Witchcraft*, to be in Savannah during the reunion to provide rides to the veterans and to the public. We were very excited to work with the incoming bomber crews, particularly with our friend Norm Ellickson who is the crew chief of the Yankee Air Museum's *Yankee Lady*. Norm had called ahead and said that he would offer a free ride on *Yankee Lady*'s press flight to one of our deserving volunteers. We held an all-hands meeting to discuss how we would work with the reunion veterans and the incoming flight crews. At the close of the meeting, we held a lottery of all the volunteers, excluding the managers, for the coveted seat on the B-17 ride. The winner was the very deserving Gil Patrick. When the day of the flight occurred, many of us were at SAV to talk to the crews and to get tours of the airplanes as they sat outside the private flight facility building. When it came time for the press ride on *Yankee Lady*, the local media and Gil Patrick climbed aboard the

Justin and Gil Patrick share a great father/son experience thanks to Norm Ellickson.
(CoS Archives)

B-17 and prepared for takeoff. Gil's son, Justin, who was also one of our volunteers, one of our father/son teams, stepped forward to take a picture of his dad waving out the waist window of the airplane. Norm noticed Justin's position near the airplane and asked if he knew any of the passengers. Justin replied that his dad was the *City of Savannah* passenger. Norm, great guy that he is, signaled for a delay in the engine start sequence and quickly ran Justin over to the waist door entrance and put him inside the airplane to ride with his dad and the press corps. Norm made a friend for life of every *City of Savannah* volunteer that day.

November was the busiest and perhaps most important month of the project's existence to that date, with the arrival of the national B-17 community leadership at the Mighty Eighth for their annual conference. Dr. Harry Friedman presided and the *City of Savannah* was officially represented by Jim Grismer, Dave Talleur, and myself. Many of the volunteers were also present, providing assistance to the families of the conference attendees and giving constant attention to all of our guests. Bill Liening was the tour coordinator for our guests and quickly charmed the families who toured the museum while the conference was underway. Bill missed his calling in the field of public relations.

Harry mentioned to Henry Skipper and me that our organization coming into existence in 2009 and hosting this meeting in only three years was unprecedented. We were all very proud of our accomplishments, and it was a pleasure to spend time in the shop and around the airplane, proudly talking about our progress and receiving very useful advice from a group of consultants who are generally not available and love to talk about airplanes, particularly B-17s.

The Co-Op meeting only lasted for a weekend, yet many of our volunteers had given up a great deal of personal time to make the event a success. Tommy Garcia had attended the meeting and then stayed in town for Garcia Week IV; so, without even one day off, it was again a very full week of work on our airplane for Tommy and the various volunteer teams.

When Tommy departed for his home in Houston, we were faced with one more all-out push for our tired volunteers, and I was hoping we weren't going to the well just one time too often when asking the volunteers to participate in another *City of Savannah*

The official 2011 City of Savannah *group photo.* (CoS Archives)

event, the 2nd Annual Flying Fortress 5K. Jane Grismer had learned several lessons from her first running of the race in 2010, and this year, she had many more sponsors and entrants. As expected, the volunteers turned out in full force, and the race was a great success with full media attention for the museum and a nice cash deposit in the bank for the *City of Savannah* project. It should also be noted that the 2011 5K saw a return to the winner's circle of our rising star, Dr. Milt "Crazy Legs" Stombler.

2011 had been quite a year. Thirty-six months into the project and we were feeling very good about what we had accomplished, and what we anticipated in our future.

2012

We began the fourth year of the project with what had now become a tradition, our annual mid-January dinner to thank the volunteers and their families on the anniversary of the arrival of the airplane in 2009. Henry Skipper addressed the volunteers, and, once again, thanked them for the amazing amount of progress that had occurred during the previous twelve months. For my part, it was an honor to stand before my colleagues and their families for the third consecutive year as the project manager. I had prepared some statistics to let the group know what they had accomplished in the past 36 months:

- The total number of recorded volunteer hours on the project now exceeded 15,000.

- A total of 120 volunteers had served during the first three years.

- Major portions of three turrets had been assembled.

- The radio team had gone active on July 13.

- We had hosted the 2011 National B-17 Co-Op meeting.

- Seventeen volunteers had recorded more than 100 hours of service during 2011.

Lastly, two museum staff members, Bruce Johnson and Jane Grismer, were both recognized for their support of the project with plaques thanking them for their service.

The dinner was, as always, a big morale booster for the volunteers as we started into the second year of actual restoration work.

The month of February might be remembered in *City of Savannah* project history as the "Month of the Road Trips." On varying days throughout the month, we had Road Warriors in the states

Miss Liberty, *the object of our affections at Barksdale AFB.* (CoS Archives)

Before the team left for Barksdale AFB, all of the wood products they would be installing were laid out on the Mighty Eighth driveway. (CoS Archives)

of Ohio, Indiana, and Louisiana, and they all had great adventures!

The big trip involved our self-proclaimed "Special Operations" team, made up of Jeff Hoopes, Bob MacDonald, John Finch, and Gil Patrick. The team departed for Barksdale AFB in a rented 12-passenger van loaded with only four passengers, but a great deal of flooring, ammunition boxes, and tools. The long anticipated mission to equip the Barksdale B-17, *Miss Liberty*, with all of its wooden interior requirements was finally underway.

Our good friend Terry Snook, the *Miss Liberty* project manager, met the *City of Savannah* team and settled them into comfortable quarters after their fourteen-hour drive. The next morning, the *CoS* volunteers arrived at the airplane with the prepared wooden floors, several boxes of tools, and a lot of spirit.

As expected, the wooden pieces that had been constructed following Tommy Garcia's Hollywood plans did not always match the fit required in the *Miss Liberty*. There was a great deal of measuring, fitting, cutting, and applying fresh urethane to newly exposed wood before the floors could be fitted. Several USAF active-duty volunteers worked with our team in the radio room, helping Bob MacDonald position his perfect-fitting metal shelf brackets. These brackets would hold the heavy radio equipment that the Barksdale volunteers were ready to install when our work was finished.

After completing the radio room, including the shelving and complex flooring/storage compartment, it took the next three days to finish the upper cockpit, lower cockpit, nose, and waist area. One bonus for our team was that Terry allowed them to bring the *Miss Liberty*'s original radio room table back to Savannah, where

Bob MacDonald, John Finch, Gil Patrick, Jeff Hoopes. (CoS Archives)

following our loaned parts policy, the table would be copied twice by our carpenters: one copy returning to Barksdale along with the original, and the other being installed in our airplane. (Historical note: When the table was unwrapped, our carpenters noted that the bottom of the table had been signed by several original members of the *Miss Liberty*'s crew.)

When the boys declared that they were done, there was much handshaking with the local volunteers and the *City of Savannah* visitors were treated to a terrific dinner by Terry and the Eighth Air Force Association. It had been quite an adventure and a learning experience for everyone involved.

While the Special Operations crowd was in Louisiana, we had another duo of Road Warriors going north and west. Darrell Schwartz and Bud Currey were sent on a double mission to Ohio and Indiana. They would bring home a treasure trove of neat stuff. The first stop was at the Military Aviation Preservation Society Air Museum (MAPS) in North Canton, Ohio. The material picked up at MAPS was the most significant lucky discovery that we encountered during our restoration effort. Further, we owe a great debt to the very generous and gracious management of that wonderful museum. Once again, Jeff Hoopes was involved. Here is his story:

Jeff Hoopes: *Tommy Garcia and I were on the phone in early 2012 talking about various technical issues and somehow the conversation*

One man's trash is another man's treasure. (CoS Archives)

came around to turrets. I mentioned that we probably never would have a complete and operational upper turret because there did not seem to be any interest in building them in the B-17 community. Tommy said it would make us one step above the rest if we did have an upper turret and that through a contact in England he knew of a G-model upper turret superstructure that was rotting in the outdoors at a naval aviation museum in Ohio. Then the conversation moved on. Later I thought about what Tommy had said and googled something like "B-17 turret in Ohio." I was amazed when I found an article from the local Aurora, Ohio, newspaper about the turret superstructure, including a picture! My first reaction was, "WOW, that's only about five miles from where my mother lives!" As soon as those words came out of my mouth, Jerry McLaughlin said, "Well, I guess we'll be paying for you to visit your mom in the very near future."

And so it came to be. I contacted the author of the story, Ms. Holly Schoenstein, who provided me with the contact information for the Military Aircraft Preservation Society museum curator, Mr. Kim Kovesci. I called Kim and explained to him who we were and asked if the MAPS museum had any plans for the turret superstructure. He informed me that they had no immediate plans and invited me to visit the museum and inspect the superstructure for myself in order to determine if the Mighty Eighth would be interested in obtaining the turret for our restoration.

Details were arranged, and off to frosty Ohio I went. I had a nice visit with Mom and drove down to meet with Kim and see the turret firsthand. They had moved the turret indoors, and I got to inspect it very carefully and take many pictures. I looked at the broken, rusted pile and the only thoughts that came to my mind were, "Man, what a waste of a trip this was; this thing is a piece of junk." How wrong I was!

After I got back to Georgia, I sent the pictures to Tommy Garcia. He went berserk! He told us (Jerry and myself) "You've GOT to get that! It's gold!" I immediately called Kim and explained that while we were cash poor, we had many WWII aircraft parts in our parts room and asked if we could trade something of value to his museum for the turret parts. A couple of weeks went by without a reply, and we were getting nervous that the MAPS board might decide that the value of the parts was more than they had anticipated and we would not be able to work out a trade. Finally, just as we were preparing a Road Warrior team to Grissom AFB on another mission, I heard from Kim. He told me that they only had need for parts for WWII Navy Corsair fighters, and since we didn't have anything even remotely related to what they needed, their Board of Directors had voted to donate the turret parts to the Mighty Eighth so that our B-17 could have original upper superstructure parts from an original B-17G when the restoration was completed. A class act!

Darrell Schwartz: *Bud Currey and I were picked to make the road trip to Ohio to bring home the upper turret structure. The Ohio portion of the trip was a last-minute addition, as we had already been scheduled to go to Grissom AFB, in Indiana, to bring back their Cheyenne tail turret. We flew to Canton, rented a truck and headed to the MAPS museum. The museum staff was very friendly and gave us a tour of the facility. When they finally showed us the turret structure, my first thought was, "We came all the way to Ohio for this? By the time we get back to Pooler, it will disintegrate into a pile of rust in the back of the truck." We left Canton as soon as we had loaded the turret parts into the truck and headed for Indiana to pick up the tail turret. It is gratifying that the upper turret parts turned out to be so valuable. They certainly didn't look like anything useful when we picked them up.*

On another area of the airplane, our most prolific volunteer, LMI Corporation's David Pinegar, really outdid himself with one of

2012's highlights, providing a unique solution to a problem. David had been trying to find some appropriate grade plexiglass for the side windows at the nose of the airplane. He finally found the rare thickness he needed, but had learned that after cutting the plexiglass to fit the windows he would have to bake each window in order to make it strong enough to remain in its position for years to come. Never shy about explaining what he needs to solve a problem, David walked into the kitchen behind the museum restaurant and approached the owner, Terri Belle, about his problem. Terri stepped up to the challenge and handed over David's request to her head baker, Linda Thompson, and the problem was solved on the spot. The pies lined up next to the oven were put aside and David's windows went into the oven. Linda got into the spirit of the day and provided David with a baker's hat as they waited for the windows to come out of the oven. The windows came out just like Linda's pies – perfecto!

While David was making windows for the front of the aircraft, additional work was being done for the interior of the nose. More Gulfstream Corporation expertise had been brought in via the corporate metal shop, with Gulfstream's Jim Moriarty supervising the

David Pinegar and our favorite baker, Linda Thompson. (CoS Archives)

building of the struts that had to be replaced as we transitioned back to the lower cockpit's original configuration. Our own John Finch was also working during his off hours in the Gulfstream metal shop to manufacture an original mounting ring for the nose turret.

Metalwork was being done at the opposite end of the airplane by other talented metal artisans, Jack Nilsen and Jim Odom, who were disassembling the Grissom turret in order to utilize its parts as templates for our new turret, and to treat the Grissom turret with anti-corrosion protection.

The highlight of the month of March was a visit from one of our favorite authors, Donald Miller. Don is the author of *Masters of the Air*, the pre-eminent book on the Eighth Air Force in WWII. (At this point in time, Don's work had yet to be selected as the third leg of the HBO WWII trilogy.) Don had spent a great deal of time in the Mighty Eighth's library while he was writing the book. I first met Don in Henry Skipper's office and then took him and his wife, Rose, for a tour of the airplane. As three transplanted New Yorkers, we all got along fine talking about WWII history, the B-17 restoration, and the commonality of our three families' histories in the Borough of Brooklyn.

A period of several weeks followed Don's visit where we caught our breath and put some effort into reorganizing the shop area and a special project, led by Paul Abare, to defog all of the airplane's fuel tanks. The slow interval period ended abruptly with the May 9 arrival of Tommy Garcia for Garcia Week V. Jeff Hoopes took Tommy through the airplane from nose to tail and wingtip to wingtip. The big issues inside the airplane were the progress with the wiring done by Rocky and His Friends and the lower cockpit and tail turret work done by the Wednesday "Night Riders." While climbing around on the wings, Tommy inspected the newly de-fogged gas tanks and the propellers, which had been scraped and painted by the Wednesday day crew. Garcia Week V evolved into more of a planning than a hands-on visit for Tommy as he met with the management team and Henry Skipper on several occasions, resulting in the development of a long-term plan for maintenance of the *CoS*'s engines as well as for acquisitions needed to keep the restoration on track. Items included: a full oxygen system, changing the airplane's electrical operation from battery to

"Thank You"to the City of Savannah *team from* Miss Liberty.
(CoS Archives)

house power and developing a strategy for several possible large trades with other projects.

The month of June brought some interesting developments, including a surprise from our good friend Terry Snook and the Barksdale restoration team. Terry had taken care of our team when they were in Louisiana, and he continued to show his appreciation for our assistance there with a very special award presented by the *Miss Liberty* project to those who have been instrumental in their progress. The specially produced wooden award is carved in the shape of the vertical stabilizer of a B-17, marked with the unit and aircraft markings of the original *Miss Liberty*. Terry told us that all of the previous awardees had been either general officers or Eighth Air Force fighter aces who had assisted the *Miss Liberty* project. We certainly appreciated being included in that kind of company.

The next events that brought excitement to the project were two superb examples of state-of-the-art engineering from Gulfstream Corporation. During the month of March, Jim Moriarty had visited us and explained that through his various engineering assignments at Gulfstream he had heard about our project and Gulfstream management's strong support for having various corporate organizations involved. He was interested in seeing if he could be of any assistance—the answer was "You bet!" After several months of consulting with our metal team on both the structural issues in the nose of the aircraft and the construction from scratch of the tail turret, Jim came through for us with two remarkable pieces of engineering perfection. The rebuilding of the nose back to its original configuration from the civilian adaptation that had been installed by Kenting Aviation was a major challenge because only the 1945 Boeing drawings were available to show the engineers how to recreate the necessary structural metal parts, unlike the tail, where actual parts were available to measure and replicate. Original drawings were just fine for Jim and his team, and he arrived with a spanking new chin turret ring that was necessary in order to mount our chin turret.

The second piece delivered by the magicians from Gulfstream came from their state-of-the-art RDC Composites Lab and was produced under the supervision of the shop supervisor, Chuck Aitkin and his team. Seventy man-hours of personal time were required to create an exact composite copy of the Cheyenne turret upper gun mount structure that had been removed from the Grissom AFB turret.

Jim Odom: *The Cheyenne turret upper gun mount is probably the only carbon fiber B-17 part in the world! It looks great and fits perfect. Jack and I had been stressing out for a long time over how we were going to build this piece. It was a major milestone to finally have this part made available. The guys in the Composites Lab at Gulfstream did a wonderful job.*

The chin turret ring manufactured by Jim Moriarty's Gulfstream metal shop. (CoS Archives)

July saw a major jump forward for the project with the arrival of Steve Grodt and Bob Dupree from Chroma Systems Solutions located in Foothill Ranch, California. Steve and Bob joined us with several important boxes of equipment that Chroma was donating to the project. Steve traveled all the way from company headquarters in California, and Bob from upstate New York to be with us and deliver two sets of Chroma power supply equipment. This equipment literally changed our

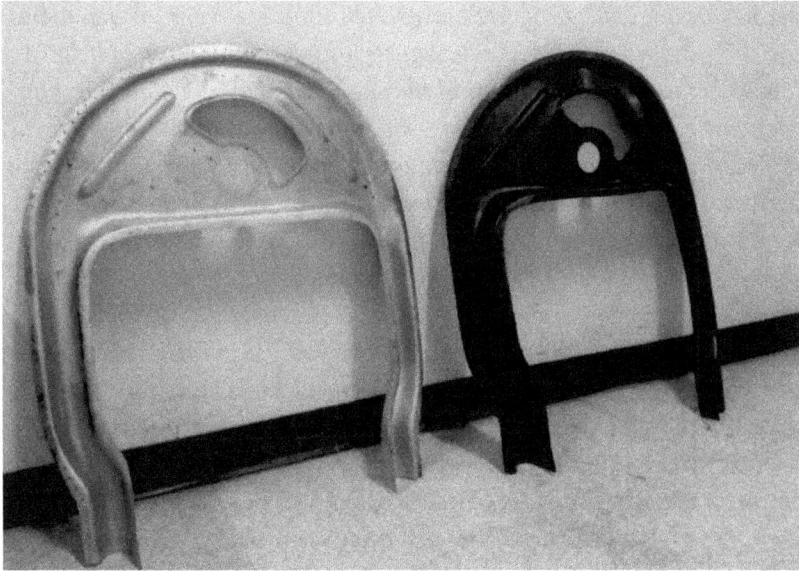

The original metal mount is on the left—the composite exact copy is on the right. (CoS Archives)

plans for the future of the project. Again, Jeff Hoopes was in the middle of this story.

Jeff Hoopes: *When we had finally come to the reality that powering our beloved B-17 strictly with a series of batteries was not going to be possible, I set out trying to find a suitable technology that would provide us with a reliable source of power. I started by consulting with Fred "The Turret Guy" Bieser as our planned turret operations seemed to be the biggest challenge in our use of electrical power within the aircraft. Fred told me he uses 24 volt, DC 50 amp power supply to power his various turrets, so I began searching the Internet for a 24 volt, 50 amp DC power supply, and found many possibilities.*

I randomly chose the Chroma Systems hyperlink, looked at their offerings, and used the "Contact Us" link on their website to send them a list of the specifics that we were looking for, a system that would provide us the power to run our aircraft's systems, along with one power turret at any given time. Several days later I got a phone call from Bob Dupree. Bob explained that he was very familiar with our project, and that he was a serious WWII buff. I was really amazed when he told me that he had actually been to our museum, after a visit to Savannah where his daughter had recently graduated from *the Savannah College of Art and Design. Bob was very excited about our project, and seemed like he was serious about wanting to help. We talked for a while, and Bob said that he would contact Chroma management and get back to me. I hoped, that at best, they would give us a decent discount on the equipment we needed. When the proposal arrived I was surprised by the sophistication of the equipment they were suggesting, which appeared to be WELL in excess of anything we would ever be able to afford, and there was no pricing on the proposal. I called Bob and mentioned both of my concerns. Bob's answer, "Don't worry, we are donating the equipment to you." I couldn't believe what I was hearing; I think I asked him to repeat himself. I went over the list of equipment one more time, and he reaffirmed: it was going to be a corporate donation. In the end, Chroma Systems donated TWO entire 24 volt 300 amp DC power supplies, worth in excess of $15,000. Our project's power source was acquired, and we knew it would meet all of our needs, and then some! Sometimes miracles do happen!*

Bob Dupree: *I had visited the museum with my family during my daughter Anna's graduation from the Savannah College of Art and Design. I was enthralled by the project and the overall presence of the museum. It is a phenomenal place, from the entrance to the chapel. Months later we received the e-mail request from Jeff Hoopes asking about a power supply. I suggested our "B" series equipment*

Steve Grodt and Bob Dupree wearing their official CoS badges.
(CoS Archives)

with its scalability for additional power as needed, and even dreamt up the idea of mounting it in the ground power cart. Steve Grodt came up with the money from his marketing budget, and the president of our group Fred Sabatine (also the son of a WWII Vet and a history buff himself) blessed the project. Steve and I made arrangements to meet in Savannah to donate the equipment. The greeting we received, including staff badges and a media ceremony, really gave me a feeling of ownership. My badge and the picture of us standing next to the airplane are on the wall of my office today. I'm proud to have been a part of saving this important piece of history.

Steve Grodt: *Bob brought the project to me and it quickly became a no-brainer to donate the equipment. My role was to manage the agreement with Henry Skipper, nurture the relationship with the museum and its staff and drive the PR for Chroma Systems Solutions. Our applications engineer, Larry Sharp, also played a critical technical role, specifying the right configuration and remotely helping with the installation. It was a real team effort and a pleasure to be part of this entire effort.*

Dave Talleur and Rocky Rodriquez were our experts on the subject of aircraft power supply. As Dave looked over the newly arrived Chroma equipment, he described it to me as a "heart transplant" for the *City of Savannah*. He explained that we would now be able to bring power to the airplane using museum house current. The house power, along with the Chroma power supply technology, would enable us to operate all of our planned on-board equipment, to include the radio room, flaps, lighting, power turrets, and the planned state-of-the-art interactive media for the museum visitors.

Several of the local TV stations came to the museum to see our first demonstration of the Chroma equipment, using our as yet un-mounted chin turret as a showcase for the power capabilities that we now had at our disposal. Another big step had been taken in our stated objective of becoming the finest static B-17 display in the world!

While the state-of-the-art technology was being tested within the Combat Gallery, there was also important work going on involving equipment that had been constructed before the birth of many of the volunteers. Road trips were now a staple of how we

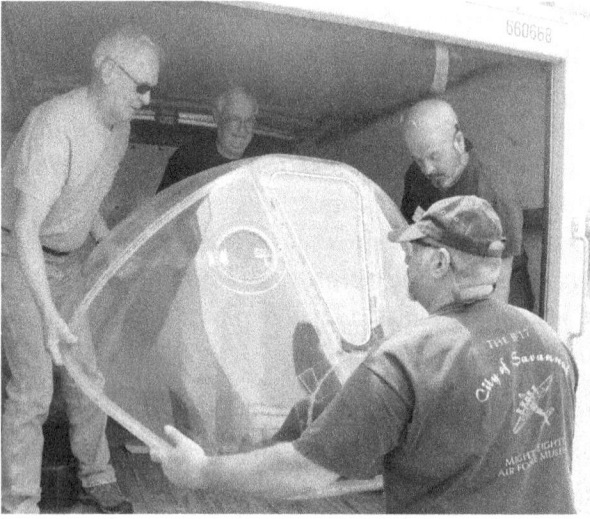

Joel Hedgpeth and Rocky Rodriquez assisting Darrell in unloading the EAA nosepiece. (CoS Archives)

were bringing home equipment to mount on the airplane. Darrell Schwartz had become one of the stalwart Road Warriors, and in mid-July 2012 he departed for Oshkosh, Wisconsin, on a solo trip to bring home a "new" nosepiece for the *City of Savannah*. The original nosepiece for our airplane was almost opaque from scratches and many years sitting in the sun. As was often the case, we had discussed this subject with Tommy Garcia, which led to a call to Norm Ellickson, our very good friend from the Experimental Aircraft Association, and once again EAA came to the rescue. In exchange for a starboard wing oil tank, Norm provided us with a not-so-perfect, but much superior, nosepiece that would serve on a temporary basis for our airplane. Darrell, once again, prevailed over administrative and logistical hurdles and brought the nosepiece safely back to Pooler, where it was immediately picked up by LMI Corporation to have several cracks repaired before being mounted on the airplane.

Early September brought a very symbolic and historical event to the Mighty Eighth and to our project. The 388th Bomb Group came to Pooler to celebrate their annual reunion around the airplane whose name was so closely attached to one of their own crews. As we mentioned previously, Lt. Kittle and his crew, but not the original airplane, were assigned to the 388th when they arrived in England in December of 1944. The 388th veterans had been very supportive of our project since its inception. On the occasion of their 2012 reunion, they forwarded two vinyl copies of the 388th

The unique "High H" insignia of the 388th Bomb Group. (CoS Archives)

"High H" group tail insignia and asked that we place them on the airplane on a temporary basis to honor the group during their reunion. Needless to say, we were more than happy to accommodate their wishes. Dave Talleur supervised the placement of the insignia and it was gratifying to see the smiles on the faces of the veterans and their families, when they entered the Combat Gallery and saw their markings on the *City of Savannah's* stabilizer.

Mid-September called for another all-hands meeting to bring the volunteers up-to-date on events affecting the project, to thank several individuals who had been making significant contributions, and to introduce what would become a very welcome tradition to the project.

The volunteers who were singled out for outstanding performance thus far in 2012 included Bob MacDonald, Jeff Hoopes, and Scott Whitcher. Bob was honored for his part in the very successful Barksdale AFB road trip and the original metalwork he completed for both the lower cockpit and the tail turret. Jeff's contributions included his leadership on the Barksdale trip and his key roles in both the Ohio Upper Turret Miracle and the Chroma Corporation Heart Transplant. Scott's efforts displayed his diverse carpentry and research skills as well as a strong dose of incentive. He constructed a board that displayed a baseball card picture of each volunteer with information as to their role on the restoration team. The board is displayed beneath the left wing of the airplane between the two display cases that Scott built for us in 2011. Still in the carpentry field, Scott constructed a sample wooden B-17 ammunition box that we hope will become the first of many that will be sold in the museum bookstore to supplement our finances. Finally, Scott did a great deal of research in the area of military Challenge Coins. These coins are carried by members of various military organizations, and they display the name and often the mission of that organization. They are given as gifts to friends and visitors and are, we hear, sometimes utilized to determine who might have to purchase beverages in selected locations that serve special libations. Scott submitted ideas for a *City of Savannah* challenge coin that was heartily approved by Henry Skipper and rushed into production. The final event of the evening was the gift of a coin to all members present and the announcement that from that day forward all new volunteers would receive a coin after having completed twenty-five hours of volunteer service.

The official City of Savannah *challenge coin as designed by Scott Whitcher.* (Scott Whitcher)

Scott Whitcher: *Having been associated with, or employed by, various military and government organizations over the past 50 years, I have quite a collection of challenge coins. After moving to South Carolina, I joined the Sun City Veterans Association and while serving as the group's quartermaster I had the opportunity to design their challenge coin. As a member of the* City of Savannah B-17 *restoration team, I saw the group grow in number, and I felt a coin was appropriate for all the reasons other groups employ them, including morale and esprit de corps. Additionally, the coin could be provided to special donors for their help with the project or sold in the museum's* *gift shop as a fundraiser. My idea was very well received by the project's management team and approved by the museum CEO for production. I am very proud that I was allowed to design the coin and that it has become an important part of the project's culture.*

The month of October meant that it was time for the 2012 B-17 Co-Op meeting. While we had been happy to be the hosts in 2011, it was a relief to only have to travel and let someone else do the hosting work in 2012. It was an additional bonus that for the second year in a row, the meeting would take place on the East Coast, this time at the Military Aviation Museum (MAM) located in Virginia Beach, Virginia, the home of the flying B-17 *Chuckie*.

I attended the meeting with Dave Talleur and Jeff Hoopes. It was another one of the great breaks that we have encountered over the years that these two highly knowledgeable professionals were with me on this trip as we found the MAM staff and volunteers to be a friendly and highly skilled group, who were more than happy to share their ideas and knowledge with Jeff and Dave.

After returning from Virginia, with a morale boost from the new friends we had made, I got an exciting phone call from Jim Moriarty. He told me that his "Merry Band of Metal Masters" at Gulfstream Corporation had completed two more projects, and that they would like to come to the museum and deliver their handiwork.

Chuckie sitting in the rain at the Military Air Museum in Virginia Beach, Virginia. (Author photo)

Looks simple, but this is actually very sophisticated work. Top: Turret well for chin turret built from scratch, using 1944 Boeing drawings. Bottom: The rotating bar that controls the arc of the tail turret gun platform. The bar was copied from the identical part loaned to us from the Grissom museum turret. Thank you to Gulfstream Corporation's metal team. (CoS Archives)

Jim's team, working after scheduled shifts and on weekends, had utilized scrap metal salvaged from Gulfstream projects, 1944 Boeing drawings, and metal examples from the Grissom AFB tail turret to create two very necessary parts for our airplane. As was the case with the previous parts that Jim's team had produced for us, these parts—the chin turret well and the tail turret rotating bar—are not available for sale in the world market. They could only be included in our restoration after being constructed from scratch by excellent craftsmen such as the Gulfstream metal shop professionals.

After the Gulfstream team arrived with the new parts, the original rotating bar from the Grissom tail turret was reinstalled and the entire turret reassembled. The rejuvenated turret was now complete and ready to be sent back to Chris Henry and his team in Indiana. Jack Nilsen and Tony Grasso did a first-class job refurbishing the turret, removing corrosion, painting the interior, and reassembling the entire structure. Bob MacDonald added some bonus work in the form of kneepad stands and several other pieces of interior work.

Apparently the word must have gotten out that Jack and company had done a particularly good job on the Grissom turret. As we were preparing to send a Road Warrior team to deliver the turret

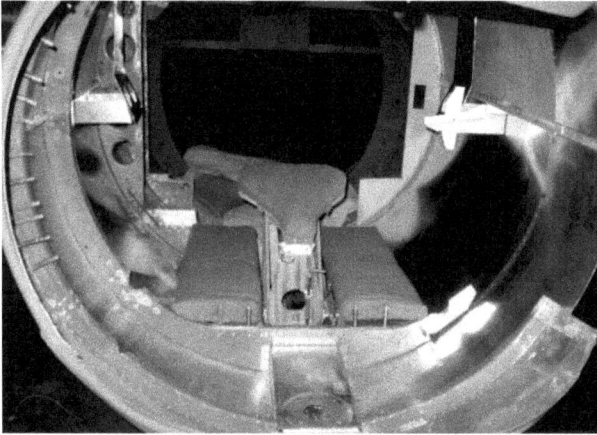

The Grissom project Cheyenne turret, painted, corrossion-free, and with the custom bicycle seat and kneepads added by Bob MacDonald. (CoS Archives)

back to Indiana, the National Museum of the United States Air Force (owner of the Grissom B-17) contacted us and asked that we send the turret commercially to their facility at Wright-Patterson AFB instead of returning the turret to Grissom. Building a crate that would hold the turret for commercial travel was something of a challenge but, as usual, our volunteers were able to complete the mission. The turret was last seen being loaded into a FedEx truck at the Mighty Eighth's shop entrance.

The windup of 2012, the fourth year of our project/adventure, left all of the volunteers feeling quite proud about what we had accomplished since bringing the *City of Savannah* home. Rocky and His Friends had completed much of the interior wiring we would need for operating the flaps, lights, turrets, and display materials. Power for those operations had been assured by the extremely generous donation of Chroma Corporation Solutions, Inc. Thanks to Gulfstream and LMI Corporations, sophisticated metalwork had been installed in the nose and tail of the airplane, and finally, who would have imagined that we would stumble across the extremely rare upper turret stanchions and cap that would, hopefully, be the basis of a fully operational upper turret. Plans were also underway to address other goals for the restoration, such as a ball turret and a new nosepiece. We felt very good about working within our limited budget and the ability of the team members to overcome the various challenges we had faced in the first four years of work. We hoped that the good work and good luck would continue into 2013. Little did we know what amazing events were in store for us in the

City of Savannah *volunteers at annual all-hands meeting for 2012.* (CoS Archives)

coming year that would move our project forward with more punch than we had ever imagined.

The final event on the 2012 calendar was the 3rd Annual Flying Fortress 5K. The *City of Savannah* volunteers, radio team

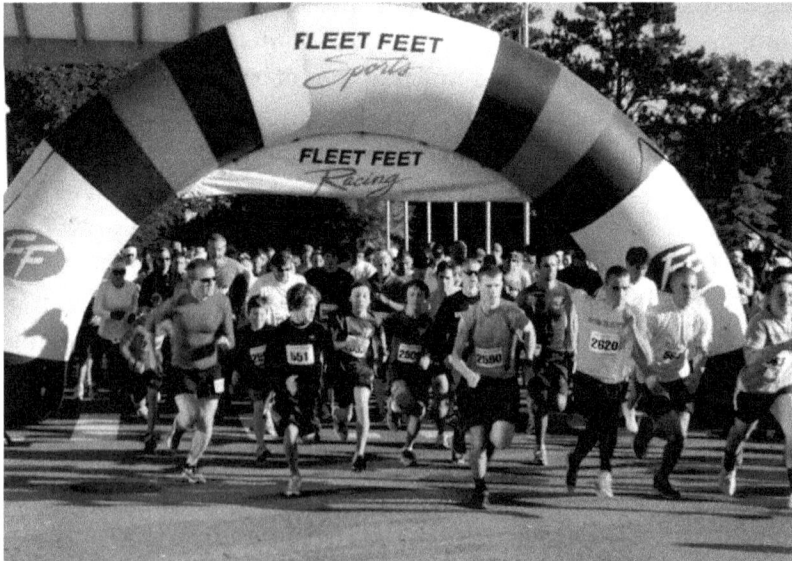

Runners leaving the starting line for the 2012 Flying Fortress 5K. (CoS Archives)

volunteers, and museum staff turned out to ensure that the project would be a financial success, and it was, with an even greater number of runners participating than in 2011. The financial success of the race was significantly enhanced by the sponsorship support of the United Parcel Service, Hilton Head Land Rover, and Fleet Feet Sports. Once again, our own Jane Grismer had put long hard hours into preparation for the race, and the payoff was a big one!

And for those of you who were wondering, yes, "Crazy Legs" Stombler was a medalist for the third consecutive year.

CHAPTER 5

Making It Work

JANUARY 2013 – OCTOBER 2014

"We have applied the best of ourselves to the task at hand."

Vince Lombardi

The fifth year of the project began with optimistic anticipation. The previous year had seen a great deal of success and everyone was ready for more. As had become the custom, we officially began the New Year with the anniversary dinner at the museum and took stock of where we were and what we planned for the future. Henry Skipper's opening remarks at the dinner did a great deal to further good expectations when he announced that one of our most distinguished board of trustees members, Donald Miller, had called to announce that HBO had signed an agreement with Don to make his book on the Eighth Air Force's WWII history, *Masters of the Air*, the third leg of their WWII trilogy, after *Band of Brothers* and *The Pacific*. Henry's second announcement was that the *City of Savannah* project had a generous new benefactor. As part of an annual appeal undertaken by the museum for financial support, a WWII Eighth Air Force veteran by the name of Joseph Glasser had contacted the museum and asked to speak to "whoever was in charge of the B-17 project." (I had received a note to call Joe and reached him at his office in New Haven, Connecticut. He explained to me that he had been a teenage navigator in the 94th Bomb Group in 1945 and that he was intrigued with our restoration. I gave him details on what we had done and what we were planning. When I finished he asked, "What do you need right now for your next step, how can I help you?" A half an hour later, Joe had agreed to provide the funds for us to purchase a ball turret that was sitting in a movie storage facility in California. He asked me how the purchase would be made, and I turned him over to Henry to complete the business end of the transaction.) Henry explained to the group that he and Joe had worked out the details of transferring funds to the museum's restoration account, and all that remained to complete the deal for a "new" ball turret was finalizing details with the owner of the turret. A big round of applause followed this great news.

After dinner and before our speaker for the evening began his presentation, I made some brief remarks to document the accomplishments of the group during the first four years of the project. More than 22,000 hours of work had been recorded, and thousands more probably were not. We had prepared a Strategic Plan that we anticipated would take 6 to 10 years to complete, and we had met all the requirements in only four years. The annual Flying Fortress 5K, organized by the museum's own Jane Grismer, had been our main source of income from 2010 to 2012. I mentioned that without the contribution of the local industrial community, particularly LMI and Gulfstream Corporations, the project would not have accomplished nearly as much as we had. Finally, the support of the project by Tommy Garcia and Harry Friedman from the very beginning could not even be measured. Recent out of town contributions from Chroma Systems Solutions Corporation and individual donors such as Joe Glasser spoke to a very positive future as the project became more well-known. In short, there were a lot of people and organizations to which we owed a salute for assisting us in our mission.

The highlight of the evening was the guest speaker, board of trustees member, Mr. John O'Neil. John's participation on the board is driven by the memory of his father, Staff Sergeant John J. O'Neil, who flew as a tail gunner in 1944 on a Pathfinder B-17 in the 482nd Bomb Group, stationed in Alconbury, England.

John presented a superb show of classic photos that his dad had brought home from WWII, depicting his service with the 482nd. He explained the importance of the museum's mission to tell the story of the WWII veterans and their sacrifice during the prime years of their youth. He mentioned how more young men died in the Eighth Air Force in WWII than in the entire Marine Corps, and how approximately 50 percent of the flight crew members who served

Author and John O'Neil. (CoS Archives)

between August of 1942 and May of 1945 were killed, wounded, or became prisoners of war. The most commented-upon portion of John's presentation was the individual pictures he showed of each member of his father's crew at their respective station on the B-17. With each picture, John gave the man's name and thanked the *City of Savannah* volunteers on behalf of that member of his dad's crew. It was an emotional and meaningful presentation that touched the hearts of everyone in the room.

Joel Hedgpeth: *I don't believe that anyone who attended the 2013 Volunteer Appreciation dinner will ever forget the presentation given by a member of the Mighty Eighth board of trustees, John O'Neil. The emotions John stirred in all of us with the presentation, especially coming from the viewpoint of each member on his father's B-17 crew, will not ever be forgotten by me. He closed the presentation by naming each crew member and his role and adding the phrase ". . . thanks you." I still get misty-eyed thinking of this. . . .*

Jim Grismer: *Good speakers make eye contact with their audience. When John O'Neil gave his closing remarks at the 2013 dinner, he somehow locked on to every eyeball in the room. It was a supremely*

153

focused presentation that riveted me in my seat. The intensity of the emotion he was exhibiting certainly got to me. As I wiped a tear from my eye I hazarded a glance around our table and noted that I wasn't alone. That moment told all of us who work on the project that we are indeed wed to the brotherhood of airmen who flew those B-17s in WWII. We honor them every day that we work to bring the City of Savannah back to life. I will always feel that way.

The year began with plenty of work to do on the airplane and in the shop. Even more important, events were going on in the museum offices that would significantly impact the entire restoration effort. Every year the museum sends out its annual appeal to all members and those associated with the museum through membership in Bomb Group Veterans Associations and similar groups. Joe Glasser was not the only person to respond to the request for financial support in 2013. Many smaller donations were made, which amounted to a good bit of help for both the museum and the *City of Savannah* project. Then the bombshell hit! Henry Skipper was contacted by a family that, on behalf of their patriarch, a WWII B-17 pilot, wished to make a significant donation to the B-17 project in order to assure its completion! A dollar figure was presented to the family that Henry felt would assure the completion of the restoration of the airplane. The family quickly agreed to the figure and a transaction was completed to place the funds in the *City of Savannah*'s bank account. Life had completely changed for those of us managing the project. We had to totally rethink how we would move forward now that we had the ability to purchase goods and services that had, to this point, been unavailable to us. Decisions were made, plans were accelerated, and some very positive events began to move the *City of Savannah* restoration down the road at a pace that none of us had ever imagined.

Looking back on events from the year 2013, one would think that perhaps we should call that period "The Year of the Donor."

Until the arrival of our new-found financial resources, we had not even imagined how we would be able to afford parts for the upper turret. Jeff Hoopes immediately began to do research and the upper turret became a realistic sub-project.

While plans were getting underway to build the upper turret, the planning for a ball turret also began to take shape, again based upon the generosity of a donor, in this case, Joe Glasser. As often happened, our good friend Tommy Garcia was at the heart of the ball turret story. Tommy had been involved with the turret in question when he was a technical advisor to the 1990 movie *Memphis Belle*. The turret had been removed from a B-17 being used in the movie so that close-ups could be taken of it in action to use in the movie. The turret had changed owners several times during the 23 years since Tommy had worked with it, and it was now in the process of changing owners once again. Midway through our negotiations with the owner, the turret became the property of the WWII Museum in New Orleans. Fortunately, all went well in discussions with the WWII Museum, and we were able to purchase the turret at the previously agreed upon price, with pickup approved at its current Auburn, California, location. Before any more changes could occur, we had Jeff Hoopes, our Chief Engineer/Road Warrior-In-Residence, on an airplane to Houston, where Tommy picked him up at the airport and they set out for California.

Jeff Hoopes: When it became a reality that one of us would be traveling to California with Tommy Garcia to pick up a near-complete ball turret, I immediately volunteered for this once-in-a-lifetime opportunity. Not only would I get to be cooped up in a pickup truck

The Memphis Belle *movie ball turret as it appeared when Jeff and Tommy arrived in California to pick it up. Note the pin-up pictures from its movie role. The pictures have been preserved and are on the ammo cans today.* (Jeff Hoopes)

for ten days with the legendary Tommy Garcia, I would meet more fa-
mous B-17 restoration veterans and have the opportunity to wander
around in warehouses full of WWII airplane parts and scrounge for
"stuff" for our beloved project.

Tommy and Jeff arrived in Auburn and immediately began
sending pictures back to us of the turret and its associated parts.
The agreement called for the final purchase to be made after an inspection by our representatives, and that the turret and associated
parts would be purchased "as is." Then a telephone call came that
brought everything to a halt! Tommy's inspection revealed that the
motors that operated the turret had been removed and replaced
with empty, look-alike covers. Tommy and I talked at length and
decided that because the rest of the turret was completely functional, and that appropriate motors for the turret, though rare, were
available, we should make the purchase under the "as is" condition
regardless of the absence of the motors. I talked with Henry Skipper, and we agreed to go forward with the purchase. The cash was
wired to the WWII museum and the boys loaded the turret onto
Tommy's truck and headed east.

When our Road Warriors arrived with our new ball turret, it
was immediately moved into the shop area and was completely disassembled for a total refurbishment.

The arrival of the upper turret in late 2012 had begun an adventure that would go on for months and years to come. The arrival
of the ball turret in 2013 set in motion a reorganization of the shop
area so that the ball, upper, and tail turrets could each have their
own work area within the shop. The fully operational chin turret
was sitting in a far corner of the shop awaiting its infrastructure to
be completed by our Gulfstream colleagues. It was at this point in
the restoration that we first began to understand that we just might
have the wherewithal to bring our project to a special level: the only
static B-17 restoration *in the world* to have fully functioning lighting, flaps, bomb bay doors, flight controls, radio room, and *three*
working power turrets on display to the public. We were truly beginning to believe in ourselves as a successful restoration team.

While the volunteers assigned to the ball turret began working with their new toy, two of our stalwart long-time volunteers
were working hard on the upper turret structure. Joe Pritchard and

The ball turret on board Tommy Garcia's truck. More than one police officer took a second look as Tommy and Jeff drove more than 3,000 miles across the United States. Picture on the bottom shows the travelers and Bud Porter, a founding trustee of the museum and WWII B-17 ball turret gunner, upon the arrival of the ball turret in Pooler. (CoS Archives)

Mort Glick were cleaning the rusted and corroded canopy and legs for the upper turret, while Jeff Hoopes was searching for parts that would eventually make the turret operational.

Jeff Hoopes: Once the upper turret structure was delivered back to Georgia, it began its restoration saga. The legs were the first items addressed with a deep cleaning and copious amounts of All Metal body filler. The canopy was first thought to be too far gone to restore, but when we pressure cleaned it and began to attack the corrosion,

157

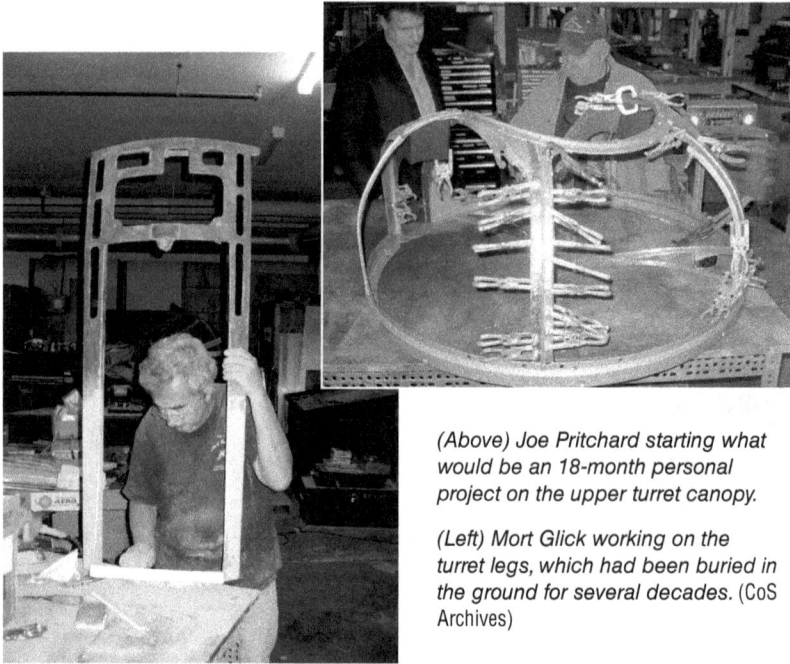

(Above) Joe Pritchard starting what would be an 18-month personal project on the upper turret canopy.

(Left) Mort Glick working on the turret legs, which had been buried in the ground for several decades. (CoS Archives)

we found that there was quite a bit of good material underneath the surface corrosion. We put our heads together in the shop and agreed that we should try to treat the metal surface corrosion with POR-15, a "paint over rust" cure that is well known in the automotive restoration world. I contacted the POR-15 Corporation directly to inquire about the suitability of their product for our situation. I was pleasantly surprised when the salesman offered to donate the material to us at no cost. He donated a gallon of their degreaser, and surface prep solution and 12 half-pints of the silver POR-15 paint product. We couldn't have been more pleased. The treatment we gave the canopy will allow it to sit proudly atop our beloved City of Savannah *forever.*

While the first quarter of 2013 had been a time of advancement and very high morale, we were hit hard by bad news in April when Shirley Shelton informed us that her husband, Skip, our good friend, resident artist, and WWII Eighth Air Force pilot had passed away. Skip was a great friend of our project, and his artwork on the *City of Savannah* will be seen by museum visitors for decades to come.

As our busy year continued, attention turned to the nose of the airplane after John Finch returned from several sessions in

Atlanta with one of our favorite contractors, Tom Wilson. John had been traveling to Tom's shop to assist in the production of parts to rebuild the nose of the *City of Savannah* back to original bomb-site/ turret configuration from the adaptations that had been done by Kenting Aviation to mount their camera equipment in the 1950s.

The everyday events surrounding the project seemed to speed up on an almost daily basis. Our Wednesday (day) crew chief, Jeff Hoopes, apparently didn't feel that he had enough to do supervising the restoration of the upper and ball turrets, so he enrolled in Savannah Technical College to learn about state-of-the-art 3-D CAD modeling. Jeff figured that with some formal introduction to this new engineering art, he could begin working with the Gulfstream Corporation 3-D engineering team to produce hard or impossible to find parts for our airplane. After a few sessions with the Savannah Tech faculty, Jeff saw an even better possibility to help our project and to add some spark to the Savannah Tech curriculum. He came to me and we discussed starting a program in cooperation with Savannah Tech whereby students at the school, as part of their coursework, would create software that would allow us to produce hard to find or unavailable parts. I thought it was a great idea and agreed with Jeff that he should bring the idea to Joseph Powell, the

Tom Wilson's chin turret parts for the City of Savannah. (CoS Archives)

159

appropriate Savannah Tech department head, and I would bring it forward to museum management. Joe Powell loved the idea, as did Henry Skipper, and we began a wonderful offshoot of the *City of Savannah* restoration project: a fledgling internship program that would work for both organizations. The educational concept that we were building was to have the students learn to apply 2013 software technology to create working parts through utilization of either engineering drawings (in this case, drawings that were 70 years old) or reverse engineering of existing parts. The students would learn state-of-the-art skills, Savannah Tech would have a much-enhanced modeling curriculum, and the *City of Savannah* project would be setting the standard for aircraft restoration parts acquisition. It was a winning combination for everyone.

Needless to say, the excitement for this new project began to affect many people involved with our project and at Savannah Tech. After careful consideration, including discussion with Joe Powell and several of our volunteers, Jeff selected three projects for the newly chosen student interns. Two of the three projects would involve duplication of parts we had borrowed from other B-17 projects: the navigator's astrodome aluminum support ring and the cheek gun K-5 gun mounts. The third project would involve the interns using 1940s drawings to create software to produce a sheet metal bombardier's control panel. From that original plan, the program developed into a full-fledged and curriculum-certified internship program. It didn't hurt that during this period Joe Powell was promoted to dean of Industrial Technology at Savannah Tech and that his support for the program continued from his upper management chair. Jeff completed his 3-D CAD Certificate and then enrolled in more classes to be certified in CNC/Precision Manufacturing, which qualified him to produce working parts from the 3-D software packages. All of these newfound skills actually hurt our project as the faculty at Savannah Tech were so taken with Jeff as a student that when they opened a new facility in a nearby county, they hired him as an instructor and he had less time to work with us because of his out-of-town responsibilities.

One of the biggest events on the schedule for the National Museum of the Mighty Eighth Air Force in the year 2013 was the July reunion of the Eighth Air Force Historical Society. The society is a national organization of Eighth Air Force veterans, many from the founding WWII generation. The annual reunions are held at various locations throughout the country. When they choose to have the reunions at their "home" museum in Savannah, it is always a special honor for everyone involved with the museum. This was the first time that the society would be holding a reunion at the Mighty Eighth with the *City of Savannah* in residence, so it was particularly important to us that the airplane look its best for these very special veterans and their families.

Months in advance we had been planning to have all four turrets temporarily installed to project the airplane with its full combat-ready silhouette to the visitors. The biggest challenge was the chin turret, a challenge that was met by the metalwork specialists of the Wednesday (night) crew, aka Bill Liening's Night Riders. The speakers at the formal meeting of the veterans would be standing beneath the nose of the airplane, and the chin turret would not only be seen by hundreds of attendees, it would appear in many pictures. As expected, the Night Riders did a fantastic job of mounting the turret cap (without the interior mechanical gear), and all the visitors and their cameras viewed a perfectly appearing chin turret. (Held together inside with ropes and 2x4s—not up to WWII standards, but it looked good to the visitors on that day!) The upper turret presentation only involved the canopy, and Joe Pritchard's team came through with a beautiful canopy that only weeks before would have been rejected as not presentable to exhibit. Finally, the dynamic duo of Jack Nilsen and Jim Odom had put together enough of the tail turret to "hang" the turret on the rear of the airplane. The pseudo-ball turret was fitted with gun barrels. Our bomber may have had a very shaky interior holding things together, but it looked really great from the outside to the visiting veterans, which was our goal.

All-hands were called for a special workday on the Saturday before the reunion, and we had a large turnout as everyone realized the importance of the upcoming event. The airplane was looking better than it had since it came in the door four years earlier. All four turrets were, at least by outward appearances, looking terrific. The aluminum skin was gleaming and Skip Shelton's *City of Savannah* artwork perfectly replicated the artwork from the original airplane on the starboard nose and port side waist area. The final touch was a special armament exhibit that was created next to the airplane showing off our newly purchased machine guns, .50 caliber ammunition belts, and the classic ammunition boxes built by Scott Whitcher.

The WWII Eighth Air Force veterans, the very people whom we were honoring, would arrive in several days, and we were sure they would be proud of our efforts.

All of the hard work in preparation for the reunion paid off when several hundred reunion participants, including 67 WWII veterans of service with the Eighth, arrived at the museum. Events began with a "formal" tour of the museum for the reunion visitors and the introduction of our B-17 at the very end of the tour. One of the main points of discussion among the visitors was learning that the *City of Savannah* radio team was actually broadcasting from the radio room as the visitors watched their activities on a TV screen and listened to the operator's conversations on a speaker system.

After their tour of the museum, the reunion group filled the area in front of the airplane to overflowing as speakers from the museum and historical society addressed the veterans and their

Armament package exhibit. Note the temporary ball turret cap under the airplane and the soon-to-be-mounted complete ball turret standing behind the display. (Scott Whitcher)

The author speaking to WWII Eighth AF veterans: "We are your children and grandchildren." (Debra Kujawa – Eighth Air Force Historical Society)

families. I was asked to present the B-17 to the veterans. It was a very emotional moment for me to stand directly in front of these men, many of whom were only teenagers when they flew in the skies over Europe. I mentioned that several of our volunteers had direct ties to the Eighth in WWII. Bill Liening's dad had been a waist gunner in the 385th Bomb Group and had been interned in Switzerland after a horrendous mission experience. Greg Kindred's extended family had received six telegrams announcing that sons were MIA, and three of those young men had died, one in the tail turret of a 327th Bomb Group B-17. Both Bill and Greg had joined us after ending military careers in aviation. I also mentioned that my uncle was a Ninth Air Force navigator who was KIA on D-Day. I emphasized that many others from our group had relatives who served all over the world during WWII. I ended my comments by stating that the passion and dedication of the volunteers to the restoration came from the fact that "we are your children and your grandchildren."

Henry Skipper made closing remarks, and the veterans and their families then began to inspect the airplane and mix with the volunteers. There was a great deal of handshaking, hugs, and congratulations from our visitors. I was standing with some of the volunteers, including Bill and Greg, when several veterans and their wives came over to our group in tears—talking about the children and grandchildren comment. I hadn't realized the effect those few words would have on that audience. The tears of "grandparents" became contagious.

After the powerful events surrounding the visit from the Eighth Air Force Historical Society, the management team (consisting of myself, Dave Talleur, Jim Grismer, and the three crew chiefs, Jeff Hoopes, Bill Liening, and Rocky Rodriguez) sat down and took stock of where we were with the project. Rocky and His Friends, the resident electricians, had made strong progress in wiring the airplane for all of the planned display activities in the future, to include the radio room, lights, flaps, the bomb bay doors, and particularly, the three power turrets. If we could get the upper turret working, it would set us ahead, as far as we knew, of any other static B-17 in the world. A lofty goal, but as we sat at that meeting we said, as a group, "Why not?" Our job had become significantly easier thanks to the Chroma power equipment that provided power to the airplane, enough to operate power turrets on an individual basis. Bill's Night Riders were also making excellent progress with the nose and tail turrets. Structural riveting was coming to completion on the nose and the tail turret's metalwork was almost finished. Jeff's Wednesday (day) crew was working full time on the upper and ball turrets and, thanks to the unexpected influx of funds, the administrative task of acquiring the operational parts for the upper turret was also well underway.

It would not be an exaggeration to say that in September of 2013 morale was sky high and we were ready to once again show off for a major audience. This time the occasion was the October arrival of the 100th Bomb Group Veterans Association and the HBO team that would be working with them in preparation for the upcoming mini-series. It was not a coincidence that we scheduled Garcia Week VI for the same week as the arrival of the mini-series team. Tommy's experience with the *Memphis Belle* movie and other West Coast film projects was part of our marketing plan to work with the HBO team.

As we prepared for October's event, spirits were dampened when we realized we would need to repaint some of Skip Shelton's work on the nose where replacement parts had taken away his original work, and that Skip had never been able to return to paint the tail number on the airplane. Both jobs would have to be completed before the upcoming reunion and Garcia Week. I called Shirley Shelton and asked if there was a colleague of Skip's that might be available to do the job. She was grateful for the call but said that there wasn't anyone she could recommend. Bill Liening found the answer for us with two colleagues from Flight Safety International, Kristine Baker and Abby Schaaf. These fine ladies had the honor of repairing Skip's original work. We told them the story, which they much appreciated, and they got the job done.

Monday, October 14, began a chaotic week, and a lot of fun, for the *City of Savannah* volunteers as Tommy Garcia arrived for the beginning of his sixth week in residence. We started with an all-hands staff meeting to let Tommy know where we were with our various sub-projects and to fill everyone in on the plans for the day's activities. We were also honored to have our chief mentor, Dr. Harry Friedman, in attendance. Harry knew how important the week's events were to not only the *City of Savannah* project, but to the entire B-17 community, and he took time off from his busy medical

Kristine Baker and Abby Schaaf repaired Skip Shelton's nose art and gave the City of Savannah *its long delayed tail numbers.* (CoS Archives)

practice to be with us. Immediately after lunch came an unusual event, particularly during a Garcia Week: most of the workforce left for the day. The cause for their departure was an unexpected bonus for all the work they had been doing for years on the *City of Savannah*. The previous week our good friend Don Brooks, a neighbor from Douglas, Georgia, and president of the *Liberty Belle Association*, had called Henry Skipper to tell him that the movie *Memphis Belle* B-17 that he was flying that year would be in Savannah on October 14 to do some publicity work in preparation for the 100th Bomb Group reunion. Don told Henry that the airplane would be returning to their home field in Douglas with only its three crew members on board, and he offered to give nine of our volunteers a free B-17 ride back to Douglas. Henry called me with the great news and then I had to figure out the logistics as well as who would get to ride on the *Belle*. After consultation with Dave Talleur and Jim Grismer, the final decision of who got to ride on the B-17 was based upon two criteria: seniority and who answered the telephone first. Finally, nine of our volunteers were selected. The lucky winners left for the airport immediately after lunch for their first ride in a B-17. Jim Grismer and Jack Hango had departed several hours earlier and would be in Douglas to meet our flyers and provide them with a ride back to Pooler in a rented van.

While half of the volunteers who showed up at the museum on October 14 departed for their B-17 ride, the rest of us were back in Pooler to finish up day one of Garcia Week. One of the most important events of that afternoon was placing the signature marking of the 100th Bomb Group, the "Square D" symbol, on the vertical stabilizer of the *City of Savannah*. The method for placing the temporary unit symbol on the airplane belongs to museum staffer Heather Thies. Heather's idea was so successful that it is now museum policy to place the realistic looking, but temporary, markings on the airplane for any visiting group that makes a request to be recognized.

The second important event that afternoon caused a few of us who had been around from the beginning to get a little emotional. One of Tommy Garcia's main goals for this visit was attained when he and our chief electrician, Rocky Rodriguez, called for attention. When everyone had gathered around them near the nose of the

The lottery-winning B-17 passengers pose with the movie Memphis Belle *B-17. (L–R) Ray Fowler (pilot), Milt Stombler, Scott Whitcher, Jim Grismer, Jack Nilsen, Tonnie Glick, Joel Hedgpeth (behind Tonnie), David Pinegar, Bill Liening, Don Brooks (host), Danny Harden, Mort Glick.* (CoS Archives)

aircraft, Rocky, for the very first time, opened and closed our bomb bay doors using the newly installed electric motors. Another special event to be noted in the history of the project!

The 100th Bomb Group reunion was being sponsored by HBO. The goal of the HBO staff was to obtain as much personal history from the group's veterans as possible for use in development of the third leg of their WWII mini-series trilogy. This episode, "Mighty Eighth" would be based on Donald Miller's history of the Eighth Air Force in WWII entitled *Masters of the Air*. HBO arranged for the veterans and their families to stay in a nearby hotel that would also be the site for individual and group interviews of the 100th veterans by HBO researchers. The NMMEAF would be the social center for the veterans with tours of the museum and a dinner in the museum rotunda to complete their visit.

The 100th veterans arrived at the museum on October 17 for their guided tours. We turned out in what had now become our Class A uniforms: *City of Savannah* golf shirts and khakis. We waited for the veterans to enter the Combat Gallery, where we greeted them individually and provided tours around the airplane, in essence giving each of them a private guide to answer questions about

The 100th BG Square D on the CoS tail. Jack Hango (R) installs the left elevator while Jim Argo supervises. Darrell Schwartz, underneath, is doing the hard work. (CoS Archives)

the restoration. We also listened to their stories and generally did our best to make them feel that they were in "their" museum as our special guests. Many of the veterans were very happy to see the 100th Group "ID" on the tail of the airplane—obviously a good decision to put the time and effort into that project.

After touring the museum and the *City of Savannah*, the group moved to the restaurant for lunch. Following lunch, all of the veterans, their families, the *City of Savannah* volunteers, and the museum staff gathered in front of the museum as the movie *Memphis Belle* B-17, which had just taken our volunteers on a wonderful trip, flew over the museum in a tribute to the visiting 100th BG veterans. I was especially honored to watch the flyover with board of trustees member John O'Neil and Dan Rosenthal, the son of perhaps the most famous 100th BG WWII hero, Robert "Rosie" Rosenthal. It was quite a day.

Although the day had been exciting, our work was not going to end until well into the evening. We had been asked to have a team on hand to assist with a special visit to the airplane from HBO producer Guido Caretto. Guido arrived in the Combat Gallery several hours after the museum had closed. He brought a great

deal of sophisticated photography and video equipment. I spent time explaining the details of the airplane to him, to include access to the interior, and listening to his questions on how he might best utilize his camera gear for his planned video tour of virtually every aspect of the exterior and interior of the *City of Savannah.* We were oversupplied with manpower, but we wanted to show him we were more than ready to help. For several hours we assisted Guido as he moved throughout the airplane with his equipment. When he was packing to leave, he asked if he could have several hours more with the airplane the following night. That was, of course, not a problem. The following night Bill Liening and Joel Hedgpeth picked Guido up at his hotel, and they assisted him for almost three hours as he repeated his video procedures from the night before, this time emphasizing the exterior of the airplane. Bill and Joel also spent time that night entertaining visitors from the dinner for the 100th BG veterans, underway in the museum rotunda.

After the departure of the 100th Bomb Group, it was time to take a break. I could tell that even this hardworking crew needed a bit of time to stand down. Once again, we assembled the management team and took stock of where the project was and what was in the immediate future.

The management team sat at a table in the museum art gallery and discussed how 2013 had been quite a year. It all started at the annual dinner when John O'Neil's presentation had inspired so many of us. Then there was the very successful museum finance campaign that resulted in Joe Glasser buying us a ball turret and the extremely generous cash donation that had completely changed how we planned and executed the management of the project. "The Year of the Donor" remained a very valid phrase, literally from the nose of

This display on the City of Savannah *tail turret was a symbol of the spirit and morale of the volunteers as 2013 began to wind down. As October ended, Greg Kindred placed a specially prepared addition to the tail turret, designed to ward off any seasonal bandits, such as witches with broom-mounted weapons.* (CoS Archives)

the airplane to the tail. Morale had peaked with the two memorable events involving the WWII Eighth Air Force Society reunion in August and the 100th Bomb Group reunion in October. Meeting with so many WWII veterans on those occasions had pushed our group

The official 2013 City of Savannah *volunteer photo. A great group of people, who did a great job.* (CoS Archives)

to make the veterans as proud as possible when they came into the Combat Gallery to see "their" airplane.

2014

We began the year 2014 more determined than ever as we gathered for the traditional annual dinner to celebrate the accomplishments of the previous year. The major difference between this dinner and the previous events was the sheer number of guests in attendance, starting with Joe Glasser. Joe flew down to Savannah from New Haven, Connecticut, to check out the ball turret that he had purchased for us. He arrived on Friday night, in time to visit with Rocky and His Friends the next morning.

Additional guests at the dinner included Fred "The Turret Guy" Bieser who drove from Atlanta to be with us, and Dean Joseph Powell from Savannah Technical College, with a contingent of six, including three faculty members and three of the four interns selected for the pilot semester of our new intern program: Jared Edie, Hahn Luu, and Jason Betts. Finally, we were honored that the Houston Garcias, Tommy and his wife, Karen, joined us for our fifth anniversary dinner.

Henry Skipper began the evening with some opening comments regarding the evolution of the project over the previous five years. He made special note of the presence of Joe Glasser and Dean Powell as well as the work that Jeff Hoopes had done to initiate the intern program with Savannah Technical College. He also

Joe Glasser, center, standing with the ball turret, along with CoS volunteers: (L–R) Jeff Hoopes, Josh, Joel, and Jeff Hedgpeth, Joe, Jack Devine, Bill Schwickrath, Dave Talleur. Mort Glick is the designated sign holder. (CoS Archives)

mentioned that during 2013, the volunteers had contributed a record 8,000 hours, 2,000 more than the previous 12-month high; and that the majority of those hours had been devoted to the Eighth Air Force Society and the 100th Bomb Group/HBO visits. He noted that a record 27 volunteers had exceeded 100 hours of service during 2013.

Henry's comments were followed by a wonderful dinner, after which he returned to the podium for some closing comments. He told us that during the sixty months the project had been in service, there had been a total of 141 individuals officially on the books as volunteers with the *City of Savannah*, but only ten had served the entire time. He asked these ten volunteers to come to the front of the room and began a new tradition by presenting each of them with a pin for five years of service to the B-17 restoration project.

The dinner ended with everyone very excited about the prospects for 2014 and, as it turned out, they were right.

The work year started with a major effort by all three volunteer crews to put the ball turret into operational service. Much as Gil Patrick had become famous for designing the "rotisserie" work stand to provide easy access to the tail turret, Bob Kinsell solved a similar access problem with the ball turret by designing what came to be known as the "gallows," which held the ball turret off the floor and provided 360-degree access to its interior.

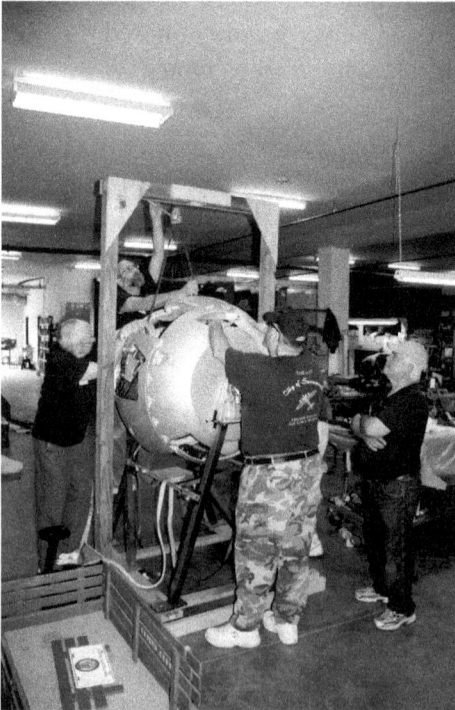

Bob Kinsell's "gallows." The designer is on the right. (CoS Archives)

Jeff Hoopes had been leading the effort on the turret's restoration ever since bringing it back from California.

By February his team was getting close to having the turret ready to mount in the airplane. Jeff's goal was to finish the assembly of the interior of the turret and conduct the final mounting during the planned Garcia Week VII scheduled for March, one year to the week from when Tommy and Jeff had brought the turret back from California.

Jeff Hoopes: When we arrived back in Pooler with the ball turret, we counted our blessings in that we actually had an original WWII ball turret. While the turret had original gear boxes that would make it turn, and Hollywood credentials, we were missing the vital motors to make the gears function. We stripped the turret down with the goal of identifying every single part depicted in our 1945 manuals. This search revealed that we were missing several other essential small parts. Luckily, after a brief search of the Internet, we discovered that the parts appeared to be available on the commercial market. Each part was cleaned and carefully inspected, and in the case of the bearings and gear boxes, overhauled, to "like new" condition. We were concerned about some cracks in the cast aluminum ball and once again the "local aviation expertise" that Bob Mikesh had told us was so important, came to the rescue when Jim Odom brought the ball to the Gulfstream Corporation welding shop for a quick repair that would have taken weeks and a big payout to have done commercially. While all the rehab work was being done, I was parts hunting. The major breakthrough came when I spoke with John Szabo, the president of a company in California named Depot 41. John put together a package that included the missing motors as well as hydraulic pumps that we needed. When John's parts arrived, we could see that the turret project was going to work and we pushed even harder. Part of that final push was going to pay off through our growing relationship with Savannah Technical College's drafting department and machine shop. Several of the final parts, the turret's support masts and their couplings, were not on any vendor's list of available parts. They simply did not exist in the commercial parts market. We also did not have any manufacturer's drawings of the missing parts, only an assembly drawing from the original parts catalogue. We gave these very basic drawings to our Savannah Tech interns, who delivered, big time, with state-of-the-art 3-D CAD models of the missing parts. The software models were then delivered to the school's Machine Tool Technology Department, which produced the final parts. Everyone was VERY happy.

Jeff and his team were pushing technology to its limits and working three different shifts to create the electrical, metal, and interior parts of the turret for its final mounting on the airplane. We had matured from "We don't know what we don't know," five years previously, to coordinating with world-class machinists and designers to construct recreations of 70-year-old parts. I spoke with Jeff and asked him if, as a statement to what he and the others had created with this operating turret, he would be willing to have us bring in the media to show off to the entire community what was

The ball turret with all its parts displayed prior to assembly. Note the movie Hollywood "pin-up" pictures preserved on the metal ammunition cans from their movie role in 1988. (CoS Archives)

being accomplished within the walls of the Mighty Eighth with the operational ball turret. He didn't even stop to think about it: "Yes," he said. "How do you want to do it?"

We decided that, to make the event as dynamic as possible, we would have the media observe the turret being moved into its dorsal well beneath the airplane and then lifted into the fuselage. The closure for the event would be when the turret would begin to rotate—a great camera image for the 6:00 news. The secret to success for our plan was that we would practice the entire process in private, before the public event.

As the date of the actual mounting of the turret came, we were utilizing almost every asset that was available to us within the museum and some resources from rather far away; that is, we were constantly on the phone to Houston with Tommy Garcia as we prepared for the big day.

The first step in mounting the turret was to get the airplane lifted to a perfectly level line. The perfect-level requirement was necessary both for the turret to fit beneath the airplane for mounting and to ensure that the mounting ring would allow the turret to turn easily.

The dress rehearsal for lifting the turret into the *City of Savannah*'s fuselage took place on Monday, March 3, the day before the scheduled media event. An all Air National Guard team of Sam Currie, Bill Burkel, and Joe Pritchard was assigned to bring the B-17 tail off the ground to achieve a zero-degree tilt, nose to tail. In preparation for lifting the tail, the team went to visit their colleagues at the 165th Air National Guard facility and returned with a 40-ton-capacity bottle jack that they had used in the past to do similar lifting work with modern C-130 aircraft. Utilizing the jack, specially cut plywood, and 4x4 studs, the three veterans got beneath the tail of the *City of Savannah* and in short order had the aircraft in a level stance that would allow the turret's mounting ring, and the turret itself, to be properly installed in the airplane.

The next step in the process was to have two mounting teams, one working inside and one outside of the airplane, mount the ring that would support the turret. Jeff supervised this process from within the airplane as the ring was lifted into the fuselage and

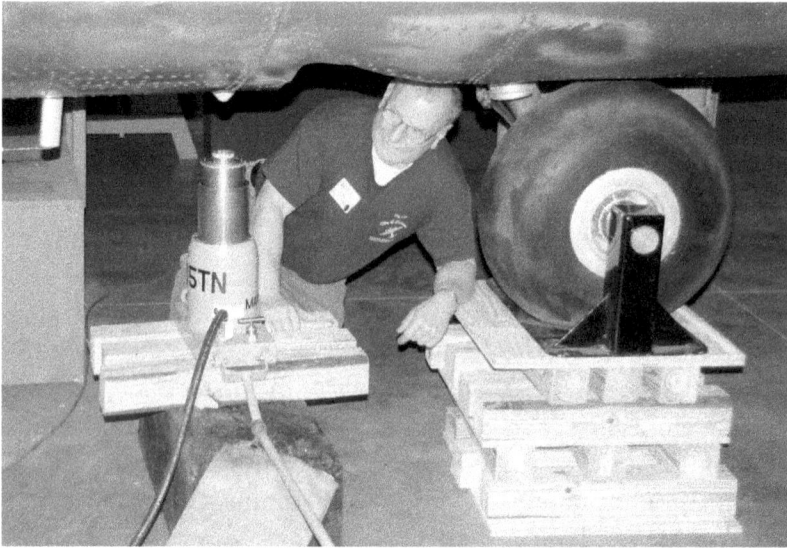

Bill Burkel inspecting the final work to level the airplane. (CoS Archives)

mounted to the airframe. After Jeff was certain that the mounting ring was secure and level, he called for the turret itself to be placed beneath the fuselage. The exterior team began using an automobile transmission jack to slowly lift the turret into the ring. After a great deal of discussion between the two teams, those of us who were only observers were informed that the turret was officially "mounted." The announcement was followed by a period of approximately 15 minutes of near silence; finally, the exterior team stood back and we all held our breath, and then . . . the turret began to rotate! The turret rotation was being done manually, with a cranking device, and everything had worked! It was quite a moment for all the volunteers and a small group of museum visitors who had learned what was going on and had stopped to watch. The cheering could be heard throughout the building.

The excellent work by all concerned, from the moment the turret ring was lifted into the fuselage until the turret itself was mounted and turning under manual power, had taken slightly longer than two hours. As soon as the cheering and hand-shaking stopped, the team began the reverse process and removed the turret and returned it to the shop. Everyone gathered around the center table, and we discussed how we would conduct the official mounting of the turret before the TV cameras the next day. All involved in

Top: *The outside team rolling the turret from the shop into the Combat Gallery.*

Bottom left: *Fitting the turret support ring into the airplane.*

Bottom right: *Safety cable holding the ball turret as it is lifted into the airplane.* (CoS Archives)

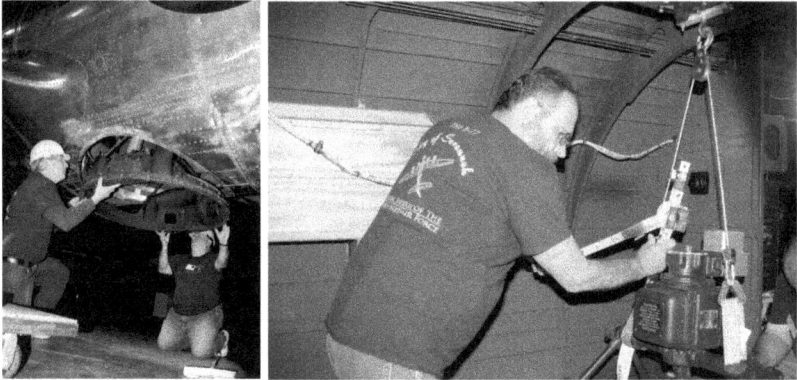

the process were sure that the elapsed time for the second mounting of the turret would be well below the one-hour mark.

The next day the ball turret team proved to everyone how good they really were. The media had gathered around the work-zone barriers surrounding the airplane and many museum visitors stood amid the cameras and reporters. Jeff signaled that the interior mounting team was ready, and I gave the exterior team the signal to leave the shop and roll the turret beneath the airplane. From that moment until the turret began to rotate before the large audience was 27 minutes! Once again, the cheering was thunderous!

Final closure for the media event involved several interviews. Proud papa Jeff Hoopes told the reporters his story of the turret from Hollywood to installation. Bud Porter was the on-site Eighth Air Force veteran ball turret gunner, and hero of the day. He gave several interviews to reporters and camera operators about what it felt like to be inside a ball turret as a young gunner in the skies over Europe in 1945. Team members Jack Hango, Paul Abare, and Joe Pritchard also got their several minutes of fame with the media. No matter from what direction the story was told, everyone had a smile on their face about what had just been accomplished.

Needless to say, we were excited after the installation of the ball turret. There was, however, a great deal more work to be done to have the turret permanently mounted and fully operational. In addition, we continued work on the tail and upper turrets, as well as the interior of the airplane, particularly the upper cockpit and waist area. There were no idle hands in the *City of Savannah* workshop as we entered the second quarter of 2014.

One of those circumstances that we didn't anticipate occurred as a result of the mounting of the ball turret. While the airplane was in the level flight attitude that was necessary for mounting the turret, several of the volunteers and visitors from an executive Board meeting commented that the airplane looked good in the level attitude as compared with standing on its tail wheel, as it had since arriving at the museum five years earlier. We decided to leave the airplane in its level position for a while—and it's still there.

April began a period in which several new people joined our group and we lost a major player. We learned that Jane Grismer was leaving the museum for a management position at a Savannah public relations firm. Jane had replaced Sheila Saxon on the museum staff in 2010 and had been an important contributor to our efforts and success. Her most significant contribution to the *City of Savannah* project was, of course, the introduction of the annual Flying Fortress 5K race, our main source of income in the early years of the project.

As was the case in 2010 when Sheila left the fold, we were all worried about who would be the next person hired as the museum's administrative officer. Once again the recruitment process was a great success with the hiring of Lynne Alexander. Lynne came with outstanding credentials and would carry us through the period from her arrival in May until the dedication the following January, keeping up the tradition of her predecessors.

At almost the same time that Lynne joined us, we welcomed the arrival of another one of those people who seemed to show up

Jane Grismer and the author. (CoS Archives)

just when the project needed them the most. In this case the right man at the right time was John Mirakian. John joined our merry band as the ultimate volunteer. He was traveling between his homes in Florida and Connecticut and stopped to visit the museum. He was admiring the B-17 near the entrance to the shop area when he ran into Jim Grismer. As the owner of a machine shop, he was interested in some of the metalwork he had noticed being done on the airplane. He stopped and asked Jim several questions. The rest is history. When John left several hours later, he was carrying a package of drawings and plans for gun mounts and other metal parts that were needed for the airplane. He got back to Connecticut and spent hours personally working in his shop to produce machine-tooled parts for us. The gun mounts which John built for us at no cost saved us more than $10,000!

John Mirakian with his superbly constructed gun mounts. (CoS Archives)

John Mirakian with the upper turret frame and with his donated lathe. (CoS Archives)

It isn't often that a man of John's ability and generosity walks in the door, and he didn't go away after producing the gun mounts; he was just getting started. John was preparing to leave his previous life as a business owner, retire to Florida, and join us as our resident machinist. Before we knew it, large shipping crates holding a full-service lathe and a "Bridgeport Machine" (whatever that is) showed up at the museum. After delivering the gun mounts, John began working with Jeff Hoopes on solving the many parts' problems of the upper turret.

While John was introducing the volunteers to state-of-the-art machinery, another one of our unsung heroes was using one of the world's oldest skills to make a major contribution to the project. Ray Willingham had retired several years earlier from his civil engineering job and started a business building canvas tops for the large boating community in Savannah. We had not realized that a great deal of canvas material was needed to complete the interior restoration of the *City of Savannah* to its true 1945 standard. When we realized the requirements, we approached several local contractors who worked with canvas to assist us with the interior work and to create the complex canvas and zipper combination required for the airplane's chin turret. Virtually every candidate said that they couldn't, or wouldn't, even attempt the required job. Enter Ray.

A friend of Jim Grismer from the local American Legion chapter, Ray came out to the museum at Jim's request. After reviewing a few sketches and pictures that we had of the canvas requirements, he walked through the airplane and was hooked. While the contractors we had contacted told us that the appropriate zippers and canvas for the various projects were no longer available, and/or that the work was too complex for them to undertake, Ray took a lot of notes and got right to work, utilizing our limited visual resources as his "patterns." He obtained period-correct military brass zippers from fellow volunteer and WWII parts collector, Paul Abare. Many of his other material requirements he found through a relentless online search of military surplus outlets. The mother lode of Ray's requirements appeared at the museum when Paul was able to locate 15 yards of period-correct, WWII tenting canvas. Ray hand-washed the filthy tenting to remove decades of soot and accumulated dust. His dedication to perfection paid off handsomely.

The tenting now appears inside the *City of Savannah* as the appropriate canvas bulkhead work in the tail compartment, the tail

Ray Willingham completing the very complex chin turret canvas/zipper project.
(CoS Archives)

wheel housing cover, seat cushions in the upper and lower cockpits and ball turret, as cockpit insulation, and spent shell recovery bags. Ray's biggest statement of accomplishment, however, was the very complex zipper and canvas package in the nose turret. The "non-existent" canvas and the zippers, located by Paul, were sewn together by Ray into the completed nose turret package in less than four hours.

No year in *City of Savannah* history would be complete without a Road Warrior story. In 2014 one of our most seasoned Roadies, Darrell Schwartz, was sent to Houston, Texas, with a very experienced aircraft parts expert, but rookie Road Warrior, Sam Currie. Their task was to visit with the folks at the Commemorative Air Force, Gulf Coast Chapter, and return with a number of parts from an upper turret that the CAF keeps in storage. The agreement with our CAF friends was that we would personally transport the parts to Pooler, reproduce two copies of each part, and then personally return the originals with the extra set as payment.

Sam Currie: *Darrell Schwartz and I were tasked to travel to Houston, Texas, to meet with some of our opposite numbers on the B-17G Texas Raider team from the Gulf Coast Wing of the Commemorative Air Force. The purpose of our visit was to borrow several difficult-to-find Sperry upper turret parts. The few B-17 upper turrets that have survived have been bought up by restoration groups many years ago. Our task was to borrow original parts and bring them back to Pooler where we would oversee the reproduction of the parts in order to complete our challenge to assemble an operational 1945 model B-17G Sperry upper turret.*

The plan since the start of the City of Savannah restoration project has been to create the finest B-17 static display in the world, including three working turrets that we can show off to the public for instructional purposes. We did not want a museum exhibit that just looked good and would be remembered with a quick photo before moving on to another exhibit. It is important to us that the visitors to the museum experience the noise and smells that our fathers, grandfathers, uncles, and brothers experienced when they flew in the skies over Europe. Darrell and I were part of that plan.

We departed 17 May and arrived in Houston the following day. Our first stop was to visit Tommy Garcia. Tommy took us on a tour of his facilities, and we spent several hours discussing how we would copy the turret parts when we got back to Pooler.

The next day, along with Darrell's son, who lives in the Houston area, we traveled to the David Wayne Hooks Memorial Airport in Tomball, Texas, the home base of the B-17 Texas Raider. We met with the Raider's shop team and were shown the turret with the parts we would be borrowing. During our discussion about the turret, our hosts told us that their airplane was leaving shortly on a charter flight, and that there were two empty seats available for us if we wanted a B-17 flying experience. The Schwartz family took the empty seats and returned to the hangar with big smiles and a great shared father/son adventure to add to their family history.

After the living history adventure, we got back to work and removed several parts from the Raider's turret and collected them together with the items we had assembled earlier. The Commemorative Air Force team, who support the Texas Raider aircraft, were extremely helpful and went out of their way to be good hosts and fellow restoration comrades during our time with them. Each of them have a standing invitation for a personal guided tour of the City of Savannah should they ever visit Pooler.

Early the next morning we began our two-day return trip to Pooler. When we got home, we had been on the road for six days, with 31 hours of driving time and over 2,000 miles on the odometer. I was proud to now be entitled to say that I was a member of the City of Savannah's elite Road Warriors' Club. Most important of all, both Darrell and I were very happy to see the smiles on the faces of our fellow volunteers when they saw the parts we had brought home to meet our ultimate challenge of constructing an operational upper turret.

The same week that the Road Warriors were bringing home upper turret parts from Texas, we received a borrowed, and much needed bomb hoist from Mike Kellner with the *Desert Rat* B-17 restoration in Illinois, again with the proviso of providing Mike with a second copy in the return package. All of this metalwork would be placed in the queue for production with a local company that had joined our project, Carolina Metal Castings. CMC was another great surprise addition to our stable of contractors. Owner Jim Harwood had contracted with us to do some work and, when he realized what we were doing, refused payment for our first job and then became our official foundry for both copying existing parts and creating parts from the 3-D CAD drawings created by Jeff Hoopes and the interns.

The period of April through June saw a lot of turret work being completed as the electricians worked to install power to the ball turret, while the machinists were doing triple duty on the tail and upper turrets, as well as the nose area updates that were required before the chin turret could be mounted.

The biggest news during the month of April was that John Finch completed fitting the new metal framing that returned the *City of Savannah's* nose to its original Boeing format. The metal struts forming the nose structure were built in Atlanta by Tom Wilson, using original Boeing drawings. The unique Kenting Aviation struts and skin that had been installed in the 1950s to fit cameras into the nose were discarded—some of the few items taken off of our B-17 that would have no purpose on another airplane.

The month of May had Wednesday nights at the museum sounding like a 1940s Boeing factory as the night crew began riveting a new skin onto the nose to replace the Kenting aluminum skin. John Finch, Jack Nilsen, and Jim Odom worked the long-standing tandem operation of one person driving the rivet from outside of the airplane and a partner inside "bucking" the rivet, or providing pressure against the rivet being driven into the metal skin. This almost-forgotten methodology would go on for weeks as the night crew worked to cover the nose area with new aluminum. It would be late June before the last piece of new skin was finally riveted onto the nose.

Meanwhile the Wednesday (day) crew was, as usual, engaged in several different projects. One of the benefits of our generous financial bonanza from 2013 was our ability to purchase 1,600 dummy .50-caliber cartridges that would eventually be placed in ammunition belts and chutes for inclusion in the interior display of the airplane. Each of these cartridges had to be cleaned and painted to appear as if it was new brass ammunition that would have been in the armament package within a WWII B-17. The lucky draftee who landed the job of preparing the 1,600 rounds for display was one of our early volunteers, and 165th ANG veteran, Danny Harden.

Danny accepted this very difficult task with good spirit and
humor as he began a chore that
would last for many weeks into
the summer.

Bullets were not the only
items on our list of ordinance
requirements. From the very
first day we had opened the
bomb bay doors, we had agreed
that we would find authentic
500-pound bombs, or replicas, to place in the bomb bay
to show our visitors the reason

Dan, Dan, the ammo man. (CoS Archives)

that these bombers were sent on
their deadly missions. Between 2009 and 2014 we researched every possible source for these prize exhibits. While we found several
vendors who would be glad to sell us their products, we found the
quality of what was being offered to be less than the quality that we
wanted. We saw WWII "practice" bombs that were clearly not what
we wanted, as they were either plastic junk or cheap sheet metal
knockoffs. In 2014 Scott Whitcher finally located exactly what we
were looking for to fill the *City of Savannah*'s bomb bay. War Relic
Replicas, a company located in California's hotbed of warbird restoration, Chino, manufactures realistic replicas of many items for
the Hollywood film industry. Jim Grismer investigated the site's
WWII 500-pound bombs, which were prominently displayed on
their website. Their bombs were neither cheap, nor did they look
fake. They came with all the bells and whistles: fuses, arming wires,
bomb tags, and even the appropriate stenciling. Once again, we had
to thank our benefactors from the previous year that we could afford to purchase eight replica bombs. Four of the replicas would be
placed in the bomb bay and four would be mounted on dollies and
displayed beneath the bomb bay, as if waiting for an ordinance crew
to load them onto the airplane.

The Wednesday (day) crew also discovered during the cleaning of the upper turret frame that there was a crack in the frame.
Normally, this would have been a crisis, but since the same thing

War Relic Replica's amazingly accurate WWII 500-pound, general-purpose bomb.
(CoS Archives)

had been a problem with the ball turret and been immediately re-paired by the welding shop at Gulfstream, we knew just how to get the problem fixed. The availability of local professional expertise cannot be overemphasized in the success of a project like ours.

Rocky Rodriquez and his Saturday crew of electricians spent much of the spring of 2014 building the wire harness that would bring power to the new ball turret. While we had basic plans for the required wiring, we could not find pictures of how it was in-stalled and there was a problem with how to mount the harness so that it would not become tangled when the turret revolved. As had been the case with all the other challenges Rocky's team had faced, this one was solved, and on June 25 the ball turret turned for the first time under its own power. It had been a long road from when Tommy Garcia told us that the turret existed, to the negotiations to purchase it, the cash donation by Joe Glasser, the 3,000-mile drive across country to bring it to Pooler, the donation of the power sup-ply equipment by Chroma Corporation, and finally, 12 months of technical work by the volunteers to put the turret into working con-dition. Lastly, we had to have a gunner to man our turret during the testing process. Bill Schwickrath met each of the unique "3-P" qualifications for the job: professional, psychological, and physical.

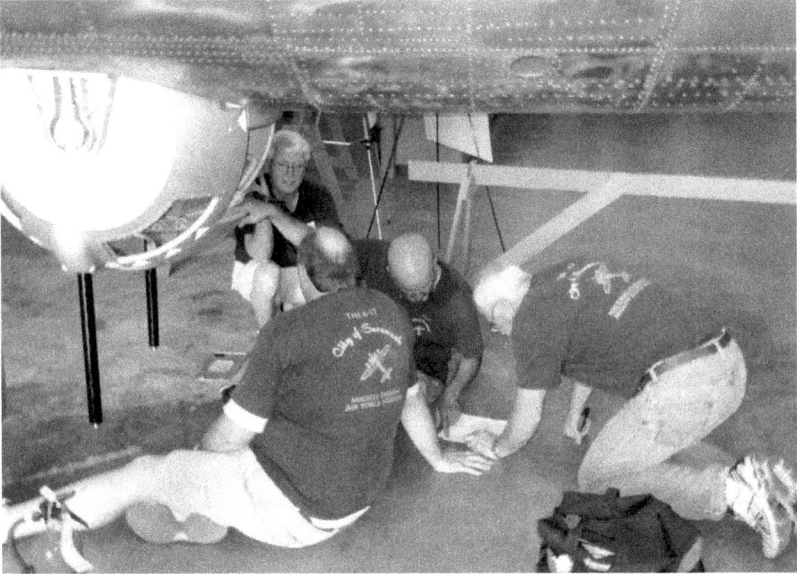

(L–R) Bill Schwickrath, Jeff Hoopes (back to camera), Rocky Rodriquez, and Sam Currie reading the electrical diagram for the ball turret. (CoS Archives)

(He's an engineer, he is not claustrophobic, and he can actually fit into the turret.) "Ball Turret Bill" had a new job.

Rendering the ball turret operational was the result of an earnest effort by many individuals involved with the project, and it constituted a major accomplishment. The chin turret was fully operational but not yet mounted. We now had two working power turrets—just one more to go!

The month of July with its summer doldrums did not slow us down. We started off with what had become another annual ritual, the radio team's broadcast from the airplane celebrating the Fourth of July. A total of 11 radio team operators, led by Bill DeLoach and Steve Jonas, worked the broadcast session beginning at 9:00 a.m. and lasting until 3:00 p.m. The team made a record 197 contacts during the six-hour activation. The contacts came from 39 states and 5 Canadian provinces—all these folks answering the broadcast of Fourth of July greetings from our call sign, WW2COS. The radio team did some of the broadcasting from a desk set up outside the radio room and found that many museum visitors joined them to hear the radio conversations. It was another grand success; the radio team, our first functioning station on the airplane, continued to make us proud.

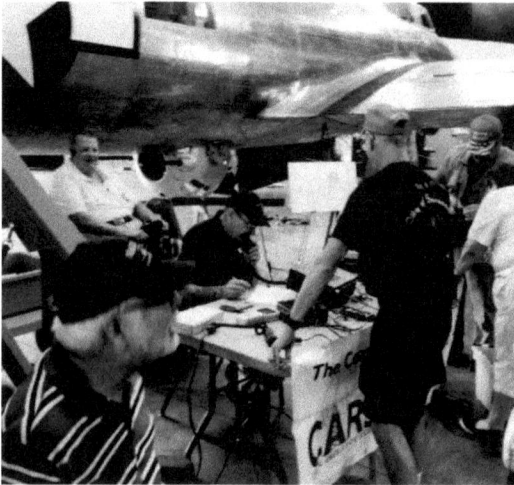

Museum visitors and fellow radio team members watch Bill DeLoach broadcast as WW2COS on July 4, 2014.

Shortly after the radio event Dave Talleur and Sam Currie began coordinating several groups of volunteers on the upper turret project. The fuselage metalwork for the turret had been built by one of the finest aircraft restoration metal shops in the country, owned by Tom Wilson of Sugarhill, Georgia. Tom's work is always of the highest quality, and we were able to contract with him for the structure piece, once again, because of the cash donation that we had received in 2013. John Finch had taken several trips to Tom's shop to work with him as the structure was being formed. When Tom arrived in Pooler to deliver the final product, he and the metal team immediately realized they had a problem. Mounting new metalwork on a 70-year-old airplane with thousands of flying hours in its logbook has its problems. Tom had built the structure to the precise requirements of 1940s Boeing drawings, but the *City of Savannah's* fuselage, after years of hard work, no longer matched the precise engineering standards it held when she left the factory in 1945. This was yet another challenge for the Wednesday Night Riders that would be solved with thought, skill, and patience.

Greg Kindred: *The upper turret structure piece was more of a challenge than the Night Riders needed in the summer of 2014. We had lost several long-time members of the crew, and we were already dividing our efforts between the tail and the nose turrets. When Tom Wilson delivered his fantastic piece of metalwork, it was the equal of the same product that our fathers had produced in 1945. The problem*

Upper turret assembly.
Another fantastic piece
of engineering by Tom
Wilson.
(CoS Archives)

was that the 30 years the airplane had spent earning a living since 1945 had bent her airframe in many ways—and her new shape did not match Tom's precisely engineered structure. We compared this to a WWII veteran trying on his old uniform and finding that his frame no longer had the same dimensions he had when he left for Europe 70 years earlier. We discovered that the gusset and the stringers on Tom's work did not nearly match their corresponding sections of the airplane. If nothing else, making the upper turret structure finally fit into the airplane was a melding of all of the related skills that Jack Nilsen, Jim Odom, and I had acquired during our aviation careers. That's the one we'll always remember.

We kept learning about the knowledge, skills, and abilities of our volunteers as special needs surfaced, and out of nowhere someone would say, "I can take care of that." One outstanding example of a volunteer having skills we didn't know about occurred when we were trying to address the complex carpentry work that would support human traffic moving between the waist area and the radio compartment.

Peter Knepton: *During the summer of 2014 I was given the assignment of finding a contractor to build the very complex floorboard area that surrounds the ball turret. The reason that I got the job is that during my working days as a mechanical engineer at Gulfstream Corporation, I had spent a portion of my career designing custom interiors*

189

for our corporate aircraft customers. During the time I was doing design work, I spent a great deal of time working with Doug Edwards, who was the woodshop manager in the Completion Center. Doug had retired and started his own custom aircraft carpentry company. I knew that he would be up to the highly technical woodwork that involved the wooden ribs of the floorboard being steamed and formed into shape to support the floorboard. Two of Doug's best employees, Tommy Morris, a master carpenter, and Brad Griffin, a mechanical engineer, were assigned the task and came out to the museum to figure out how they would get the job done. The computer copies of the original Boeing drawings we had on hand could not be printed large enough to be full scale. But by using the dimensions on the original drawings, Brad constructed a computer-generated, three-dimensional scale drawing. After manufacturing the floorboard we check fitted and trimmed and check fitted and trimmed again until the platform finally dropped into place. Our restoration crew had to wait until the final electrical work was done on the ball turret before we could install the brackets that mounted the floorboard to the aircraft. Only after we installed the floorboard did we discover that the original material thickness for the floorboard would not hold up to the day-to-day foot traffic through the aircraft. So we increased the floorboard thickness to support the individuals we knew would be walking through the airplane in the years to come.

During August of 2014 we had two important visitors who were with us to move our turret program down the road: Tommy Garcia was going to be in-house for Garcia Week VII, and Fred "The Turret Guy" Bieser from his Atlanta stable of WWII turrets and parts was also present.

The first two weeks of August saw each crew prepare for the arrival of Tommy and Fred. On the morning

Fred Bieser's upper turret stand. (CoS Archives)

(Above) Bill Schwickrath painting
the interior of the tail turret during
Garcia Week VII.

(Right) Tommy Garcia pondering
the upper turret motor with Danny
Harden, Jeff Friend, and Fred Bieser.
(CoS Archives)

of Monday, August 15, we held a management coordination meeting and then joined a large group of volunteers from all three crews at a breakfast provided by the wonderful ladies from Miss Sophie's, the museum's restaurant. It was the beginning of a very special week that would advance us down the road to a complete set of turrets on the *City of Savannah.*

Fred had arrived with big plans for the upper turret—literally. He presented Jim Grismer with drawings for a wooden stand that would be perfect for working on the upper turret ring. Bud Currey, Milt Stombler, and Bill Schwickrath were assigned specific tasks in preparation for the interior painting of the tail turret, and Jeff Hoopes brought a team inside the airplane to work on a myriad of electrical problems that were still haunting the ball turret.

When Garcia Week VII was completed and "The Month of the Turret" came to a close, we had made quite a jump forward, and progress continued on both the nose restoration and the necessary preparation for rebuilding the upper turret.

The end of the summer brought about several personnel adjustments when three long-time volunteers in leadership positions left the project: crew chiefs Bill Liening and Jeff Hoopes and the leader of the nose restoration John Finch. All three of these long-time volunteers left very big shoes to fill. Each had contributed to our success with their skills, leadership, and initiative. In trying to plug these major holes in our workforce, we kept up our tradition of utilizing retired military NCOs in leadership roles as Sam Currie (ANG) and Greg Kindred (USN) stepped up to the crew chief jobs. Machinists like John Finch are hard to find. Jack Nilsen and Jim Odom now had to divide their efforts between the nose as well as the tail turret. The vacuum with the Wednesday Night Riders staffing was met when Mort Glick and Bill Schwickrath, from the Saturday crew, and the long-time helper-wherever-his-services-were-needed, David Pinegar, all volunteered to work with Greg's Wednesday (night) crew. The extra hands on the night shift, along with Jack Nilsen and Jim Odom moving from the tail turret to the nose, allowed for the chin turret well and the final support frame to be mounted in the nose; this in turn allowed the Wednesday (day) carpenters to begin construction of the lower cockpit floor. As a side note here, during a telephone conversation, I mentioned the progress on the nose compartment to our benefactor Joe Glasser and he immediately sent us a check to cover the bombardier station expenses, matching the check he had previously sent to cover the navigator's station. We can't thank Joe enough for his support!

Mid-September brought a very welcome message from Greg Kindred that he wanted to meet with me. He was declaring the structural nose restoration as being completed! While we had overcome many challenges during the restoration up to this point, none had come close to the technical skill-set requirements and creativity needed to build the new frames and skin for the nose reconstruction. It was typical of the culture and pride that the volunteers had been exhibiting since the very beginning of the project that as Greg, Jack Nilsen, and Jim Odom stood under the nose of the *City of Savannah* explaining the finished product, they were very quick to mention the contributions of Bill Liening and John Finch, who had worked on the nose restoration, literally for years, but were no longer with the project. They also mentioned the work of Peter Knepton, one of our cadre of retired Gulfstream professionals, who had spent many hours searching through original Boeing drawings so that copies of the original supports and skin could be created.

While a big job had just come to a close on the nose of the airplane, much more activity was also underway as we all kept an eye on the calendar with regard to the upcoming January dedication date for the airplane.

Rocky and His Friends were addressing a myriad of assignments following the installation of power to the ball turret. With lessons learned from the turret, the bomb bay doors were now fully operational, and Rocky's crew had taken on an additional non-electrical job and had finished preparing the bomb racks for their final mounting.

The Wednesday (day) crew, as was usually the case, had several projects underway. Each week part of the crew was dedicated to making sure that a portion of the exterior of the airplane was freshly polished and ready for the upcoming dedication. Meanwhile, Joe Pritchard continued his work on the upper turret cap, restoring the metal and molding the plexiglass windows.

All of this activity going on with the airplane did not stop Sam Currie and me from accepting the difficult task of traveling to Palm Springs, California, to attend the 2014 B-17 Co-Op meeting at the Palm Springs Air Museum. The annual Co-Op meeting is always a pleasure to attend as it is a unique opportunity to talk about our airplane with others who understand the subject. Most of those who attend the meeting are operating flying aircraft, and their issues are very different from ours, but we are always made to feel welcome and the good will that we have developed with our flying partners has resulted in a great deal of mutual benefits from trades and knowledge that we are able to bring home. Our contribution to the meeting was to discuss our success with the development of 3-D printing to produce new parts and a description of the visit from the 100th Bomb Group veterans and HBO with regard to the upcoming *Masters of the Air* mini-series, which was of major interest to everyone in the room because of its impact on their individual projects. I also mentioned the upcoming plans for the dedication of our B-17. After making my remarks, it was very rewarding to receive several congratulatory comments from the members, two of whom went out of their way to compliment me on the success of the *City of Savannah* since 2009. That certainly made my day.

Sam and I arrived home, tired and also reenergized, as we had used much of our travel time to discuss the approaching dedication and the final push to make the *City of Savannah* the finest exhibit possible in order to address the mission of the National Museum of the Mighty Eighth Air Force: to honor the men who had flown those deadly missions from 1942 to 1945.

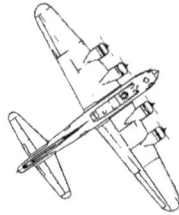

CHAPTER 6

The Last 90 Days

NOVEMBER 2014 – JANUARY 2015

"It isn't the start that matters. It's the finish line."

Lt. Gen. Julien C. Smith, USMC

November 1, 2014, began the three-month countdown to the scheduled January 28, 2015, dedication of the B-17G, now known to one and all as the *City of Savannah*. This final run was quite a milestone for all the volunteers, particularly those of us who had been involved for the full six years.

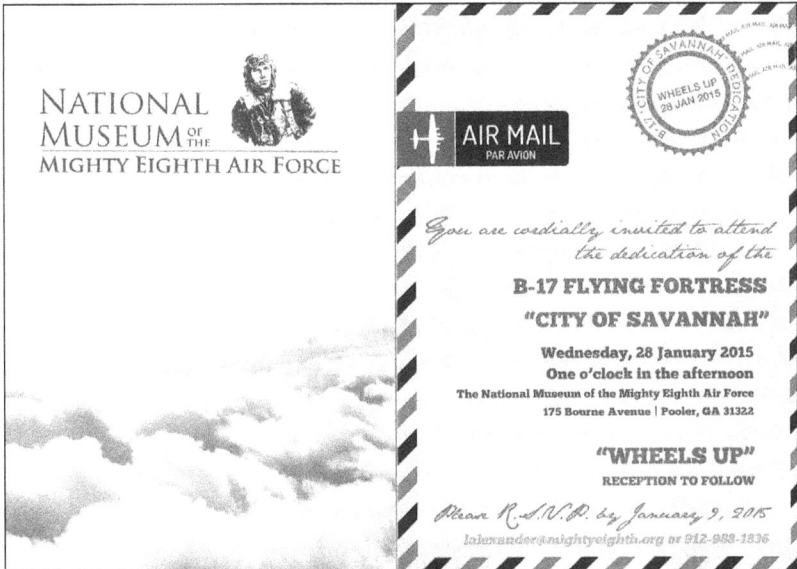

Invitation to the dedication of the City of Savannah. (NMMEAF)

The final 90-day, all-out endeavor was one of the few times we had ever put pressure on the volunteer team with regard to having work complete by a certain date; there was just no choice in view of the publicly announced dedication date. Preparing for the big event did not become a chore; it was a job that the volunteers assumed with pride. We all knew the primary mission of the museum was to honor the individual veterans who served in the Eighth Air Force, and we were more than ready to show off what we had accomplished in their honor.

One major effort we emphasized in order to ensure that the airplane would make an appropriate impression on those attending the dedication was that all of the turrets would be in place in order to properly display the thousands of hours of work that had gone into their restoration, or in the case of the tail turret, almost total in-house fabrication. Once again we organized a special out-of-towners group to work on the turrets and brought Jeff Hoopes back to Pooler along with Fred Bieser for a five-day stretch in which those two experts were dedicated to the turrets, assisted by a support team that provided the backup they required. Much of the work was focused on having the upper turret's cap mounted and displaying the superb glasswork that Joe Pritchard had been creating for over a year. Similar plexiglass work had been formed and mounted in the tail turret by David Pinegar.

Tail turret with David Pinegar's custom windows. (CoS Archives)

David Pinegar: *As the tail turret came together, the need for windows was a serious challenge. The complex curves of the tail section suggested a complicated mold and expensive project. I agreed to see if I could solve the problem. All the windows I had made for the nose of the airplane were made with materials I obtained from Nor-Dam Corporation,one of LMI's partners in the aerospace industry. It›s not hard to get an aerospace supplier to come on board to support a project like ours. In this case, however, NorDam did not have material that would bend to the serious degree required. Using experience from my aircraft modeling background, I was able to locate a commercial outlet that provided a thinner material that was both crystal clear and would bend to the compound radius.*

The technical highlight of the fall of 2014 was the arrival of the impossible to purchase upper turret pedestal constructed under the supervision of Nick Meinhardt at Gulfstream Corporation. Nick's role as both the supervisor of the Gulfstream 3-D print shop and a faculty member of Savannah Tech was a double play that allowed his students to develop the software needed by the Gulfstream 3-D printing operation to produce a resin copy of the original pedestal.

(L–R) Sam Currie holding the original upper turret support pedestal on loan from the Texas Raiders and Nick Meinhardt with the resin copy produced in his lab at Gulfstream Corporation using software prepared by Savannah Tech interns. (CoS Archives)

After Nick delivered the resin copy to us, it was taken by Dave Talleur to our Carolina Coastal Foundry partners in South Carolina, where an exact metal copy was made for us, along with a second copy that will be returned to our benefactors at the Gulf Coast Chapter of the Commemorative Air Force in Texas who loaned us the original pedestal.

On the non-technical side in the autumn of 2014, the most significant event was the now-famous annual Flying Fortress 5K race. The race had become more popular each year, and the financial reward for the project increased correspondingly. As always, the volunteers turned out in full support. While Jane Grismer was no longer with us, several other museum staff picked up where Jane had left off, and the race was logistically, financially, and socially another great success.

The radio team also turned out with their usual fervor and kept all the course monitors in direct communication. The highlight for the volunteers was when Milt "Crazy Legs" Stombler, yet again won an age-group medal: the only *City of Savannah* volunteer to run in every Flying Fortress 5K and bring home a medal every year!

A special highlight of the 2014 race was the presence of Jack Rude as the official starter. Jack, a tail gunner in the 493rd Bomb Group in 1945, was visiting Savannah and the Mighty Eighth from his home in Arizona. During the previous week, he could be seen holding court around the *CoS*'s tail turret and talking with visitors to the museum wearing an official *City of Savannah* uniform T-shirt. Jack was officially adopted by the *CoS* volunteers and will always have a place at the table with us when he returns to Savannah.

Milton "Crazy Legs" Stombler, PhD, waving to his adoring public.
(CoS Archives

Following the annual race, it was traditional that the project would go into a slow period as the volunteers became more involved in family activities from Thanksgiving through the first week in January. This was also the time of year that includes the anniversary of the arrival of the airplane in 2009 and the annual dinner for the volunteers. The management team used this period to evaluate what had happened during the previous 12 months and provide a yearly report to both the project membership and the museum's board of trustees. The end of 2014 was no exception.

Our review of the 2014 calendar year seemed to be dominated by the word "turret." Starting in the nose of the airplane, John Finch, Greg Kindred, and Jack Nilsen had done such exceptional work in restoring the structure of the lower nose area that we were now ready to install the chin turret and begin working on the restoration of the lower cockpit. The same Night Rider trio, working with Jeff Hoopes and his upper turret team, had installed the fuselage support work for the upper turret as well as the restored interior support structure salvaged from Jeff's famous Ohio road trip. The ball turret had gone from "California dreamin'" to a fully operational example of the ingenuity and determination of the entire *City of Savannah* team. Finally, the tail turret stood ready for mounting. This turret, a truly astonishing creation, was 95 percent constructed in the project shop area under the supervision of Jack Nilsen, along with many other volunteers, including the night crew stalwarts and David Pinegar. There is one strut within the turret that was salvaged from the original Alaska turret brought to us by Tommy Garcia; all the rest of the turret was created by our master craftsmen. As the management team discussed the four turrets, we realized that we did not have to take second place to anyone when it came to the display that would soon be presented to the museum's visitors.

Other issues that we discussed included the arrival of Ray Willingham and John Mirakian during 2014 and the amazing contributions both these professionals had added to our efforts, and how David Pinegar had spent months building and installing the flat plexiglass windows in the nose compartment and the very challenging navigator's dome, not to mention the tail turret windows. Finally, the formation and development of the intern program with Savannah Technical College and its connection with the 3-D printing facilities at both Savannah Tech and Gulfstream Corporation were significant accomplishments. With those two programs producing molds for the production of unavailable and necessary parts

As fine a group of volunteers as can be found. Official 2014 photo. (Matt Stephan)

needed for our airplane, along with our foundry partners at Carolina Coastal Foundry, we felt that the *City of Savannah* project had now moved from being the new kids on the block to a state-of-the-art leader in the warbird restoration community.

We were proud of how far the project had come as we finished our sixth year of work, and we were ready to present the *City of Savannah* to the world with a formal dedication scheduled for January 28, 2015.

2015

When we returned to the museum in early January, we had a list of tasks that absolutely had to be completed before the January 28 dedication, and we prepared a schedule to get those tasks accomplished.

The first thing on my personal list was to take care of a very important public relations assignment. We had been informed by our good friends from Gulfstream Corporation that the renowned aviation writer, Stephen Pope, would be traveling to Savannah to write an article on Gulfstream's newest airplane, the G-600, for *Flying* magazine. Thanks to encouragement from a member of Gulfstream senior management, who happened to be a member of the museum's board of trustees, Stephen would also be visiting the museum with the possibility for a story involving our restoration appearing in the internationally famous magazine. I was at the appointed place and time to meet Stephen in the museum rotunda along with John Telgener, a member of the museum board. John and I would be Stephen's guides throughout the day, with my role mainly being to provide an in-depth description of the *City of Savannah* project and answering any questions. Stephen, John, and I toured the museum for over an hour and then sat down for lunch in the museum restaurant. After lunch Stephen and I toured the airplane and then adjourned to the library, where he interviewed me at length about the project. It was a great day and Stephen did publish a wonderful article about us in the January 2015 issue of *Flying*.

While I was busy entertaining our visitor, Dave Talleur and Jim Grismer had worked out a schedule whereby we had volunteers working as individuals and teams almost every day in January. The primary goal was to complete the profile of the airplane by installing all of the turrets and the newly arrived nosepiece that we had acquired through a trade with our neighbor, Don Brooks, of the *Liberty Belle* project in nearby Douglas, Georgia.

On Tuesday, January 13, 2015, Henry Skipper called a meeting at the museum for every segment of the museum operation, including the restaurant. Dave Talleur, Jim Grismer, and I represented the *City of Savannah* project. Several members of the museum administrative staff had carefully choreographed the dedication ceremonies from the early morning gathering of all concerned, to supervision of parking, to the final handshakes as honored guests left the building in the late afternoon. It was an excellent plan. Dave, Jim, and I listened, saluted when required, and agreed to everything. No one was more excited about the upcoming events than we were.

Our major workday on the January schedule was set for Saturday the 17th. Every resource, human and otherwise, was brought together on that day. The mounting of the tail turret was to be the highlight. Although we did not formalize the event, word had gotten out as to when it would occur and there was a full cadre of volunteers on hand to witness and participate in one of our proudest moments: mounting a turret that was truly ours, built and prepared entirely by *City of Savannah* team members under Jack Nilsen's leadership.

(Above left) Tail turret sitting on its cradle. (Above right) Jack Nilsen supervises from floor; Sam Currie on the cart.

(Above) Lifting the turret into place. (Right) Fitting the turret against the fuselage. (All photos on this page are from the CoS Archives.)

A great deal of planning went into the final move of the turret from the shop to its mounting on the airplane. It was decided that the best way to have the turret fitted in its proper location against the airplane fuselage was to lift the turret on an electric cart that was used by the maintenance staff to replace lights in the museum's ceiling. The cart's platform can rise up and down, and the people who knew what they were doing felt that the turret could be lifted by the cart to exactly the height needed for it to be placed against its connecting points on the fuselage.

The turret was carefully lifted from its custom cradle, on which it had been sitting for many months, and was temporarily placed on two padded 2x4s that had been secured to the platform of the cart. Sam Currie, our most experienced cart operator—he had driven it once before—then VERY carefully drove the cart out of the shop, stopping with the turret just short of the fuselage. Needless to say, there was hardly a sound in the gallery as Sam slowly moved the cart and Jack Nilsen provided direction from the floor. Jack directed Sam to slowly lift the turret to the required height. From this point on, a great deal of communication was required between Jack, on the left side of the turret, Sam, on the cart, Greg Kindred, inside the fuselage, and Joel Hedgpeth, on the right side of the turret. As if they were a seasoned team of turret movers, they made it work. There were several sighs of relief as Greg called out from inside the airplane that the mounting holes had matched up against each other!

As I stood to the side and watched these great guys work together to place the turret on the airplane, I remembered when the

Done! Jack Nilsen below; Greg Kindred looking out from the turret window. (CoS Archives)

airplane itself had come through the same entrance between the shop and the museum's Combat Gallery six years previously, almost to the day. I realized that of all those present in 2009, I was the only one present at this event. An honor, to be sure, and even more, reflective of how the organization had grown into an outstanding group of talented craftsmen. It was quite a moment.

While I had been daydreaming, the people with the technical skills were getting things accomplished. At one point Greg, who was now tightening bolts inside the airplane, explained to those out on the floor that the turret needed to be slightly tilted from outside to match the upper mounting points of the turret and the fuselage. Discussion about using the mechanical power of the lift to bring the turret upward caused some concern with Jack and Sam, and it was decided to do it the old-fashioned way, with muscle. Several volunteers stood beneath the outer portion of the turret and gave it a slight upward push with their backs until Greg gave the signal that they had reached the correct angle for him to tighten the bolts connecting the turret to the fuselage. Finally, as both a test and a signal that all was well with the final connection between the turret and the fuselage, Greg appeared in the turret—and it didn't fall off! I looked over at Jack Nilsen. The proud papa of the *City of Savannah*'s tail turret was a very happy guy.

There was no time for cheering after the tail turret was mounted. Attention was moved to the nose of the airplane, where the chores included mounting the cap on the chin turret and our newly acquired nosepiece. The operating portion of the nose turret had been purchased in 2011 from Fred Bieser. After we played with it for several days, it had been put in storage to ensure that too much playtime did not result in us having to hire Fred to repair our toy. The Night Riders had pulled the system out of storage and installed it the previous week. On this day we mounted the fairing behind the turret cap, and the cap itself. The canvas work that had been done on the cap by Ray Willingham looked particularly handsome. The beautiful new nosepiece was mounted and, as it had been tested previously and adjustments made as necessary, it fit perfectly, and completed the profile of the *City of Savannah*'s nose. David Pinegar's windows in the lower cockpit and the navigator's dome completed the picture.

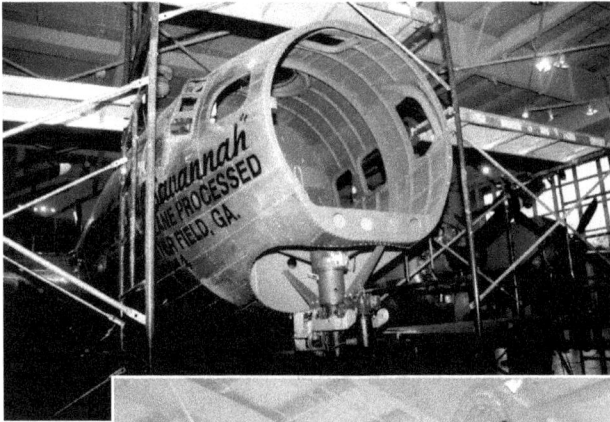

Before and After.
(CoS Archives)

The final turret chore of the day was the upper turret. This installation would be totally static for the dedication, with the dome placed on top of its supporting ring and its two guns sitting in their proper mounts, with Joe Pritchard's new gleaming plexiglass windows shining brightly. Joe's dome would put the final touch on the B-17G profile that we wanted our guests to see as they inspected the B-17 from the floor of the museum on dedication day.

The end of this very long day was one of significant accomplishment. All four turrets were mounted, at least temporarily, so that the historic B-17G profile of our airplane was complete. It had been quite an effort by all hands. There was one more step to be taken in our preparation for the dedication . . . to make our airplane shine.

CoS ready for its upper turret.

Reclaimed upper turret interior.

Upper turret installed on the City of Savannah. (All photos on this page are from the CoS Archives.)

Milt Stombler, on the wing, demonstrating the "Stombler Shoe Shine Method" for cleaning airplanes. Helpers are Jim Barry and Darrell Schwartz. Museum guests often ask the volunteers if they can take pictures of the process. (CoS Archives)

One of the major chores, which would go on until the very last minute, was the cleaning/polishing of the airplane's aluminum skin. In the early years of the project, cleaning the exterior of the airplane had involved a crew of five to six volunteers with large janitors' floor mops and a lot of soft towels working for several hours. All of that effort had disappeared several years previously when our resident physicist and 5K champion, Milt "Crazy Legs" Stombler, came up with a terrific solution that allowed two individuals to clean the entire exterior of the airplane in under one hour, using the "Stombler Shoe Shine Method."

Milt used a 25'x3' piece of flannel and simply threw the cloth over the portion of the airplane to be cleaned. Another volunteer on the opposite side wing, fuselage, or stabilizer took the opposite end of the cloth and they worked the flannel cloth back and forth, like shining a shoe, as they walked the cloth the length of the area being cleaned. Two cleaners could polish the entire airplane, with the exception of the vertical stabilizer, in under an hour. Many visitors watch our volunteers polishing the airplane with Milt's flannel cloth and ask the volunteers to pose for pictures. The shoe shine polishing method is yet another example of the unique ingenuity that lives within the *City of Savannah* team. Milt's idea might not catch on in other parts of the aviation community, but it has certainly become part of our culture.

The final 10 days before the dedication were full of activity for all of us. I was asked to speak at the monthly Eighth Air Force Historical Society on January 20 and began my remarks by asking the group how many of them were at the meeting when Brenda Elmgren had announced that a B-17 had been gifted to the Mighty Eighth by the Smithsonian. A bunch of hands went up, but not many remembered that it was the six year and one month anniversary of that December meeting in 2008—a good way to introduce my remarks that included a review of the restoration over the last six years and comments about work that would remain for the months and years to come, including finding or manufacturing the elusive parts that would allow us to render our upper turret operational.

Four days later the museum held the annual dinner for the *City of Savannah* volunteers. This year, in addition to CEO Henry Skipper, we were joined by the chairman of the board of trustees of the museum, Al Kennickell. This was our most rollicking annual dinner to date. Everyone was in high spirits and very much looking forward to the dedication events that would follow in three days, on the 73rd anniversary of the founding of the Eighth Air Force in Savannah. The preparation work on the airplane was complete, and we were all ready to present our work to the world. When it was my turn to speak, I broke tradition and, instead of describing events from the past 12 months, I asked the group to tell us what they considered the highlights of the previous six years, noting that there were only eight of us at the dinner who had been part of the 2009 roster of volunteers. The stories told were mostly funny. Several volunteers spoke of significant obstacles that were overcome, the teamwork that had accomplished so much over the years, and the bonding of the group that had evolved during our time together. It was an upbeat conversation amongst almost 100 people, and we all felt good when we gave each other a round of applause at the end.

Tuesday, January 27, was a busy day as we prepared for the dedication and worked on the long list of last-minute tasks. After completing our chores at the museum, a small group of us gathered at a local restaurant to welcome some special guests who would be attending the ceremonies the next day. Jim Grismer organized the dinner to welcome the out-of-towners to Pooler by bringing them all together for introductions and hopefully some story-telling. We assigned a volunteer to each visiting group to ensure that they were picked up at the airport and found their way safely to the restaurant.

The group gathered, with everyone introducing themselves and discovering what role their fellow diners had played in the history of our B-17. In addition to our volunteers, the guests included the Kittle and Watkins families, representing the original crewmembers who had been Georgia natives. Maurita Autry and her husband Gene represented the Kolb family, specifically, Maurita's dad, the last civilian owner of the B-17, and her brother Nathan, our airplane's last pilot. Steve Grodt, who had delivered the power supply from Chroma Systems the year before, attended with the president and CEO of Chroma, Fred Sabatine. Also in the group were Harry Friedman and Tommy and Karen Garcia, whom we consider to be family. Several members of the All Coast team that moved the airplane to Pooler were in town to attend the dedication, but unfortunately could not make it to the dinner.

When everyone had finished dinner, I asked if one member of each group would make some remarks regarding how that family or organization was related to the dedication. I had hoped that some polite words would be expressed, and we would begin to see who was representing each group. The result was much more than expected. The large group of Kittle family members was represented by Kit Kittle Jr., the son of the original *City of Savannah* pilot. He introduced his extended family and told everyone how excited they were about attending the dedication, having gathered from all over the country. Kit's cousin, Pat McMillen, then told the group the story of how, as a two-year-old in November of 1944, he had been present when Kit's dad brought the original *City of Savannah* to Lovell Field near the family home in Ringgold, Georgia, and he had his picture taken sitting in his uncle's pilot seat.

Next to speak was Margaret Watkins, the daughter of the original crew's navigator. Margaret explained that the Watkins family members are still Georgia residents and told the story of how her cousin had noticed the picture of his uncle, and how the Watkins family had officially adopted the restoration project and visited the museum on several previous occasions to follow the progress of the restoration.

Maurita Autry told us of how her dad and brother had delivered our B-17 to the Smithsonian at Dulles airport in 1984 and how happy the restoration project of his former airplane had made her father before he passed away in 2011.

Fred Sabatine, the president and CEO of Chroma Corporation explained that this was his first visit to Savannah and the National Museum of the Mighty Eighth Air Force and how emotional he had found the visit to be thus far. He spoke of his dad's service in WWII and how proud he was that Chroma Corporation had been able to play an important part in the restoration.

As the various stories and comments were shared by the group, I noticed people leaning between tables to talk: the group was very interactive with their excitement. I figured it was time to end the organized portion of the dinner and quickly thanked everyone for attending and let them know that the bar remained open. It was another hour before people began to leave as everyone seemed to want to share stories and ask questions. It was a great event, and for Jim and me, a long, long time from when the two of us sat in a similar local restaurant and wondered how we were ever going to get this restoration off the ground.

Finally, it was dedication day, January 28, 2015! We all felt like kids on the first day of school: excited, but nervous about what was soon to happen. Everyone arrived very early at the museum to take care of the necessary last-minute organizational work. Dick Gorman and I met the Watkins and Kittle families when they arrived and escorted them to the library where Dick interviewed several members of each family with the assistance of museum staffer Sam Martin, who videotaped the interviews for both the families and the museum archives.

The museum staff had completed an enormous job in setting up the rotunda for the estimated 500 guests who would be attending the events. The ceremonies were scheduled to begin at 1:00 p.m. We had asked the volunteers to arrive before that time so we

The "thank you" picture to our families on the day of the City of Savannah *dedication.
(NMMEAF)*

could take a picture next to the airplane of all the volunteers along
with our families. So many of the family members understood how
important the restoration had become to our group. We had been
sharing our lives for several years with the airplane, and it was appropriate that our families be part of both the ceremonies and one
unique picture of all of us.

Because of the size of the anticipated attendance at the dedication ceremonies, the museum staff had planned that the speakers would address the entire group in the museum's rotunda, where
seating could be made available for everyone. After the speakers
finished, everyone would be asked to move into the smaller Combat
Gallery, where the airplane was located, for a brief ribbon-cutting
ceremony. A large group of WWII veterans would be in attendance,
and seating was reserved for them directly in front of the stage that
had been placed next to the airplane.

Saying that I agonized over what I would say in my remarks at
the dedication would be a gross understatement. Summarizing six
years of work accomplished by more than 100 people you consider
to be good friends into only five minutes can lead to a great deal
of anxiety. I had put many hours of thought into what I would say
when I was introduced. I was the third of three speakers, behind

Henry Skipper and Major General Scott Vander Hamm, then commander of the Eighth Air Force. Although I had my notes with me and had rehearsed many times what I would say, I can honestly state that I did not hear a word that Henry Skipper or General Vander Hamm said in the minutes before I was introduced. I have done a great deal of public speaking, but this occasion was very unique and intimidating.

When I finally stepped up to the podium, I began my remarks by saying how grateful I was to have been given the honor of being the project manager for the *City of Savannah* by Walt Brown. It was important to me that Walt's name be mentioned to this audience. Then I asked the question, "How did this project come to where it is today?" I began with Jim Grismer's statement, "We don't know what we don't know," our mantra as we tried to figure out how to go about a major aircraft restoration. Now, with hindsight, I was able to tell the audience that there had been three main factors that had resulted in our success: utilizing the expertise in our own Savannah aviation community, reaching out to experts in the national aircraft restoration community for help, and assembling a group of volunteers who truly believed in the mission of the museum to honor the veterans of the Eighth Air Force in WWII.

I continued by describing how, as we were struggling to get started, Marshall Brooks had contacted his boyhood friend Bob Mikesh, the man who literally wrote the book on how to restore airplanes when he had been curator of aircraft restoration at the Smithsonian. Bob had given us the four "must haves" to make the project succeed. Over dinner, he told Marshall and me that there are four keys to success in restoring aircraft: (1) first, the airplane must be inside an environmentally controlled building; followed by (2) stable management; (3) the ability to raise money to fund the project; and (4) access to active local aviation expertise. Well, I explained to the audience in the museum rotunda, our airplane had been inside the building from day one, our management team had been intact for six years, the museum had a very active fundraising plan, which had paid off handsomely for us, and finally, we had started from day one to involve the Savannah aviation community in our cause. I mentioned the entities from the local aviation community that had played major roles in our success: Gulfstream

Corporation, Flight Safety International Corporation, the Air National Guard's 165th Airlift Wing, and LMI Corporation, led by a one-man support team by the name of David Pinegar. Then I mentioned how while we were addressing Bob Mikesh's four requirements for success, we had stepped onto the national stage to seek specific assistance in the restoration of B-17 aircraft by contacting the National B-17 Co-Op, which had brought Dr. Harry Friedman, the Co-Op's leader, and Tommy Garcia, onto our team.

I told the audience that the most significant key to our success had been the men and women who arrived at the museum to volunteer in making our B-17 meet the standards of the museum founders for a first-class exhibit that would honor the WWII veterans of the Eighth Air Force. I mentioned some statistics: almost 150 volunteers had served over the six years the project had been in existence, for a total of 45,000 hours of service, and that on the day of the dedication there were 38 active volunteers, eight of whom had served from the start of the project, and that it was no mistake that the majority of the crew chiefs who had led the on-site supervision of the restoration had emerged from the volunteers who were retired military non-commissioned officers. These men had literally earned their stripes in Military Occupational Specialties relating to aviation.

I also added that as a statement to the skill and dedication of the volunteers to make our B-17 the finest tribute to the Mighty Eighth's veterans, we had made a commitment to build a completely operational upper turret in our airplane, making it the ONLY static B-17 exhibit in the world that would have three working turrets displayed to the public. It was very gratifying that it was necessary for me to pause after making that statement because of the applause that followed. I mentioned that other restorations were reported to have the capability to operate three turrets for public display, but that did not, for fear that the turrets would eventually fail. I stated, very clearly, that we would operate our turrets because we had built them, and if they broke, we knew how to fix them!

I concluded my remarks by stating that I was often asked where the obvious enthusiasm of our volunteers came from, and I said, "Let me tell you about some of the volunteers who have worked on this project." As I had with the Eighth Air Force veterans several months earlier, I mentioned how Bill Liening's dad, a B-17 gunner, had crashed in Switzerland and escaped from internment to return to his unit in England, and how Greg Kindred's family had received six telegrams informing them of missing sons, three of whom were killed, one in a B-17 tail turret, and Jim Odom's dad who had loaded bombs into B-17s and had despaired for the rest of his life at the number of his friends who did not return, and Jack Devine's father who flew 58 missions in the nose of a B-24. Lastly, I told them that the 48-star American flag flying above the *City of Savannah* at that very moment had been presented to my grandmother by the United States government when her son, my uncle, was declared KIA after his C-47 was shot down while dropping paratroopers in Normandy on D-Day. Again, I reiterated what I had said to the Eighth Air Force veterans: "Those men I just mentioned are only several examples of where our enthusiasm comes from," and I looked directly at the section of WWII veterans in the audience and said, "We are your children and your grandchildren, and we honor you with the restoration of this B-17."

Near the end of my remarks I have to admit I was becoming emotional. This event, after all, was the culmination of six years of very impassioned hard work. When I was finished, I stepped away from the microphone and two things immediately came to my attention: my wife, Denise, had a smile on her face a mile wide, so I knew I had spoken well, and General Shuler stood up and took several steps forward to shake my hand as I returned to my seat. Those two reactions were as big a paycheck as I could ever receive for those six years of effort as the project manager of the *City of Savannah* restoration team.

Henry Skipper finished the speaking portion of the ceremonies, which were officially closed by a Retirement of the Colors ceremony by a team from the 165th Airlift Wing.

The final ceremony of the day was the ribbon cutting, which was held next to the left waist area of the B-17, where Skip Shelton had painted the airplane's name precisely as it had been on the original airplane in 1944. All of the work during the previous several weeks to prepare the airplane for its public introduction was paying off, as the guests, staff, and volunteers gathered around the waist area and saw a B-17 that looked just as it had when it rolled off its

Ribbon cutting for the dedication of the B-17 City of Savannah. *(L–R) Author, Henry Skipper, Major General Scott Vander Hamm, Lt. General (Ret.) E. G. Shuler, Al Kennickell. (NMMEAF)*

assembly line in 1945. The airplane looked magnificent! It was an extremely proud moment for all of us who had worked so hard to present the *City of Savannah* as tribute to all of the young men who had served our country during World War II in the Mighty Eighth.

Henry Skipper, General Vander Hamm, General Shuler, Board of Trustees President Al Kennickell, and I were all given scissors, and with a command from Henry, we cut the ribbon simultaneously. I couldn't help but think back to the day 73 months previously when the *City of Savannah* had rolled into this very room with a gutted interior and covered with matted plastic, gunk, and guano—it had been an incredible, once-in-a-lifetime journey!

CHAPTER 7

Special Stories

"Some things are true, some are not, but they are all good stories."

Hilary Mantel, English Novelist

During the six-year time period covered in this work, many, many interesting, mysterious, funny, sad, heartwarming, and unexpected stories were heard and recorded in various forms by our volunteers. Some of them are well documented; some are not. Some took place at the museum during the project's time period. Some took place 70 years previously. Some are best described as "urban legend." What follows are the most interesting stories. These stories have become part of the culture of the *City of Savannah* project, in which we are all so very proud to have participated.

Jim Argo: (Volunteer) *Very early in 2009 a woman came into the museum on a Saturday morning and approached several of us with a very concerned look on her face. Behind her were what appeared to be her family—a man her age, two younger men, and an infirm older man. She explained that the older man was her father and that he had been a B-17 pilot in the Eighth Air Force during WWII. She said her father was terminally ill and had asked his children to bring him to see our B-17 before he died. She asked, "Is it possible that he could get into the cockpit?" We all answered at the same time, "Sure," and then we walked over to meet the man, his son-in-law, and grandchildren. We took him to the forward hatch and with several of us inside the airplane, several outside, and a stepladder, we got him into the lower cockpit. It took quite an effort, but we got him into the upper cockpit and then, into the pilot's seat. He began to cry. Then, of course, we began to cry. There wasn't a dry eye inside or outside of the airplane during those few minutes. Finally, he composed himself, looked around, smiling, and then asked, "Do you think you can get me out of here?" It wasn't as hard getting him out of the airplane and we finally were able to lower him to the gallery floor. Everyone was laughing and congratulating the old gentleman. After a lot of shaking hands and hugs, the family said their good-byes and started to leave—then the pilot's daughter came back to us and hugged everyone. She said, "Nobody else in the world could have done for that man what you just did! Thank you from the bottom of my heart." That visit had a big effect on all of us. We realized what we meant to those veterans.*

Jack Devine: *(Volunteer) One Saturday around noon, Bill Schwickrath and I had just finished working in the bomb bay when we noticed a boy around 10 years old accompanied by a woman too old to be his mother; they were standing at the nose of the plane, and he was pointing something out to her in a very animated way. It was a quiet day for spectators and we had finished our project, so we decided to go speak with them to see if they had any questions. Not only did this young man have several very insightful questions, but he exhibited a very impressive knowledge of the B-17 and WWII aircraft in general. His knowledge was not limited to general information but also indicated that he had memorized certain specifications and capabilities of the various aircraft and in particular the B-17. Because of this, we offered to show him the bomb bay area and he quickly accepted the offer. While under the plane's belly, he continued to impress us with his knowledge and interest. We looked around and, not seeing any other spectators in the gallery at the time, decided to offer to take him inside the plane. Bill gave him a tour as far as the radio room and I took his photo a few times, including one shot of him standing at the waist gunner's station with the biggest smile on his face. While he and Bill were still inside the plane, I struck up a conversation with the woman with him. She was his grandmother and she informed me that the young man has autism and that he has, as we had seen, a very deep interest in and love of flying, especially WWII planes. She added that this would be not only the highlight of his day or his week, but that he would be recounting his experiences that day for months if not years to come. We realized then, more than ever, that this project was not only about honoring the men and women who fought in that war but* *also about preserving whatever possible to educate future genera-tions and remind them that their freedoms aren't free.*

Joe Glasser: (Friend of the *City of Savannah* project – Joe's story appears as he described it to the author along with written materi-al.) *Like most people who served in any war I have a date that will be with me always. Mine is February 26, 1945. I was 19 years old and the navigator for the B-17 My Ideal. We were flying our 25th mission with the 94th Bomb Group out of Roughham, England, when our luck ran out. Returning from a raid on Berlin, a target at our maximum range, our group encountered severe head winds. I began calculating our fuel consumption and told the pilot I doubted that we could safely cross the channel on the fuel we had left. The problem was exacerbated by the fact that there was a 10/10 cloud cover beneath us, and I could not calculate our exact position in order to determine if we were over Al-lied- or German-controlled territory. The pilot tried to drop through the clouds in order to determine our position, but we couldn't get below the cloud level, and he pulled up again. I did my best estimation and told him that I believed we were now over Allied territory, and well short of the English Channel, and almost out of fuel.*

Joe Glasser (top, second from left) and the crew of the My Ideal. (Joseph Glasser)

He decided that he would put the airplane on automatic pilot, head it towards the North Sea, and that we would jump. I made my way to the exit door behind my desk and wondered if I was going to fit through such a small opening wearing my parachute. Truth was, I didn't know anything about how to make a parachute jump; I had never had any training. I tucked my arms around the chute, curled myself up as tightly as possible to avoid hitting the propeller, and just fell through the hatch. There was no yelling, "Geronimo," just abject fear. I came down through the clouds and fog, which were so thick that I hit the ground before I even knew I was landing. Luckily, I landed in a newly plowed field and did not get hurt. I gathered up my parachute and began to walk in the direction where I could hear vehicle noise, holding my breath that the vehicles were not German. I finally got close to the road and saw a good old US Army truck with the white five-pointed star on the door. I ran to the road waving, and the driver of the next truck in the convoy stopped and picked me up, and then dropped me off a few miles down the road at a battalion headquarters. Eventually, all of the enlisted members of the crew showed up at the same location. Both of our pilots had not had the luck I did with their landings and had been injured. I did not get to meet them as they were handed off to a medical unit. I was now the 19-year-old leader of the sergeants from our crew and was given orders that took us to Paris for an overnight stay. We were issued new uniforms and the next day we were on our way back to England. We all got a short rest and then were assigned two new pilots, with whom we flew 10 more missions before the Germans surrendered in May.

Paul Grassey: (Note: During the time I was writing this book, I would occasionally have breakfast with Paul, a neighbor, friend, member of the Mighty Eighth board of trustees, WWII B-24 pilot in the 446th Bomb Group, and fellow Long Island storyteller—this is one of the better stories he told me over the years.)

We were just kids when we were in training. I was one year out of high school, only 19 years old, and flying as a copilot in one of the biggest warplanes in the world in 1944. One day we were on a cross-country training flight and we saw a squadron of B-17s flying below us. There was always a rivalry between B-17 and B-24 crews about who were flying the better airplanes. My pilot and I talked it over and we decided to show off for the B-17 guys. I fire walled the throttles and we began a gradual descent from above and behind the B-17s. As we came up beside them, we must have been going well over 200 miles an hour, much faster than the cruising B-17s. Before we blew past them, I cut the power and feathered the two outboard engines—so we flew past them, going about 70 miles an hour faster than their cruising speed, on what appeared to be only two engines. My pilot waved to them, and then peeled off to the right. Everyone in our crew was hysterical laughing. I still wonder what the B-17 guys thought of us.

Paul Grassey in pilot training, 1944. (Paul Grassey)

Joel Hedgpeth: (Note: Early on in our restoration Joel earned a reputation as a man who is a true ambassador for the project with museum visitors. Because of this proclivity he has many stories to tell. Three of the best are below; others have been placed within the preceding chapters.)

Story #1: *Some of my most memorable moments at the museum are not in the aircraft restoration but in the interaction I have had with the men and their families who flew this airplane and the other aircraft of the Eighth Air Force. The one that stands out was when I was talking to a B-17 crew member (he was a pilot) near the nose of the aircraft. He was with his family. As we chatted about the airplane, I could see in his eyes he was reliving some of the memories he had. I noticed a tear rolling down his cheek, and I asked a simple question—"Good or bad?" His response, "Both." We chatted a while longer. As they moved on, one of his sons came up to me and said, "Thanks for talking to my dad, and for what you are doing with the B-17. You don't know what seeing this aircraft means to him." After multiple encounters like this during my time on the restoration project, I am beginning to understand.*

Story #2: In early June of 2015, Susan and Wayne Lewis came to the shop door and Susan told us that her father, Lt. Robert Miller, had been a B-17 pilot in the 486th Bomb Group in WWII. I introduced myself and said, "Come with me," and as is our policy with WWII Eighth Air Force veterans and their families, offered them a personal tour of the interior of the airplane. I showed them the tail compartment and then we began moving forward through the waist area. They had a camera and were taking a great many pictures. After passing through the bomb bay I helped Susan into the cockpit, and she became very emotional as I explained that this was her father's station in the airplane. She told me that his plane had been shot down on December 6, 1944, and that other crews reported seeing no parachutes escaping from his airplane. After the telegram saying that her father was MIA, the family was despondent until early 1945 when a postcard from her father arrived saying he was alive and a POW in Stalag Luft I. He survived the war and lived a long life, only passing away recently. Susan told me that she had been very close to her father and spent many hours flying with him in several types of aircraft.

Several weeks later, I received a phone call from Susan, who told me that their camera had malfunctioned and they had lost all of the pictures they had taken during their visit. She told me that she was very upset, and asked if they could come back and take the photos again. I replied, "Absolutely." They showed up the following Saturday and were at the door of the museum before it opened. When I greeted them they both began crying, hugging, and thanking me for the opportunity for a second tour. We then spent two hours covering every inch of the airplane, accompanied by tears of both remembrance and

Joel and Ben Hedgpeth are one of several father/son combinations on the project. (CoS Archives)

relief. This became a very personal experience for me from the moment I met these wonderful people, and it was an honor to help them realize a connection with their WWII Eighth Air Force family history.

Story #3: *There are several of us who have had a son also volunteering on the* City of Savannah *project, but I believe I am the only one who has two sons volunteering. My oldest son, Joshua, lives in Longview, Texas, where he graduated from my alma mater with an Associate of Science in Air Traffic Control. When he gets the opportunity, he comes to Savannah to visit us and help on the B-17. My youngest son, Ben, also volunteers on the B-17. As a high school student, he often has other priorities, but he enjoys helping when he can and has learned much from working with the other volunteers. I offered them this opportunity to work on the B-17 for two reasons: (1) it's a once-in-a-lifetime opportunity to be part of the restoration of a WWII aircraft; and (2) most importantly—they get to meet some of the men who fought for our country during WWII and their families. There will not be many more opportunities to meet these men, and I wanted them to be a part of this project and to develop an understanding of our country's past and why we enjoy the freedoms we have. It has been a great experience for me sharing this opportunity with my sons.*

Jim Jones: (Nephew of Lt. John Watkins, navigator of the original *City of Savannah*, in an e-mail to the author.) *I will try to describe my recollection of discovering the* City of Savannah *photo of my uncle, Lt. John Watkins. In 1971, at age 12, I came to live with my Aunt Katherine and Uncle John Watkins, along with my cousins Margaret and Robert. Uncle John instilled in all of us his love of WWII era aircraft. As a teenager, I knew almost nothing of his military career, as he, like so many WWII veterans, rarely spoke of those events in any length or detail. He passed away from cancer in 1978. When the Mighty Eighth museum was constructed in the late 1990s, I began to glean from Aunt Katherine, Margaret and Robert, that Uncle John had flown on a plane named* City of Savannah. *I cannot clearly recall the time line, but it seems to me we made our first trip as a family to the museum in 2000. I remember pulling information from the Missing Aircrew Report we obtained in the library on that visit, which confirmed the anecdotal stories – indeed my Uncle John was the navigator on the* City of

Savannah. *In March of 1945 the crew, while flying another airplane, was shot down over Czechoslavakia. John, who parachuted out of the plane, and the eight surviving crew became POWs until war's end in May. Fast forward a few years – during either a business trip to Gulfstream, or a pleasure trip to Roebling Raceway, my interest was reignited and we came to learn a B-17 aircraft would be coming to Pooler for restoration and display. We had seen some details via Internet news stories and had seen the small B/W photo of the "5000th Airplane" with its crew. Back in 2009, I became reacquainted with an old college friend who was a pilot and an airplane owner. He had recently flown chase in his King Air to the Liberty Belle B-17 across the North Atlantic. Reinvigorated by my friend's flight, I searched the net finding a link to a Savannah newspaper story with that same tiny B/W photo, but this time when I clicked the link it opened a fairly large, high-res photo. When I scanned the faces of the crew, I knew immediately – front row, second from left was Uncle John. I printed a large copy and walked down to his son Robert's office who also immediately confirmed that was indeed his father in the photo. I am really proud of Uncle John's service and staggered that he was actually in "the" photo defining the crew. I am especially grateful that we discovered all of this while his wife, Katherine, was still alive and we were able to contact the museum and visit during the restoration.*

Greg Kindred: (Volunteer/Crew Chief) *When Jim Odom and Jack Nilsen and I were severely challenged to mount the upper turret's well, we spent more than several shifts trying to figure out how to successfully mount the well to the airframe. At one point we discussed how the Rosie the Riveters must have had many challenges such as ours and that they faced their problems with a great deal less training and experience than the three of us had accumulated over the years. We all remain in awe of what those young women accomplished.*

Ralph Kittle Jr.: (Son of the original *City of Savannah* pilot) *My father spoke very little about what had happened to him in WWII. Once, at Christmas in 1975, my family was flying to Austria to see my sister during her junior year abroad. My father was staring out the window of the 747 at a mountain pass in the Alps, completely absorbed. We were wondering what had fixated him. Finally,*

I sat next to him and asked if something was wrong. He told me, "We would fly just this course during the war, and would ease right above that pass at 25,000 feet, on our way to the bombing run of Munich." For the next 40 minutes he told me a little about what had happened to him on his last bombing mission. The basic facts were laid out in the award of the Distinguished Flying Cross to my father for his last bombing mission:

"Ralph W. Kittle, 0828187, First Lieutenant, Army Air Forces, United States Army. For extraordinary achievement while serving as pilot of a B-17 aircraft on a heavy bombardment mission to Plauen, Germany, 5 March 1945. While in-route to the target his aircraft was hit by flak which knocked out one engine, but despite this difficulty he continued on to the target. While on the bomb run another engine failed, but Lieutenant Kittle pressed on until the bombs were released. Just after leaving the formation another engine failed, and seeing that it was impossible for him to reach friendly territory, he ordered the crew to bail out while he skillfully maintained level flight. The flying skill and courageous devotion to duty displayed by Lieutenant Kittle on this occasion reflect the highest credit upon himself and the Army Air Forces."

What my father told me on that flight was that after the bombs were dropped, he told his crew to lighten up the B-17, and they proceeded to throw the guns, bullets, and everything else off the plane. Suddenly, the ball turret gunner ran up to him with his open parachute. I still remember how shocked my father looked just remembering this, 30 years later. Somehow, they found another one on board. He told the crew that they were going toward the Russians to the east, because there was no way they could get back to England. Then the third engine failed. He ordered the crew to prepare to bail out. When they entered a bank of clouds, he gave the order to jump. All of his crew were taken prisoner and survived the war, with the exception of Bob Warren, his tail gunner, who said he would never be taken alive and was an expert marksman. He was killed. Now my father was alone in that plane, looking at the mountains ahead of him. It almost looked like he could make it over the mountains, but as he watched, he realized—not quite. He bailed out of the plane and opened his parachute and as he glided down he watched his plane fly on toward the mountains. He landed softly in a tree, and it took him awhile to get down to the ground. He stepped out onto a big, flat field covered in snow, his .45 caliber pistol in his hand. He wondered—what is this Georgia boy doing out here? I don't think that he had realized before that his left leg had been injured by flak, but now he had a hard time walking. He tried to head east toward partisans in Czechoslovakia. Along the way, he ran into three other American fly- ers from another airplane, also shot

Ralph Kittle's German POW picture, 1945. (Ralph Kittle, Jr.)

down. He told me that they entered a barn. The other flyers were eager to keep going and tried to get my father to go with them. But he was too injured to join them. He remained in the barn and wished them well. Some members of the Volkssturm, the German home guard, were tracking him with dogs. They found him and beat him. Some soldiers of the Wehrmacht saw what was hap- pening and stopped them. One soldier gave him a cigarette, which he never forgot. They rounded him up with other flyers they had picked up and marched them through the town to the train station. There, on the main street, he saw the bodies of the three Americans that he had been with the day before, strung up on lampposts. They also had been captured by the Volkssturm, who did not appreciate being bombed. He was transported across Germany to Frankfurt where all pilots were interrogated. The Gestapo questioned him. Something that he remembered so clearly was the trim of their black uniforms, so perfectly made. He was there for a few days. The Germans then put him in a boxcar to a Stalag near Nuremberg. He was there for less than a week. Patton was closing in from the west. The Germans emptied the POW camp and started a long march for the prisoners back across Germany.

My father had a difficult time walking and needed a cane to keep going. He was struck by a brick thrown by a civilian and was

badly hurt. The column of prisoners was strafed by American fight-
ers. His feet became perfectly flat from the march. He lost 30 pounds.
They finally arrived at another German Stalag in Schweinfurt. By this
time, the Germans had little to feed their prisoners, just soup once
a day. He talked about a pilot who had been imprisoned there for
years and helped him keep going. After a few weeks, the prisoners got
up one morning and all the guards were gone. One of Patton's tanks
rolled right over the barbed wire and they suddenly realized they were
free. The war in Germany ended a few weeks later. (During an interview with Dick Gorman at the NMMEAF at the B-17 dedication,
Ralph Jr. and his cousin Pat McMillen also revealed that Ralph Sr.
was awarded two Purple Heart medals upon his return from being
a POW. The first was for a shrapnel wound he received from the
original flak hit on the airplane, and the second for a head wound
that he received after being hit by a brick thrown by a German civilian during the POW march.)

UPDATE: While visiting the Czechoslovakian crash site of his
father's B-17, Kit Kittle, Jr., learned from a local historian that tail
gunner, Sergeant Robert Warren did not die in a confrontation with
German police, as had been reported, but from the malfunction of
his parachute.

Arnold Kolb: (Long-time owner of 44-83814) I called Arnold
during the summer of 2009 to speak to him about the history of
44-83814. During our conversation, he told me several things regarding the trip from Arizona to Dulles airport in 1984 when he
and his son Nathan delivered the airplane to the Smithsonian. Arnold told me that the flight was uneventful until he and Nathan
were nearing Dulles and were informed by air traffic control that
a storm was lingering over the Dulles area and diverted them to
a holding pattern over the Atlantic. Our conversation had started
with my question as to why there were a large number of apparently
mathematical calculations written on the wall of the co-pilot position in the cockpit. Arnold explained to me that he had been flying
in the co-pilot seat and that the numbers were the calculations that
he made when he and Nathan discovered that a fuel transfer valve
had failed, and that they would not be able to access the final fuel
tank that they planned to use if the flight became extended for any

reason. He explained that his figuring resulted in a decision that in order to stay in their holding pattern for the period that air traffic control was telling them would be necessary, they would have to shut down one of 814's engines to save fuel. They shut down the #3 engine and feathered the propeller, as was standard procedure to reduce wind drag. Finally, they were released by air traffic control to land, and did so, with 814's last landing piloted by Nathan Kolb, age 21, on three engines. For that reason, the *City of Savannah* will be presented to the public with its number three propeller in the feathered position – a question that is frequently asked of Mighty Eighth docents by knowledgeable museum visitors.

Sam Martin: (NMMEAF Archivist; assisted the CoS project on many occasions.) *The aircraft that the Kittle crew was flying on their 13th, and final, mission (42-97542), had been flying combat missions since 1 April 1944. Its final mission was its 44th. "542" was originally assigned to the 482nd Bomb Group as a radar pathfinder command aircraft (H2X). It was then briefly transferred to the 96th Bomb Group, and finally, to the 388th. After 25 missions, on 5 November 1944, 542 had its pathfinder radar removed and was returned to combat duty on 13 January as a standard bomber with the 388th Bomb Group. The aircraft's final mission, with the Kittle crew, was its 44th combat operation, and took place on 5 March 1945.*

Jack Nilsen: (Volunteer) *I have always worked in the aviation industry, and had a particularly strong interest in WWII airplanes. Working on the City of Savannah has allowed me to talk with several people who flew on those airplanes during the war. I consider that a gift. Here are two stories of WWII B-17 crewmen that I had the honor to meet during the project.*
    Story #1: *This story took place at the start of a shift one Wednesday evening, when we noticed an elderly couple looking up at the nose of the airplane. This was very unusual, as we don't start work until the museum is closed for the day and the visitors are gone. I exchanged some pleasantries with the couple and learned that he had been a pilot in the Eighth Air Force during WWII. He looked up at the airplane and said, "Seventy years ago today, I was bombing Bremen in one of these." Eventually, our entire evening crew was gathered around the old pilot and we listened to his stories. The one that stands out most*

vividly is how he described a German fighter attacking his plane head on. He described how terrified he became when he saw the flashes of the fighter's guns. He knew he was about to die. He said that the German pilot must have been as scared as he was because all of the tracers from the fighter disappeared below the B-17. In the course of our conversation, he mentioned that he had written a book about his WWII service. As must be the case with all authors, he just so happened to have a bunch of the books in the trunk of his car. We all bought an autographed copy.

__Story #2:__ I was working on the tail turret one afternoon, and a museum visitor stopped and began watching me. We introduced ourselves, and he told me that he had been a WWII Eighth Air Force tail gunner in a B-17 like ours and managed to survive a full tour of missions. I mentioned that he must have had some view of German fighters attempting to come up behind his airplane. He said that several times fighters had come in close, but they had all failed to down his plane. He said that his closest call was when an attacking fighter's round had penetrated the turret, taken the heel off of his flying boot, and traveled up the rear of his flight clothing and exited the top of the turret. His only wound was a frostbitten foot. He said, "They were only one digit away from having my number."

__Jim Odom:__ (Volunteer) This is my special story. One Saturday morning I was at the museum working on the tail turret. It was at the time when there were a couple of World War II airplanes visiting Savannah, and one was a B-17. Some WWII veterans were there to get a ride. I was standing beside the tail working, when this small in stature, grey-haired man walked up to me and said, "That's where I used to sit." I said, "Oh yeah? You were a tail gunner?" The gentleman said, "Yep, I saw the world backwards." I said, "Well thank you, sir." I had to take a couple of steps away to set something down and kept an eye on the guy. He walked over to the tail and placed his hand on it. I watched him mouth the word, "Wow." Then he slowly lowered his head and began to cry. I backed a little further away to give him some space. After a moment he recovered and walked over to me, shook my hand and said, "Thanks for restoring this old girl." I was pretty choked up but managed to say, "No sir, thank you." In that one powerful moment, I realized that all my efforts and all the work I had done up to that point were worth it. I knew then why I was here. James Collins Odom Jr. (Jim's dad was a WWII Eighth Air Force veteran.)

David Pinegar: (Volunteer) *Early on in the project I often spent my lunch hour working at a bench under the wing of the B-17. There were always questions and comments on the project from visitors. Folks would speak about their dads who flew in the war, or tell stories of the planes they saw when they were younger. One day, while I was scraping paint off of an old part, a little old lady shuffled up to me and with a very deep German voice she asked if this was a bomber. I replied, "Yes." She asked if this was a World War II bomber. Again, I replied, "Yes." She said that a bomber like this had dropped bombs on her! Startled by her comment, I asked her where she had lived. She said "Frankfurt!" She went on to tell me that when she was a little girl in Frankfurt, bombers like this had dropped their bombs on her city many times! I assured her that this particular bomber had not taken part in the war and had no part in dropping bombs on her. She thanked me and walked away. I stood there in disbelief. All the stories I ever heard while working on the airplane were of brave family members or crewmen that fought for our country in the war. I had never heard a story from the other side, by an innocent little girl. In all my years working on the* City of Savannah *project I have never heard a story like that!*

Bud Porter: (WWII ball turret gunner, member of the board of trustees of the NMMEAF.) *I spent a great deal of time in several schools at the beginning of my career in the Army Air Force. They finally decided that I should become a radio operator on a bomber crew. After radio school in Sioux Falls, South Dakota, I was sent to MacDill Field in Tampa, Florida, where bomber crews were put together. I remember that several hundred of us—both officers and enlisted men—were gathered in the base theater and names were called to assemble crews. My name was never called as the radio operators were assigned. Finally, my name was called—as a ball turret gunner! I went over to my new crew and explained to the pilot that I wasn't a gunner, but a radio operator. He asked how tall I was. That sealed the deal, they were looking for people who were less than 5'7", and I was 5'6". That's how the Army works. All that time in radio school was down the drain because of one inch in height. The next day I was in* *a classroom for ball turret gunners with an instructor who had just returned from 25 combat missions with the Eighth Air Force. The first thing he said was that the ball turret was the safest position in the airplane. Since not one of us had volunteered for the job, we were all convinced that he was just trying to make us feel good. In addition, he said that in combat, when the flak is coming up thick and heavy, a rotating turret would deflect any shrapnel hitting the turret. All my later experience proved otherwise.*

Darrell Schwartz: (Volunteer) *While working on the airplane one Wednesday, I met a couple who were walking together and look-ing very carefully at the airplane. He told me he had been a B-17 crewman in the Eighth Air Force during WWII. His wife jumped into the conversation and told me that she was a German and that he had bombed her home. Then they walked away and I didn't get any more of the story. I'm sure it was interesting.*

Jack Stiff: (Canadian Author and ex-RCAF pilot) *I first saw the B-17G 44-83814 in 1956, when she was flying for Kenting Aviation, Toronto, an international aerial surveying company. As a young Air Cadet and pilot-in-training under the sponsorship of the RCAF, I was based at their training facility at Oshawa. Across from the RCAF han-gar was a facility owned by Kenting Aviation. When the B-17 wasn't on aerial surveying missions, the airplane, painted in Kenting's red and white colour scheme, was parked in front of their hangar. As I had a working knowledge of WWII aircraft, I recognized this model as a WWII era B-17. I loved to watch the B-17 rumbling down the runway, her mighty Wright rotary engines roaring on take-off. A few months after my flight training was completed, I forgot about Kent-ing's old kite, and didn't think about her for many years.*

I was researching a potential magazine article in 2011 and found an article profiling Dave Hadfield. Dave had been involved with these early aircraft and was indeed flying them on occasion, for Vintage Wings of Canada, an organization that restores and flies heritage air-craft. In this piece, Dave mentioned his dad, Roger, who had piloted a former WWII-era B-17 out of Kenting Aviation. I then realized Dave was talking about the same plane I first saw at Kenting in 1956.

That was incentive enough for me to do considerably more re-search on the background and whereabouts of that bird. Research led me on a paper trail to former Kenting pilot, Roger Hadfield, who'd been difficult to trace due to the extreme popularity of his son, Chris, who'd recently returned from his mission as commander of the International Space Station. Dave Hadfield was a member of Vintage Wings of Canada, as was I. I contacted Dave to explain what I was doing regarding his father. Dave gave me the information I required. I then called Roger at his Milton, Ontario, home and had a long chat with him. He provided invaluable provenance on 814's history after it was sold by Kenting in 1971.

Milt Stombler: (Volunteer) *My special story involves Paul Abare sharing some of his extensive B-17 knowledge by teaching me, and Danny Harden, how to fling ourselves into the forward hatch on the airplane just like Gregory Peck in the movie* Twelve O'Clock High. *The three of us were standing near the front hatch and Paul asked if we knew how the crew got into the aircraft by holding the top of the forward hatch and swinging their legs up into the fuselage. I mentioned that I had tried it and that my attempt was awkward. Paul said that the trick was to use your heels to walk your body up the airplane after you raised them up and through the hatch. Using Paul's method, both Danny and I were able to perform the Gregory Peck move flawlessly. Paul also explained that while entering the hatch by springing off the ground looked good in the movies, a flight crew leaving on a mission would be wearing too much gear to fling themselves into the airplane, and each ground crew had a ladder for the use of those crew members who entered the airplane though the forward hatch.*

Terri and Her Ladies: During the entire restoration process of the City of Savannah, there has been a special relationship between the B-17 volunteers and the staff who work in the museum restaurant. Terri Belle is the owner of the company that operates the restaurant and has served many a meal to the CoS team, officially and unofficially. This group of fine ladies has given out just a few cookies and "leftovers" to hungry faces at the kitchen door. In December of 2012 the volunteers made a special effort to thank Terri and her ladies, inviting them to take a tour of the airplane, and surprising each of them with a yellow rose when they gathered after the tour. Thank you, ladies—you are a great part of our story.

Terri Belle (top row, 2nd from left) and Her Ladies with their roses.(CoS Archives)

Margaret and Robert Watkins: (Margaret and Robert are the children of the navigator of the original *City of Savannah* crew. What follows is from their interview with Dick Gorman on January 28, 2015, in the NMMEAF library.) Margaret and Robert discussed their father, Lt. John Watkins, in very warm terms. John died when he was 59 years old and both Margaret and Robert were teenagers. He had spoken only briefly about his WWII adventures to his children. One fact that emerged from this interview was documentation that the original *City of Savannah* did not arrive in England along with the Kittle crew. The Watkins children agreed that their father had told them that the airplane had engine trouble, and that the crew left the airplane in Iceland while they continued on to England (no further details). John did discuss with both Robert and Margaret that his relatively short time on the ground in Europe between March 6, when the crew was shot down, and the German surrender on May 7, was very difficult. When he landed John tore ligaments in both his knees, which left him in considerable pain.

He was captured by local police the day after he landed. As was the case with almost all the *City of Savannah* crew, John was forced by the Germans to march for days away from the advancing Russian army. He said that he knew if he fell out of line because of the pain in his knees he would be killed and that on at least one occasion the marching prisoners were attacked by Allied aircraft who mistook them for German forces. Finally, he and the prisoners in his group were liberated by a unit from Patton's advancing Third Army. When he was repatriated to England, he weighed only 98 pounds.

Mystery story: It isn't very often that you get documentation for a story, but nobody to actually tell the story—this is just such a case. Sometime during 2013 the museum got a call from a woman in Hazen, North Dakota. She wanted to know if the B-17 at the Mighty Eighth was the same B-17 that had been a war memorial in Hazen in the late 1940s. None of the current volunteers can re-member who took the call, but word was sent down to the shop that a woman had called and that she told the museum staffer that she and her boyfriend had carved their initials on the airplane in front of and slightly below the airplane's left horizontal stabilizer. What we do know is that Bud Currey was asked to verify that the initials

Bud Currey pointing to the initials of the young lovers from the 1940s, who remain a mystery.
(CoS Archives)

were, in fact, carved into the metal. Sure enough, there they were, "JEL MEK." The local Hazen newspaper was contacted and asked if they could help to find who it was that had made the call and carved their initials in the airplane so many years ago. No one came forward to explain. The initials are still there, but the story doesn't have a name attached . . . yet.

Urban legend #1: During the summer of 2012, a man visited the museum and began regaling visitors at the tail of the airplane about having "over 400 hours in this airplane." Considering the individual's age and the events he was describing, it would be very difficult to believe that he could have spent time as aircrew in the *City of Savannah*. He would have had to be a child when the airplane was flying for Kenting Aviation, as he was describing. Finally, he explained to his audience—he *was* a child. His father had been the pilot, in the 1950s, when the airplane was mapping portions of the Andes Mountains in South America on contract with Kenting Aviation Corporation. He said he was ten years old and had spent the summer with his dad as the crew of 814 slowly flew over the mountains taking pictures for map-makers. He said that most of the 400 hours were spent sleeping in the radio room. He promised to send documentation of this story to the museum. It has yet to arrive.

Urban legend #2: Most Americans have heard the expression "the whole nine yards," which, loosely defined, depicts an endeavor that was given a full measure of effort. During 2014 another undocumented visitor tipped us off to the origin of that phrase, and when we called other B-17 friends we had the story confirmed several times. It seems that the standard ammunition box in a B-17 Flying Fortress engaged in combat in the Eighth Air Force in 1944–1945

"The whole nine yards" of .50 caliber ammunition on the floor of the museum Combat Gallery. (CoS Archives)

held a load of .50 caliber ammunition that when stretched out in a straight line would be nine yards long—hence, when a gunner expended all of this ready ammunition, he would have given "the whole nine yards." There may be other versions of the story, but that's the one we like.

One final story from the author: Over the years I heard each of the stories that you read in this section, and, of course, many more, most of which I have related in the narrative. I do have, however, one final story of my own that will stay with me forever because it is so unique, and unlike many of the stories from the veterans, is not based on sadness. The storyteller would not reveal his name or the unit that he served with while he was in England. The gentleman in question showed up at the museum in the summer of 2012. He told one of the volunteers that he had been a radio operator in the Eighth Air Force during WWII and wanted to see the radio room. I noticed that he was not wearing the WWII veteran card that is given to all WWII veterans who visit the museum. Our policy with regard to access to the airplane is that if a WWII veteran shows up, he can have whatever he wants. So, despite the lack of a WWII veteran card, I took him into the airplane. He followed me to the radio room, where he sat down in the operator's chair and slowly took in the entire scene. He looked at me and said, "You got it right!" That was the best feedback that we could hear, and I thanked him for his approval. We talked for a while and as we were leaving the airplane, I asked him to fill out one of our veteran's contact sheets. He said he'd rather not—which was unusual—but I didn't make an issue of it. After we got out of the airplane, he said to me, "The reason I don't want to leave my name or any contact information is personal, but I am going to share it with you, since you don't know who I am."

Then he told me his story: He had arrived in England as a replacement radio operator, not assigned to a crew, in early 1945. After flying with several crews on missions as a last-minute substitute, he had gotten into a dispute with a pilot and was busted to private and taken off of flight status. At first he deemed his new status as a blessing. He would not get shot at if he remained in England instead of flying missions. He told me he was assigned only menial duties, such as sweeping the hangars. When the war ended in May of 1945, everyone was looking forward to going home. Soon the aircrews were being released and flying B-17s back to the United States. Each aircraft would carry several long-service ground personnel with them. More and more airplanes departed, filled with aircrews and selected ground personnel. Our visitor was not one of them. He began to get worried that he would be the last man left at the base. Finally, while sitting in the squadron office, he noted that one of the aircraft was flying home in several days with a stop in his native Boston. He approached the pilot and explained his problem. The pilot was a genial guy and told him, "I never go aft of the cockpit. If you are back there, on the manifest or not, I could care less." Somehow, the visitor told me, he talked his way onto the airplane and flew with them to Boston. (He implied that some cash might have changed hands.) When the airplane landed in Boston, he jumped out onto the tarmac as it was refueling, and several hours later was having dinner with his astonished parents in his boyhood home. It was a good story, but before it could sink in, he gave me a big smile and said, "And I never had any contact with the Army again; I've been AWOL for 69 years! And that's why I'm not going to give you my name and unit." Then he smiled, shook my hand, and walked out of the museum. Who knows if the story is true, but it sure is a great one.

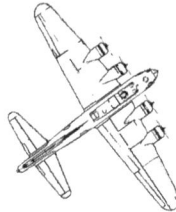

CHAPTER 8

The Tails of Two Cities: Of *Savannah*

43-39049 AND 44-83814

"When once you have tasted flight, you will forever walk the Earth with your eyes turned upward: from there you have been, and there you will always long to return."

Leonardo da Vinci

The original City of Savannah *43-39049, departing Savannah on December 4, 1944.* (Savannah Morning News)

The current City of Savannah *44-83814, arriving at the Mighty Eighth, January 15, 2009.* (CoS Archives)

The crew of the B-17G, tail number 43-39049, flew the first airplane named *City of Savannah* out of Hunter Army Airfield, Savannah, Georgia, on December 4, 1944.

The National Museum of the Mighty Eighth Air Force welcomed the B-17G, tail number 44-83814, also named *City of Savannah*, to Pooler, Georgia, on January 15, 2009.

What follows is the story of those two airplanes, their histories, and some accounts of the men who flew on the aircraft. There are two stories—of two airplanes that shared the same name, but with two different numbers painted on their tails.

The material for B-17G/43-39049 was obtained through the efforts of our original project historian Douglas Reed. Doug was assisted by Dick Hennegler, the historian for the 388th Bomb Group, and by a veteran of 26 missions over Europe with the 385th Bomb Group, William Varnedoe. Local history documentation was contributed by one of our original volunteers, Tonnie Glick. Museum staff member Brenda Elmgren provided editing.

The Original B-17 *City of Savannah* (Tail Number 43-39049)

The first *City of Savannah* B-17 story starts in late 1944 at the height of World War II, when the residents of Chatham County, Georgia, raised $500,000 to pay for the production of one B-17 bomber and the training of the 10 men who would make up its crew. During much of WWII, new B-17s and recently graduated aircrews were brought together at Hunter Field. The crews would be temporarily assigned a specific aircraft, and they would fly that aircraft over what was known as "the northern route" to England. After their arrival the crews would attend additional training and be assigned to an operational bomb group. The aircraft would be sent to the next unit in line for a new aircraft. Seldom did a crew continue into combat with the aircraft that they flew across the Atlantic.

The *Savannah Morning News* reported that shortly after Thanksgiving in 1944, the US Army Air Corps matched the crew piloted by Lt. Ralph Kittle with B-17 43-39049, the 5,000th airplane to be processed through Hunter Field to support Allied forces in Europe. The airplane was formally named *City of Savannah* to honor its Chatham County fundraisers. More than 2,000 guests at the ceremony watched as Lt. Kittle and his crew were photographed with the airplane and received a blessing by Army Air Corps Chaplain Alfred A. Williams.

That's the official story. A great deal of research and several meetings with the families of the pilot and navigator of the crew brought out much more detail about what happened to the crew and their wartime experiences. A separate story follows the fate of the original *City of Savannah*, that the crew flew as far as Reykjavik, Iceland, on an aborted trip to Europe in December of 1944.

After reviewing several sources that provided conflicting information, it appears that the B-17G/43-39049 was built under the Construction Number 10027, which indicates that it was manufactured at the Boeing facility in Seattle, Washington. The airplane received its airworthiness certificate/tail number of 43-39049, indicating it was built under a 1943 contract, and was flown to Hunter Field in late November of 1944, where the aircraft was matched with Lt. Ralph Kittle and his crew. Kittle, a native of Ringgold, Georgia, was 23 years old in 1944, when he was given command of his crew and assigned to 049. After completing combat crew training at Avon Park, Florida, the crew was transported via train to Hunter Field, arriving on November 20, 1944, and temporarily attached to the 302nd Unassigned Base Unit for their short stay in Savannah.

We know that the *City of Savannah* 43-39049, and her crew departed Savannah on December 4, 1944, and flew up the East Coast of the United States to Grenier Field, located near Manchester, New Hampshire. They departed Grenier on December 6 for Goose Bay, Labrador, and finally Reykjavik, Iceland. The airplane developed mechanical issues prior to its arrival in Reykjavik, and it was decided that the crew would continue to England and that the airplane would remain in Reykjavik until it could be repaired. Thus the original *City of Savannah* and the Kittle crew parted after their short, but interesting, time together.

While we do not know details of how the Kittle crew arrived in England, we can assume that they followed the usual steps for arriving crews and that they were transported by train to the

Combat Crew Replacement Center located at Bovington, England. After completing their additional combat crew training, Kittle and his crew were assigned to the 563rd Squadron of the 388th Bomb Group at Knettishall, in East Anglia.

Records indicate that the *City of Savannah* arrived in England several weeks behind the Kittle crew and was placed in the technical upgrading queue for all B-17s arriving in England. On January 12, 1945, 43-39049 finished its combat upgrades, including RAF compatible communications gear and was assigned to the 389th Squadron of the 487th Bomb Group in Lavenham, England. According to English historian Graham Simons, the identifying signage that had been painted on 43-39049's nose and waist identifying the aircraft as the *"City of Savannah"* was most probably removed while the aircraft was being upgraded for combat.

On May 7, 1945, five months after 43-39049 arrived in Lavenham, the war in Europe ended. Two months after the victory celebration, 43-39049 was flown back to the United States, landing at Bradley Field, in Connecticut, on the 12th of July. Several days later the aircraft was flown to a storage facility in Independence, Kansas. On December 14, 1945, almost one year to the day after its dedication as the *City of Savannah*, B-17G/43-39049 was declared surplus equipment and apparently ended its career with thousands of other WWII aircraft that were sold for scrap.

The Story of the Original Crew

Lt. Ralph Kittle and his crew were chosen for the honor of being assigned to the B-17 43-39049, the 5,000th airplane to be processed through Hunter Field in 1944. From their arrival in Savannah on November 20 until their departure on December 4, 1944, the crew had very little time that was not spoken for with official duties. They trained as a crew in 049 and drew all of the personal combat gear that each flyer would take overseas. There was one unscheduled event that occurred when a severe winter storm approached and each aircraft commander was ordered to move his bomber from Hunter Field and to seek a safer landing field inland. Lt. Kittle knew a good opportunity when he saw one. After calling his family in Ringgold, Georgia, he flew to his hometown, buzzed his mother's house, and flew on to Lovell Field, located in nearby Chattanooga, Tennessee. Kittle's nephew, Pat McMillen, told a rapt audience in 2015 how he still vividly remembers that day as one of the most thrilling of his life as the family drove to Chattanooga and he, a two-year-old little boy, was lifted by crew members into the B-17 and placed in the pilot seat where his uncle sat when he was flying the airplane.

The Kittle crew shortly before departing Hunter Field. (Margaret Watkins)

Kittle and his crew returned to Hunter the next day and watched as Hunter Field soldiers painted the name *City of Savannah* on the nose and left waist of the airplane prior to their departure. Shortly after 3:00 p.m. on December 4, the crew was assembled in front of the aircraft, pictures were taken, and several speeches were made by local dignitaries, thanking the residents of Chatham Country for providing the funds for the airplane and training for its crew. Finally, a blessing was given by Chaplain Alfred Williams, and at 4:00 p.m. the 2,000 people who witnessed the ceremonies applauded as Lt. Kittle started the engines of 049 and taxied to the main runway. He powered 049 into the sky and departed Savannah for the first stop on the trip to England, Grenier Field in Manchester, New Hampshire.

There had been some idea during early research into the original aircraft's history that there might have been some mechanical difficulties with the airplane as the crew flew through the various stops in their Atlantic crossing. It wasn't until the airplane dedication in January of 2015 that what actually happened was confirmed in an interview with the family of navigator John Watkins. Both of his children, Margaret and Robert, confirmed that their father had told them that the airplane developed mechanical troubles serious enough for it to be left in Iceland as the crew continued on to England, most likely as hitchhikers on other B-17s flying the course behind the *City of Savannah*. The crew never again saw the B-17/43-39049, named the *City of Savannah*.

The operational history of the Kittle crew was typical of the danger and suffering endured by many Eighth Air Force veterans. They underwent additional combat crew training in England and were assigned to the 388th Bomb Group. They were never assigned a "permanent" aircraft and referred to themselves as the *City of Savannah* crew—after the only B-17 they ever identified with as a crew. They flew their first mission with the 388th on January 28, 1945, followed by 11 more successful sorties. Their 13th and final mission took place on March 5, 1945. That day the Kittle crew flew a very battered F model B-17, tail number 42-97542, that had flown 43 previous missions.

History of Kittle Crew Missions

(Courtesy of the 388th Bomb Group Association)

Groups preceding the 388th Bomb Group on the Kittle crew's final mission discovered that the original targets, the cities of Chemnitz and Plauen, were covered with clouds. The groups further down the bomber stream, including the 388th, were advised to do their bombing utilizing radar in lieu of visual sighting of the targets. The 388th was assigned targets in the city of Plauen. While making their bomb run toward the target and awaiting the signal from the lead bomber to drop their bombs, they were suddenly hit simultaneously by several flak shells.

Mission#	Date	Target	A/C Tail #	Outcome
251	28 Jan 45	Hohenbudberg	43-37806	Completed
252	29 Jan 45	Bielefeld	44-6524	Completed
253	03 Feb 45	Berlin	44-6574	Completed
254	06 Feb 45	Chemnitz	44-6574	Aborted
257	15 Feb 45	Cottbus	42-97105	Completed
258	18 Feb 45	Hamburg	43-38385	Aborted
260	20 Feb 45	Nuremburg	44-6102	Completed

261	21 Feb 45	Nuremburg	44-8301	Aborted
262	22 Feb 45	Ulm	42-10698	Completed
263	23 Feb 45	Ansbach	-38869	Completed
265	25 Feb 45	Munich	42-97210	Completed
266	26 Feb 45	Berlin	44-6102	Completed
268	01 Mar 45	Ulm	42-97542	Completed
269	02 Mar 45	Dresden	44-8594	Completed
270	03 Mar 45	Gotersloh	44-6106	Completed
272	05 Mar 45	Chemnitz/Plauen	42-97542	Lost—Flak

Mission #272 – March 5, 1945
388th Bomb Group Formation

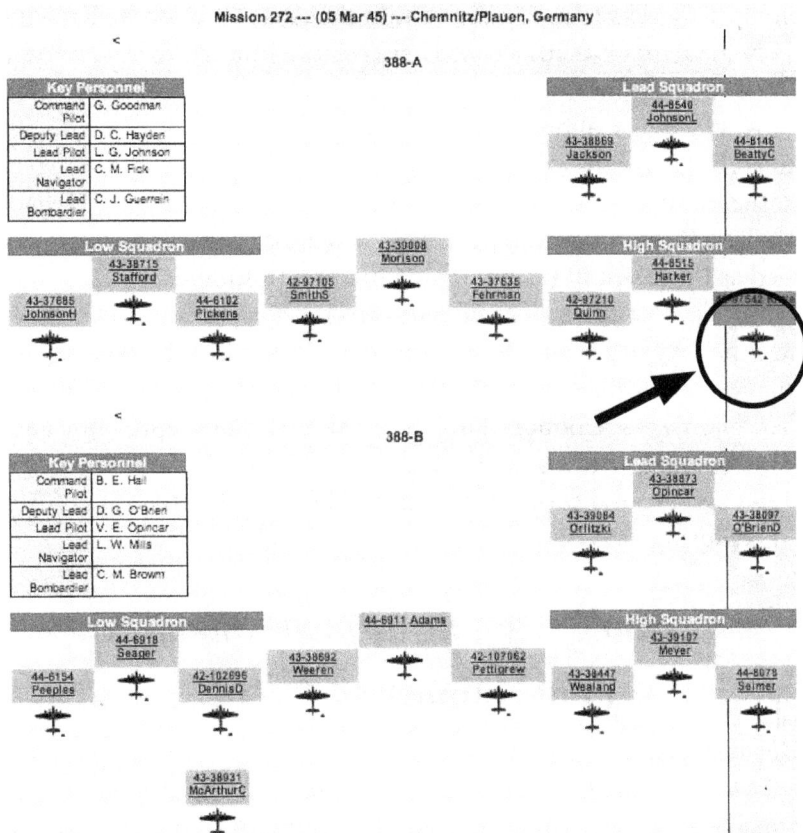

Mission 272 --- (05 Mar 45) --- Chemnitz/Plauen, Germany

(Courtesy of the 388th Bomb Group Association) Arrow indicates location of the Kittle crew in the 388th BG formation on 5 March 1945.

The immediate result of the hits was that two of the B-17's engines caught fire and had to be shut down by Kittle and co-pilot George Rutt. Almost immediately a further problem occurred when the pilots were unable to stop the propeller on one of the engines from windmilling and causing additional drag against the stalling bomber. As the pilots worked frantically to stop the propeller and keep the aircraft in the air, a third engine failed. There was now only one order for Kittle to give his crew: the order to buckle on their parachutes and jump. He held the plane as steady as possible and, after engaging the automatic pilot, was the last man to leave the bomber. With one tragic exception, the crew landed safely. During the next 48 hours they were captured by German military and civil authorities, became prisoners of war, and returned safely to American military control when the war ended six weeks later. Until a visit to the crash location by Kit Kittle Jr. in October of 2015 it was believed that the crew's tail gunner, David Warren, who had always told his fellow crew members that he would never allow himself to become a prisoner of war, was killed by German police while resisting arrest. During Kit's visit to the rural area in Czechoslovakia where his father's B-17 had crashed, he learned from a local historian that Warren had, in fact, died as the result of his parachute malfunctioning.

Ralph Kittle Sr. died in 2005, but the story of the Kittle crew and the *City of Savannah* lives on today in the Combat Gallery of the National Museum of the Mighty Eighth Air Force in Pooler, Georgia. We were honored to have the families of Ralph Kittle and John Watkins with us at the dedication of the airplane to all the crews and ground support personnel who served in the Eighth Air Force during WWII.

Today's B-17 *City of Savannah* (Tail Number 44-83814)

Of those Flying Fortresses that did survive into the postwar period, 44–83814 is one of the last B-17s built at Douglas Corporation, Long Beach, California. Accepted for service on June 20, 1945, it was flown directly to Syracuse, New York, and placed in short-term storage. It was declared excess to military requirements on

October 12, 1945, and flown to the Reconstruction Finance Corporation disposal lot at Altus, Oklahoma, where it remained until late 1947.

As is the case with much of the history of the two aircraft that are associated with the *City of Savannah* project, the early history of 44-83814 is abundant with contradictory, confusing, and in some cases, quite colorful stories. When we compared the stories, we finally came up with the probable history of the airplane from its manufacture in May of 1945 through its gifting to the Mighty Eighth in January of 2009:

Owner	Time Period	Home Location
Manufactured	May, 1945	Long Beach, California
US Government Storage	1945–1947	Altus, Oklahoma
N. Dakota Public School #3	1947–1951	Hazen, North Dakota
California-Atlantic Airways	1951–1953	St. Petersburg, Florida
Kenting Aviation	1953–1971	Toronto, Canada
Black Hills Aviation	1971–1981	Spearfish, South Dakota
NASM (Pima Air Museum)	1981–1984	Davis-Monthan AFB
NASM (Storage)	1984–2009	Chantilly, Virginia
Mighty Eighth Museum	Jan. 2009 – Present	Pooler, Georgia

Notes:
California-Atlantic Airways was an aircraft broker. Kenting Aviation and its subsidiaries ran a worldwide air survey operation. Black Hills Aviation operated the aircraft as a fire bomber. NASM = National Air and Space Museum.

The first non-governmental stop for 814, as noted above, was as a war memorial in front of Public School #3 in Hazen, North Dakota. According to the Hazen Star and other sources, two Hazen, North Dakota residents, veterans who had flown B-17s during their wartime service, became aware in 1947 that a fully functioning B-17 could be purchased from the United States government for only $350 if that airplane was placed in a location where it would serve as a war memorial. The two pilots, Rudy Froeschle and Lyle

Benz, decided that they would raise the $350 to purchase a B-17 and the additional funds for the necessary gasoline and oil to fly a surplus bomber back to their hometown. There it would serve as a memorial to all the Hazen veterans who had served in WWII. Froeschle never got to participate in the adventure as he was accepted to medical school and departed to begin his studies. Lyle's brother, John, while not a military pilot, did hold a civilian license, and joined his brother, taking Froeschle's place as the second required pilot of a B-17 crew. The Benz brothers traveled to Oklahoma, presented their money and pilot certifications to the proper authorities, and took possession of the B-17G with the tail number 44-83814. As a result of their efforts, 814 ended up parked in front of Hazen Public School #3 in late 1947. It remained at that location until 1951, when a second set of events took place, resulting in the airplane leaving North Dakota for a new home in Florida with its second civilian owner.

The display of WWII aircraft as monuments was apparently not unusual in the late 1940s, but difficulties would ensue in subsequent years as communities and schools sought to dispose of what had

John and Lyle Benz standing in front of 44-83814 in an undated photo. (Hazen Star)

become eyesores or liabilities. Many local jurisdictions assumed they owned the aircraft and attempted to sell them on the civilian market, which was the case with 814. In 1951, after four years in Hazen, the fortress was purchased from the school district by Owen F. Williams, a representative of Atlantic Airways of St. Petersburg, Florida.

Williams was able to neatly side-step the title problem by offering the school board a relatively big payday for a small rural school district that had no idea what the airplane was worth, and then turning a nice profit when reselling 814 to a Canadian survey company named Kenting Aviation. According to Doug Reed's research, when the airplane arrived at its new home on May 12, 1953, it was given the Canadian designation of CF–HBP, with a note on its record that the airframe had a total of 855 hours logged flight time.

Kenting Aviation employed CF–HBP in a variety of projects over the years, including air survey operations in the Canadian arctic and around the world. It was reportedly used during 1955 in support of construction of the Distant Early Warning (DEW) Line in Canada and Greenland. CF–HBP remained active on the Canadian aircraft registry until April 1, 1971, when it was sold to Arnold Kolb of Alamogordo, New Mexico. The FAA reassigned the airplane its original US civilian registration number of N66571.

Kolb operated Black Hills Aviation at Spearfish, South Dakota, and later at Alamogordo, New Mexico, and owned a number of B-17Gs, all of which he used as firefighters/air tankers. N66571 remained active as a tanker through 1981 when Kolb traded it to the National Air and Space Museum (NASM) for two US Navy surplus P-2 bombers.

Ownership was transferred to NASM on January 19, 1981, at Davis-Monthan AFB, Tucson, Arizona. N66571 was stripped of its civilian paint and registration and as part of the agreement with NASM, had its original military service serial number, 483814 painted on the tail. The airplane was then placed on temporary display at the Pima Air Museum, immediately adjacent to Davis-Monthan, where it remained for the next three years, until the Smithsonian could find available space for interior storage. In 1984 a place was found at the NASM facility in Chantilly, Virginia. Arnold and his son Nathan flew 814 to Dulles Airport and formally delivered 44-83814 to the Smithsonian in April 1984.

The airplane was placed in storage by the Smithsonian and would remain in that status until January of 2009, when the Mighty Eighth team arrived in Virginia to bring it to its final home at the National Museum of the Mighty Eighth Air Force.

Harry Friedman: *It was the winter of 1992 when we of the B–17 Co-Op entered an out-of-the-way storage hangar belonging to the National Air and Space Museum in the suburbs of Washington, DC. Through layers of dust and plastic sheeting, we saw the outlines of a B-17 Flying Fortress. On closer inspection it was clear that time and climate were taking their toll. As members of the B-17 Co-Op swarmed around the aircraft, there was much expression of remorse over the deterioration of the airplane. We speculated then about the fate that awaited it. Tommy Garcia and I had no idea how this aircraft would become such an important part of our lives.*

Photo History of 44-83814

814 and Betty Jensen, student, Hazen, ND, 1950. (CoS Archives)

814 with photographer Ralph O'Keefe in Kenting Aviation colors, 1957. (Ralph O'Keefe)

814 practicing a water drop. (Maurita Kolb-Autry)

814 in Black Hills Aviation colors, 1976. (Maurita Kolb-Autry)

The last pilots of 814, father and son, Arnold and Nathan Kolb, Dulles Airport, 1984. (Maurita Kolb-Autry)

814 parked next to the space shuttle Enterprise, in a National Air and Space Museum storage hangar, 2008. (Jim Grismer)

CHAPTER 9

Folks We Met Along the Way

JANUARY 2009 – JANUARY 2015

"Friendship consists of forgetting what one gives,
and remembering what one receives."

Alexander Dumas

This list of individuals who helped us out along the way includes some folks you read about in the book and others who played a role behind the scenes. Each of them was important to our success.

Thank you one and all!

Chuck Aitken – Supervisor of the Gulfstream RDC Composites Lab. Chuck is one of the professionals from Gulfstream Corporation who enabled us to use state-of-the-art technology to produce parts necessary for our restoration that are no longer available on the world market.

Lynne Alexander – Lynne is the third museum administrative assistant to do a great job in supporting the City of Savannah project. She was always there when needed and brought a special spark to the monthly update we sent to our members and followers.

Harlan and Dorothy (Xena) Avezzie – A very professional and friendly husband and wife team from Westfield, Massachusetts, who have a national reputation for producing first-class working turrets and parts for WWII aircraft. When Harlan Avezzie sends you a part for your turret, you know you are getting a quality piece of machinery.

Carroll Baker – A member of the CARS (Coastal Area Radio Society) team that did such a wonderful job with the *City of Savannah* radio room. Carroll's donation of the transmitter that he paid for himself, and spent a full year restoring, was above and beyond in support of the project. Carroll is the classic example of the many low-profile volunteers who made significant contributions to our success.

Kristine Baker – One half of the talented Flight Safety International painting team that repaired the nose art and painted the A/C tail numerals on the City of Savannah.

Terri Belle – Our Lady of Great Food! Terri is the restaurant contractor at the Mighty Eighth. Over the years she has catered our annual dinners and all-hands meetings. She is a great person, to include understanding that even grown men like to eat snacks out of kitchens. Terri also has a track record of hiring really great staff.

Jason Bess – One of our all-star interns from Savannah Technical College. Jason produced our bombardier control panel in final form using 1944 Boeing drawings and state-of-the-art 3-D technology. He also was a major player on the upper turret parts development. Well done, young man!

Fred the Turret Guy – Also known as Fred Bieser, he is a Georgia boy with an unusual nickname. He probably knows more about WWII bomber turrets than anyone in the world! Really! Fred has been a contractor, friend, benefactor, consultant, and drinking buddy with us since 2010.

Don Brooks – Our Georgia neighbor and president of the Liberty Belle Foundation, Don has been a good friend of our project from the very beginning. We have done several major transactions over the years, and of course, he gave 10 of our volunteers the thrill of a lifetime in 2014 when he gave them a free ride in the movie *Memphis Belle*. Don Brooks is a true Southern Gentleman.

Whitney Coyle – Whitney worked with us installing the stanchions, manufactured by American Aero Services Corporation, that support the *City of Savannah* on the floor of the Combat Gallery of the NMMEAF. Let there be no doubt that he was the right man at the right place when a decision was needed as to the final position of the airplane on the floor. The man is a leader!

Bill DeLoach – Bill is one of the CARS radio team who always seemed to be there when we needed him, particularly during the broadcast sessions.

Bob Dupree – The east coast half of the Chroma Corporation team that provided the power for the *City of Savannah*. Bob got the whole relationship started when he visited the museum while visiting Savannah for his daughter's graduation from Savannah College of Art and Design. When Jeff Hoopes' inquiry for help arrived at Chroma's California office we already had a corporate connection. Bob and his Chroma Corporation partners will always be part of the *City of Savannah* family.

Doug Edwards – Retired as woodshop manager of the Gulfstream Corporation's Completion Center, a group that produces the final woodwork for Gulfstream's world class aircraft interiors. Doug applied his high-level technical and professional skills to completing the woodwork surrounding our ball turret. A job well done!

Norm Ellickson – Crew Chief of the *Yankee Lady*. Norm provided us sage advice, some important parts, and a sincere friendship when it was needed.

Jim Fletcher – It is difficult to find a place in the narrative of this work to describe Jim's significant contribution to our success on the *City of Savannah* project. He participated in all of our social functions, but spent 95 percent of his efforts in our office by himself, on days when the rest of us were not at the museum—he was not available on Wednesdays and Saturdays when the rest of us worked. BUT, his contribution was enormous! Jim kept superb records on the Human Resources aspects of the project. He constantly updated who was active and who was not, and his record keeping on volunteer hours was exceptional! We were constantly utilizing his files to locate former volunteers and contractors. Several other volunteers tried to work this important function, and threw up their hands in frustration—Jim got the job done. He was so good at the job he was honored with the nickname "Radar"—after the immortal M*A*S*H company clerk who made that name famous.

Eric Fournier – Eric is one individual who truly understands the computers at the National Museum of the Mighty Eighth Air Force. Even more important, Eric's default answer to every question is "Yes, I can." Our kind of guy.

Harry Friedman – Harry's telephone call in 2009 launched the *City of Savannah* project into the world of aircraft restoration. Harry was the only person in the United States of America who could have answered all the questions that we needed answered in 2009. The words you read previously in this manuscript only begin to accurately portray the feelings of the City of Savannah team for our own "Doc" Friedman.

Tommy Garcia – As with Harry Friedman, there is no more that can be said about Tommy and the contribution and camaraderie that he provided to our project from his first visit until today, and hopefully for many years to come.

Joe Glasser – It would be very hard to find a finer gentleman and a stronger supporter of his fellow young flyers in the Eighth Air Force during WWII. Joe was a 19-year-old Eighth Air Force navigator in 1944 and later made quite a name for himself in the business world, and with us, as a major financial supporter—purchasing our ball turret and financing the lower cockpit—and as a true friend who believes in our mission.

Dick Gorman – One of the many Gulfstream employees who joined our ranks. Dick was the editor/publisher of the Gulfstream in-house journal, and worked with us on public relations issues, the monthly Update, and stress reduction. His assistance and guidance with regard to the professional and logistical requirements of publishing a book were a wonderful gift. Brother Gorman is a good man.

Jane Grismer – An administrative whiz, founder and director of the highly successful Flying Fortress 5K, a major player in completing this book, a good person—and Jim's daughter. Quite a list of credentials!

Steve Grodt – One of the Left Coast team of Chroma Corporation, the wonderful people that provided the power for the *City of Savannah*. Each of his visits, or e-mails, brings out what a fine gentleman he is. I wish Steve lived in Savannah so we could have him as our in-house power wizard.

Ron Gunnells – One of our original Gulfstream volunteers. Ron's knowledge of airplanes and his leadership skills were very important to putting us on the right road when we were getting started. Professional and family priorities prevented him from being with us for an extended time. He made his mark, and we missed him in the later years.

Tony Hall – The Louvre has Rembrandt. The Sistine Chapel has Michelangelo. We have Tony. We wouldn't let just anybody paint our airplane.

Jim Harwood – Owner of Carolina Metal Corporation. We contracted with Jim for a $2,500 parts fabrication job in 2014. When he realized what the part was for, the restoration of a B-17 bomber, he refused to take our money for his work and volunteered to do as much additional gratis work for us as he could fit into his very crowded schedule. Jim is a special contributor.

Chris Henry – When we first met Chris he was an air traffic controller at a local airport in Indiana and the volunteer project manager for the restoration of the B-17 *Miss Liberty* located at the Grissom Air Museum. Today he works for the Experimental Aircraft Association as a Tour Educator—he literally found a way to take his hobby and turn it into a career. A great guy, generous beyond words, and always with a smile on his face. Chris is a good man to call a friend.

Susan Isacson – A fellow Long Island native, Susan was Our Lady of Events during our restoration. She organized every one of our all-hands meetings and gave some excellent direction with regard to our annual dinners and the major museum events that we participated in over the years. It is always a pleasure to work with professionals.

Dick Jackson – Lucky for us, Dick retired in South Carolina. How many people in the entire country have actually built a B-17 ball turret? Dick is one of only several. He was in the area for a short time, but made a major contribution. Thanks, Dick.

Bruce Johnson – Bruce became the chief of maintenance at the Mighty Eighth shortly after we began the City of Savannah project. He was always there when we needed him, which was a lot! A retired US Army NCO, Bruce always understood our mission.

Steve Jonas – Another terrific CARS radio team member. When I called Steve with a question or a request, it was always taken care of immediately. Those are things you never forget. Thanks, Steve.

Don Keller – Owner of an airplane parts business by the name of "B-17 Air Depot" in Beaverton, Oregon. I found Don after seeing an advertisement for his business in *Air Classics* magazine in April of 2009. During an extended opening conversation Don suggested that I contact Dr. Harry Friedman for assistance in putting our project together. His suggestion was the most important piece of advice I received in the six years I was the project manager for the *City of Savannah*. Don is very friendly, very professional and a very important part of our history.

Mike Kellner – One of the really nice guys we met along the way. Mike runs the *Desert Rat* B-17E restoration taking place in Marengo, Illinois. He loaned us his hard-to-find bomb hoist with no questions asked, for which we are very grateful.

Ralph Kittle, Jr. – The son of the pilot of the original *City of Savannah*. The entire Kittle family has been very supportive of our project and Kit Jr. has gone out of his way to be a good friend of the project, to include donating a copy of a painting that was done of the original airplane by a local artist by the name of Alberta Barber. The Kittle family is very much a part of our *City of Savannah* restoration family.

Arnold Kolb – Arnold was the last commercial owner of 44-83814 before he traded the B-17 to the Smithsonian for two surplus P-2 aircraft. I had the honor of speaking to him on one occasion, when he explained to me that the numbers written on the wall of the cockpit of the airplane were his computations on how long he and his son Nathan could keep the B-17 in the air after they experienced a fuel transfer valve failure when delivering the airplane to the Smithsonian in 1984.

Maurita Kolb-Autry – Maurita is the daughter of Arnold Kolb and the sister of its final pilot, Nathan Kolb. She has been a staunch supporter of our efforts in supplying historical data for 44-83814 and its time with her family business. Her greatest achievement was obtaining her father's logs for 44-83814 from the Smithsonian and delivering them to us. The Kolb family is an important part of the *City of Savannah* family and Maurita is the Lady-in-Charge.

Sonny Koski – Sonny is a Saturday docent at the Mighty Eighth. He is known as "The Pizza Guy" to Rocky and His Friends as he has been buying morning donuts and noon-time pizza for the Saturday crew for years. Thanks Sonny!

Kim Kovesci – Kim is the curator at the Military Aircraft Preservation Society museum in North Canton, Ohio. Kim's role in having the MAPS museum donate the upper turret structures that Jeff Hoopes located on their property was a major step in fulfilling our goal to be the only B-17 restoration with three working power turrets. We owe Kim, and the folks at MAPS, a big favor!

Sam Martin – Sam worked in the archives at the Mighty Eighth for several years while also doing research on a book about the Eighth in WWII. He served our country in the Marine Corps and was a very good friend of the *City of Savannah* project. Semper fi, Sam.

Ron McDonald – Ron is an artist. Really! He works for Disney Corporation as a professional artist. He designed the *City of Savannah* patch and thus will always have a literal stamp on our project. Ron's dad and my uncle, Lt. Joe Sullivan, were on the same C-47 crew in the 435th Troop Carrier Group in 1943–1944. Two weeks before D-Day Joe was transferred to another crew and died with them in a Normandy hamlet named Clainville, just outside St. Mère-Église. Ron's dad made it home, and years later Ron and I became friends when he contacted me after reading D-Day +60 Years, the book that I wrote about my uncle and the circumstances of his death in Normandy.

Nick Meinhardt – A double-play guy for the project. Nick is an R+D engineer at Gulfstream Corporation and an instructor at Savannah Technical College. Both of those job titles paid off for us in a very big way. It doesn't hurt that he is also a very nice guy.

Don and Rose Miller – Don is the author of *Masters of the Air*, the ultimate work concerning the Eighth Air Force in WWII, and a member of the board of trustees of the NMMEAF. He and his wife, Rose, are wonderful people with whom I spent a great afternoon touring the *City of Savannah* and discussing our common New York City roots.

John Mirakian – A Connecticut Yankee in Savannah's Court. John travels between two homes, in Connecticut and Florida. He is also a highly skilled toolmaker level machinist, who just happens to also own a machine shop. John stopped by the museum in 2013 to take the tour and started a conversation with Jim Grismer. The rest, as they say, is history. John personally manufactured six of our gun mounts, and several other very complex operating parts of our turrets, saving us—literally—tens of thousands of dollars. It is hard to find enough ways to thank John for what he has done for us. Did we mention he has the world's greatest smile?

Jim Moriarty – Another one of those Gulfstream engineers who kept showing up after Jim Argo would tell him we had a problem. Jim always seemed to be able to solve the problem of the day, particularly when we needed struts to rebuild the nose of the airplane. His amazing group of professionals followed up the work on the nose, with the chin turret well and the bar and gun mount for the tail turret. Jim and his team are very high on our heroes list!

Chuck Mosely – President and owner of All Coast Aircraft Recovery, Chuck and his team moved the *City of Savannah* from Chantilly, Virginia, to Pooler, Georgia. Chuck runs a great team of professionals, and we have stayed in touch over the years. It was most appropriate that he and several of his team that delivered our airplane were also present when she was dedicated.

Paul Moure – Paul is the CEO of a company by the name of War Relic Replicas located in Upland, California. His company made our fantastically real-looking WWII 500-pound, general-purpose bomb replicas. Early on we referred to him as our "bomb guy." After a while we thought that might cause some consternation in certain circles, so he became our "California ordinance contractor."

Gary Norville – President of American Aero Services, located in New Smyrna Beach, Florida. Gary was a big help in getting us started, including several gratis consulting trips to Pooler and the building and mounting of the stanchions on which the *City of Savannah* now rests.

Frank O'Keefe – Frank is one of the few people we met along the way who could actually claim time flying in our airplane. While in college he spent the summers of 1956 and 1957 working as a camera operator for Kenting Aviation in Toronto, Canada, and spent literally hundreds of hours in the lower cockpit of the airplane, designated CF-HBP, by the Canadian government. In 2010 Frank donated a model of the airplane in its Kenting colors to the museum. The model is on permanent exhibit to the public in a display case next to the airplane.

Bruce Orriss – An ex-"Joisey" guy who has taken up with the West Coast aviation and movie crowd. Teamed with Tommy Garcia, Bruce has been a good friend and a big help with regard to locating very large hard-to-find airplane parts—as in our ball and tail turrets. He is also an author and a good man to talk with about airplanes.

Jeff Phillips – Our own personal general officer. "General Jeff" was willing to be an acting private when it came to cleaning the airplane in the early days of the project. He was a good friend and worker with Rocky and His Friends on the Saturday crew during his tour with the 3rd Infantry Division at Ft. Stewart. We were proud of him when he arrived in uniform at the dedication wearing a very impressive second star!

Joe Powell – Our connection to the academic community in Savannah. Aircraft restoration projects are not noted for involving academia in their work. Thanks to Jeff Hoopes, Joe led the effort at Savannah Technical College to develop an internship program that worked for everyone.

Don Price – As the leader of the Commemorative Air Force Gulf Coast Wing, Don arranged for us to borrow upper turret parts for re-engineering in our upper turret construction project.

Frank Quirk – One half of the original Gulfstream painting team, Frank is a "get the job done" professional.

Doug Reed – Doug is one of the folks we met along the way who walked into the museum, saw what we were doing, and asked if he could help. His chosen profession is researching and documenting historic homes. Airplanes are, apparently, not that different. Doug became our first official historian. Much of the historical data regarding the B-17 44-83814, aka the *City of Savannah*, that you find in this book was researched and forwarded to us by Doug from his home in Maryland.

Dylan Russell – Another exceptional Savannah Tech intern who found a home with the *City of Savannah* project.

Fred Sabatine – President/CEO of Chroma Corporation. Without Fred's OK for the gifting of two sets of power equipment, we would have been in big trouble. Fred's dad was a WWII veteran. He understands our mission!

Sheila Saxon – Best described as Our First Girlfriend. Sheila's organizational skills, stability, and just plain good sense, kept us on track as we got started on the *City of Savannah* project and "didn't know what we didn't know." She was special assistant to both Walt Brown and Henry Skipper during the first year we were working on the airplane. You never forget your first girlfriend!

Abby Schaaf – One half of the talented Flight Safety painting team that repaired the nose art and painted the A/C tail numerals on the City of Savannah.

Terry Snook – Terry is the manager for aircraft maintenance of the several airplanes on display to the public at Barksdale Air Force Base in Louisiana. He bonded with the *City of Savannah* volunteers at several B-17 Co-Op meetings due to his being involved with static display aircraft and the fact that the current Eighth Air Force is stationed at his location.

Tim Steele – Another one of those amazing specialists from Gulfstream Corporation. Tim put together much of the signage on the *City of Savannah* and mounted the major star decals, donated by Tommy Garcia, on the airplane's fuselage and wings.

Matt Stephan – Matt is the photographer who took the great cover picture for this book. He is yet another Gulfstream employee who contributed to our effort.

Jack and Faith Stiff – Jack is an ex-Royal Canadian Air Force pilot and author. While in RCAF flight training he watched our B-17, in Kenting Aviation colors, using the same runway from which he and his classmates practiced their new flying skills. Jack wanted to know what happened to that old B-17 and did an Internet search. He was amazed to find that it was sitting in our gallery. Jack and his wife, Faith, traveled from Canada to Florida in 2014 and stopped by to say hello and check out that once familiar B-17. Jack is our source for the information that the father of the famous Canadian astronaut Chris Hadfield was one of the pilots who flew our B-17 during the 1950s for Kenting Aviation.

John Szabo – One of those California guys you never get to meet in person. It doesn't matter. We like John and he likes us. You can be sure that if a box shows up and says Depot 41 on the return address that there is a quality product inside.

Dave Talleur – Dave needs to get one more mention because of all the work he did behind the scenes as my chief advisor with regard to technical issues. His contributions in the radio room and interaction with the Chroma team assured success in those two sub-projects. Dave's most significant role involved various sheet metal issues, to include locating original drawings and supervising the construction of sheet metalwork with out of town contractors. Finally, he provided his fine baritone voice as the narrator for our in-house videos that run next to the *City of Savannah* to explain the status of the project to visitors. It is "behind-the-scenes" people, like Dave, who keep projects like ours on the road to success. Thanks, Big Guy!

Linda Thompson – Who knew we would need a professional baker to make our windows fit on the airplane? Linda is the baker from Terri Belle's kitchen at the NMMEAF who volunteered to bake David Pinegar's plexiglass for the *City of Savannah's* lower cockpit windows. She has also been known to send a cookie or two out the door of the kitchen to a hungry volunteer.

Phil Turner – Is a member of the 388th Bomb Group Association and has visited the project many times since 2009, videotaping various events. Just to show you how much we appreciate Phil, when he is at the museum he wears one of our shirts and a *City of Savannah* project badge.

Steve Ward – Steve showed up at the museum as a visitor and became much more to the early project work when he succeeded in having his employer, International Aerospace Services, provide a professional cleaning and polishing of the entire exterior of the *City of Savannah* in 2009. He later joined us for several months as a volunteer, until he accepted a new, out-of-state job. One of the great ones, who just stopped by for a while.

Margaret Watkins – Daughter of Lt. John Watkins, the navigator who guided the Kittle crew from Savannah to England and on 13 combat missions. Margaret and the entire Watkins clan live in Atlanta and have been part of the *City of Savannah* family from the very beginning.

Tom Wilson – When Tom walked, unannounced, into the *City of Savannah* office in 2010 he introduced himself as the finest aircraft restoration sheet metal man in the country. Now we agree.

Jay Wisler – The owner of a company by the name of Warbird Parts and Memorabilia located in Tampa, Florida. As described by Jim Grismer in the narrative of this book, and by virtually everyone who has visited his facility, "WOW!" Thousands upon thousands of parts spread over multiple buildings—and Jay knows where every one of those parts is located. Jay's business is a true American aviation treasure, and instrumental in our success.

Jim Woodford – Chief of Maintenance for the Commemorative Air Force. Jim gave the OK for us to borrow upper turret parts from the CAF Gulf Coast Wing for reproduction. Without that OK, we would have been out of the upper turret business. Jim is on our "A" list of good friends.

CHAPTER 10

Why I Am Here

THE VOLUNTEERS IN THEIR OWN WORDS

"The passion and dedication that the volunteers bring to this project come from the fact that we are your children and grandchildren."

Our Message to Visiting WWII Veterans

Many times during the period between January of 2009 and January of 2015, we would ask each other, "What brought you here?" Almost invariably the answer involved the *City of Savannah* project having a special meaning for each volunteer. We were not looking for something to do—the project found us and brought each of us into the fold! The reasons for coming to the project became such an important piece of the history and culture of our effort that I felt it was appropriate to ask the volunteers to put their words on paper. Here is what they said:

Paul Abare: *I have been an aviation person from the time I was a small boy and my mother put me in a helicopter with Santa! I grew up with a father who flew a Piper 180. We would go flying all over New England. When I got interested in World War II memorabilia, it changed my life. A group of guys who restore World War II airplanes, the Atlantic War Birds, took me in. We restored a C-54, a C-47, a C-45, and a B-25, and then a B-17, which was later used in the movie* Memphis Belle. *Some of the best times of my life were at air shows when the vets would tell me their stories. I was honored to listen as they described their adventures in the skies over Europe.*

One day I found myself in Pooler, Georgia, the home of the National Museum of the Mighty Eighth Air Force. I went out to visit the
museum, saw the City of Savannah, and asked how I could sign up to
be part of the restoration. Now is the time to pay my debt for all of the
joy I received as a young man listening to the stories of the veterans.
The team at the Mighty Eighth is one of the best, from the top down.
I want to thank everyone associated with the project for providing a
place where I can give back.

Jim Barry: *Just before I retired from a 48-year career
in corporate aviation as a captain and instructor, one
of the volunteers at the* City of Savannah *project, Dave
Talleur, came to me and said I needed to come over and
take a look at what the B-17 restoration group was doing at the National Museum of the Mighty Eighth Air
Force. I told him that my technical skills amount to not much more
than polishing. "We could use a good polisher," came the reply. I then
backed off and said that I was a polisher, but couldn't claim to be a
GOOD polisher. Regardless, the next Wednesday I showed up at the
Eighth Air Force Museum and was given a* City of Savannah *T-shirt
and name badge. Wow, I was part of the restoration team. I immediately became involved in the many chores that the volunteers were
working on at the time: building a staircase to the waist door, cleaning
70-year-old gunk, polishing 1,200 .50 caliber bullets, polishing the de-
icing boots, installing the oxygen system. The welcome I received from
the volunteers, and the ability to contribute to this great endeavor has
exceeded all my expectations. What a thrill. I was very gratified to
be given a leadership position in the internship program the museum
operates with Savannah Technical College.*

*More importantly, this airplane has made a lasting impression
on me—more than I expected. Experienced restoration technicians
say that these WWII warbirds start "talking" to you as they get close to
completion. Every part I touch or install brings my thoughts to 1944:
Who built this or put that together? Who designed and engineered
all the intricate parts? Were they like my dad, a radio technician who
worked on P-40s in China during the war? Or, like my grandfather, a
machinist at GE who built the stator blades for America's first jet engine? If yes, they were great people and I wish I could have met them
and thanked them for their efforts. The WWII veterans come in and*

want to see and talk about the airplane they flew as crew members: pilots, bombardiers, radio operators, and gunners. This airplane's soul is flesh and blood. As I look to all the creature comforts of present-day flying and all the hardships these men went through, I am in awe at their bravery and sacrifice. What a great honor it is to be a small part of this restoration project! I hope this airplane "talks" to visitors for generations to come.

Bill Burkel: *I remember going out to the Mighty Eighth soon after the airplane arrived. Much to my surprise, the fuselage had already been moved inside. I looked at the wings still sitting outside and said to myself that I just had to be a part of restoring this airplane. I filled out an application to be a restoration volunteer and a few weeks later I got the word to come and join the restoration team. I remember looking at it the first day I got there with Jerry, Jim, and Marshall and looking at all the protective coatings that had been put on the outside of the fuselage and wings and thinking this was going to be a lot of work, just to clean the airplane. Eventually we did get it clean, and then the real fun began.*

Jack Devine: *My dad, 1st. Lt. John J. Devine, served with the Army Air Corps, 5th Air Force, in the South Pacific during World War II as a B-24 bombardier. He flew 59 combat missions and, although he never discussed his service, we discovered after his death that he had been awarded many medals, ribbons, and commendations. So, it is with much humility that I am doing my small part to honor his bravery and service to his country and to assure that the heroism and accomplishments of all who served during that war are not forgotten.*

Carl M. Finney: *I believe that we are all put on earth for a purpose. My whole life I have tried to do things that would make a contribution. I come to Savannah from Jackson, Georgia, to work with the volunteers who are restoring the B-17* City of Savannah *because they are doing the right thing. I served in the USAF as a mechanic servicing B-47 bombers. I now have the honor of serving as a volunteer on the* City of Savannah *restoration team because I believe*

we need to honor those boys—and they were boys—for all the sacrifices that they made so we can live a free life here in the United States.

Jim Fletcher: *My hometown in rural Missouri has only about 1,000 inhabitants. And yet from that speck on the map with its tiny population, there came two B-17 Flying Fortress crew members during World War II.*

My father was in training as a navigator on a B-25 bomber as the war came to a close. My son, a graduate of the U.S. Naval Academy, flew Persian Gulf combat missions as a flight officer in F-18 Super Hornets off of the USS Harry Truman.

Growing up in the 1950s, one of my thrills as a small-town boy was to watch airplanes land and take off from Lambert Field when we'd visit St. Louis. During my teen years my dad obtained a pilot's license and I flew with him in his single-engine Mooney.

As a restoration project volunteer, I have felt a sense of satisfaction derived from my admiration for those two men from my hometown who survived combat missions over Europe, my pride in my father's and my son's service, and my life-long fascination with airplanes—and especially with military aviation. I am also pleased to be a small part of preserving a magnificent historical item for the younger generation, including my own grandchildren.

Jeff Friend: *I am fortunate to have some family history with aviation. One of my grandfathers flew TBF Avengers off of the USS Yorktown in the Pacific during WWII. He would tell my brother and me stories of heroism and how hard it was to land an airplane on an aircraft carrier. After visiting the Yorktown myself, I believe it! My other grandfather worked in research and development for Aeroproducts in Dayton, Ohio. His job was necessary to the war effort so he was unable to enlist to fight. He ran the testing facility where they tested propellers and all sorts of engine/propeller combinations. I remember Grandpa telling the story of meeting Orville Wright when Wright visited the Aeroproducts factory. They actually held a conversation about the "pitch" of the propellers my grandfather was working on.*

My uncle was a military pilot, but did not see combat. He flew T-6s, T-28s, T-33s, F-86Ds, and the F-102s. My dad's cousin was also a pilot who flew F-9F Panthers and Cougars for the Navy. My father himself was a metalsmith in the Navy and worked on A-4s.

I have very fond memories of trips to attend air shows throughout my childhood. Of course, the acrobats were the "stars" of the shows, but my favorite part was walking around with my dad and marveling at the engineering feats that had been brought from drafting board concept to full-blown, real-life works of art. He taught me to see the real beauty in these machines. Being a machinist by trade has taught me a true appreciation for the concept of "art to part" and these machines are absolute marvels in that sense.

I haven't served in the military or had any real connection to B-17s in my life. The reason why I am a part of the project is that I love to hear all the stories from the men who lived through those tough times. I can only hope to pass these stories along to anyone who is willing to listen in an effort to preserve the history of those who lived them. I don't think of work on the City of Savannah as "work." I feel a deep sense of honor in working on the airplane and being able to meet these great men in the process. That's why I'm here.

Tonnie Glick: I have always been fascinated by aviation. I grew up in Dearborn, Michigan, a few miles from Willow Run Airport where they made the B-24s. We used to go out to the airport and see the planes take off and land. I can still remember those big planes that my father said were going to Europe to fight the war. I didn't understand what a war was yet, but it sounded serious. As an avid reader of nonfiction, I read biographies and "real" stories growing up. I wanted to become a pilot like Amelia Earhart and drove my mother crazy about taking flying lessons.

When I saw the article in the Savannah Morning News about the City of Savannah, I was very excited. I knew I did not have the skills or strength to clean and repair that plane like my husband, but I had to find a way to get involved.

Jerry McLaughlin is a neighbor. I asked him what I could do. He said "just wait" and the next thing I knew I had a dining room table full of papers and articles about our procuring the B-17. Now I could make my own historical scrapbook of the history of our plane! I went to the historical society downtown and researched the airplane that was the 5,000th to be processed through Hunter Field before it flew to Europe. I helped solve the mystery of two different planes with the City of Savannah *name.*

It is a once-in-a-lifetime experience to see the progress of our B-17 and work with the talented men restoring our plane. It has been exciting for me to see so many companies and people here in Savannah, as far away as Texas, and many other places in the United States step up to assist us.

Jim Grismer: *The reason I'm here working on the restoration of this classic warbird can be found in a decision I made 11 years ago. I answered an ad looking for volunteers at the National Museum of the Mighty Eighth Air Force. They were looking for docents. I wasn't quite sure what a docent really was. When I was enlightened, I decided it wasn't for me. I wanted a hands-on job. It so happened that the Archives were looking for help in cataloging items that were donated to the museum. BINGO! I was that square peg for the square hole! The major interest throughout my life was military history, and I grew up in a virtual war relic museum. My dad was a serious collector of militaria. I did know a thing or two about medals, weapons, patches, and such.*

Going through musty footlockers and duffel bags was right up my alley. These artifact boxes and bags were arriving at the museum's doors at a very high frequency. Widows and surviving children of our deceased Mighty Eighth airmen were delighted to see their heroes' wartime relics find a respectable and secure home after 60-plus years in the attic or garage. Just touching their cigarette packs, photos, and letters from home gave life to these inanimate objects. These young men were regular guys like us. I read through scores of combat and POW diaries in the Archives. Each word served to imbed itself in me and paint a clear vision of what they had done. The staggering losses, the level of pain, and the years of captivity for an enormous number of them became the reason and the focus for us every day we labored on the restoration. I would think of those kids who fought, died, were wounded or captured as they brought the air war to the hated enemy. These recurring thoughts were shared by all of us and kept us hammering through the restoration process. We must honor them with every nut, bolt, rivet, and screw that brings us closer to completion.

Jack Hango: *I wanted to volunteer to restore the B-17 because I love aviation, I'm semi-retired and I needed something to do. It is a very interesting project and the people are great to work with. I am amazed at the workmanship being done by every crew. These guys know what they are doing!* One aspect of the project that never occurred to me was interacting with the veterans visiting the museum. They marvel at the plane they flew and tell great stories! They have had very interesting lives, and I love to listen to them. It is sad to think that in the near future they will all be gone. I am happy that I have had the chance to work on this project.

Danny Harden: *My career in aviation started in 1965 when I joined the 165th Air National Guard. I was assigned to the 165th Maintenance Squadron/Reciprocating Engine Shop. I worked in the engine shop for several years where I had the opportunity to operate one of the largest reciprocating engines in the Air Force inventory. Just to smell the smoke and oil coming from those engines at crank up is something I will always remember and, of course, you can't leave out all the noise! What great memories!*

As to why I am here: well, it's the memories of the last era of propeller-driven aircraft and the history that they made. Working with the City of Savannah project has been one of the greatest honors that I've ever had. Just to have been involved in watching this aircraft come to life after being in storage for so many years and to play a part in honoring those aircrews that flew those missions during World War II—some that returned and some that didn't—makes me proud!

This project has been history in the making, and I am very proud of what all of us have accomplished over the past six years. Without a doubt, it has been a labor of love and a great ride.

Joel Hedgpeth: *My interest in aviation began when I was seven years old. I was bitten by the aviation bug as a result of a project I was given to build a model of an historical vehicle and write a report as to why it was significant to history. This fire was further fueled in history class in junior high school when we were assigned a*

report on some aspect of World War II. Since I already had built several models of WWII aircraft, I chose to write my report on aviation in the war. Researching this subject opened a whole new aspect of my love for aviation and how it was used in WWII.

I made a choice to study aviation in college. I graduated with a number of qualifications to enter the aviation industry: a Bachelor of Science in Aviation Technology, FAA certification as both an airframe and power plant mechanic and a commercial pilot certificate with a multi-engine rating. The way things worked out, my aviation career has stayed mainly on the ground. My first job was as a maintenance analyst and supervisor at Interstate Airlines. I was hired by Gulfstream Aerospace Corporation, here in Savannah, as a reliability engineer in 2008.

I joined this restoration team to help restore a B-17 bomber, which is a once-in-a-lifetime opportunity. But, as I learned about the aircraft and was able to interact with the museum guests, the more I realized that this restoration project is more than the aircraft itself. It is about the men who flew the B-17, the families who supported them, and the memory of those who did not return.

Several of my fellow volunteers have a son also volunteering on the project, but I am the only one who has two sons volunteering. I offered them this opportunity to work on the B-17 for two reasons: it's a once-in-a-lifetime opportunity to be part of the restoration of a WWII aircraft, and most importantly, they get to meet some of the men and their families who helped keep our country free. There will not be many more opportunities to meet these men, and I wanted them to be a part of this project and to develop an understanding of our country's past and why we enjoy the freedoms we have.

Some of my most memorable moments at the museum are not in aircraft restoration, but in the interaction I have had with the men who flew in the Eighth Air Force.

Jeff Hoopes: *I grew up in the 60s as a huge fan of WWII, arguably, the ultimate battle of good (US and Allies) vs. evil (Axis). I was especially enthralled with the aviation action. I recall watching endless episodes of* Rat Patrol, Twelve O'Clock High, Hogan's Heroes, *and later,* Baa Baa Black Sheep *(always loved the curves of the Corsair). I would dream about being a fighter pilot, and that's*

how I would respond to the age-old question of "What do you want to be when you grow up?"

After graduation from high school, I attended college at the University of South Carolina, majoring in engineering. At the suggestion of my dad, I signed up for Navy ROTC. After my first semester, I came to realize that the professionalism and camaraderie of the military really spoke to me. I was fortunate to earn a four-year NROTC scholarship after my first semester and never looked back.

Upon graduation I was commissioned an ensign in the United States Navy and received orders to report to the Naval Flight School at Pensacola, Florida. After going through various selection and request procedures, I was told I could not become a pilot because of my eyesight. After getting over that disappointment I requested and received an appointment as a flight officer in a land-based, maritime, anti-submarine patrol squadron, flying in P-3 Orions.

I very much enjoyed my time in the Navy, but now I'll fast-forward 13 years. Having transferred back to civilian life, attained a masters degree in business administration, and finding myself between jobs, I needed something to keep me occupied during my job hunt and joined the City of Savannah *restoration team in February 2010. I didn't know anything about B-17s, other than being able to recognize the airframe, but the opportunity allowed me to have an aviation experience and to, hopefully, use some of my engineering skills. At first, I enjoyed being a grunt as we were still cleaning the 25+ years of grime from the airplane. As we got her cleaned up, I found that I could offer more than labor work to the project. I'd take the parts manuals home with me and study them, learning what all the parts were and where they belonged. Then I started looking for parts on the Internet and became intimately involved with the supply and logistics side of the project. After several months I was asked if I would lead the Wednesday day crew. I was proud to take the job. Along the way, I enrolled at Savannah Technical College to learn state-of-the-art, three-dimensional CAD technology. This began a relationship with Savannah Tech that turned into a very successful cooperative effort when I brokered a deal between the museum and the school to institute an internship program, which worked for everybody. The interns are drafting students. They use 1940s drawings and 3-D CAD technology to produce software copies of aircraft parts that are no*

273

longer available on the open market. We then use their software to provide local machine shops with the CAD models, and a brand new part is produced exactly to its 1940s specifications.

Working on the City of Savannah *project for the last four years has become not only an honor and a privilege, but has become my therapy. I do it because I love to build and make things. I do it because I want to honor the men who so gallantly flew and fought in these beautiful machines to save the world from evil. I do it because it all means something to me, and I want it to be on display for a very long time so that none of us forget the sacrifices that have been made by so many men and women of our great nation. Oh, one more thing, I am now a faculty member of the Savannah Technical College. As I said, it worked for everybody!*

Arlen Juergens: *As a young boy I enjoyed building model airplanes and was fascinated by the movie newsreels and news articles about our servicemen in action during WWII. I especially was interested in the reporting of our military in the European theater. The bomber and fighting missions over Germany always captured my attention. I was thinking that as I grew older, I would be drafted into the military. I was drafted into the Army during the Korean conflict.*

Later in life I met and befriended John Humting. John was a mechanic for TWA. I was a private pilot, and with that aviation background, we struck a long-lasting friendship. John did not speak much about his military experience until much later in life, when I learned that he had served as a flight engineer and gunner with the 96th Bomb Group in the Eighth Air Force in England during WWII. I started working on the City of Savannah *after it was assembled in the museum. I learned about the restoration while visiting my son in Florida and immediately volunteered. I worked with Jim Grismer on the first crew to start cleaning the aircraft. Even though I live in Illinois, I have accumulated over 100 hours working on the B-17 during my annual trips to Florida. Over the years I have met many dedicated volunteers on the* City of Savannah *project. It has been a pleasure to meet and work with them. Several years ago I was asked to help a lady into the cockpit. Her grandfather had been a B-17 pilot and she wanted to honor him with a visit. When I was helping her out of the airplane, she had a tear in her eye and thanked me for the work we* had performed on the B-17. *There were other times when museum visitors would stop and say, "Thank you for your work on the B-17." Those comments made this volunteer feel very proud. My family was with me at the* City of Savannah *dedication. It made me proud to share the results of six years of work at the museum. That is why I volunteer to work on the B-17.*

Gregory Kindred: *I was drawn to the project by the B-17 itself. I had a great-uncle who was a tail gunner in a B-17G in 1943–1944 with the Mighty Eighth. I was "all in" for any kind of opportunity to see, touch, and restore a B-17! The initial draw to this project was to be able to literally relive days in the lives of those who had gone before us, while at the same time building and preserving a monument to them for future generations to see and touch. I have found this project to be rewarding on many levels. While there is an organizational chart and various titles, this group has PhDs assisting dogface soldiers, retired senior military working a broom, and the project manager bagging the trash—all of us drawing the same imaginary paycheck!*

I joined the Wednesday evening crew, dubbed the "Night Riders," because we make our noise after dark, as in, we have daytime jobs and come to work on the airplane after we finish working for a living. We are all aviation professionals, which epitomizes everything that is right about this project. We are descendants of B-17 flight crews, military minded, aviation oriented, OCD perfectionists! This group couldn't cut a corner if they tried. Every detail is thoroughly researched and manufactured to B-17 specs and even then, often remanufactured to look period/model correct. This methodical attention to detail makes any visible progress painfully slow, but incredibly satisfying. The men and women who originally manufactured, crewed, and maintained these aircraft are all represented by us in our completed work.

I think, now that I have gotten to the point where I need at least two boxes of candles for my birthday cake, that in my youth I should have listened better to my grandparents and the older generations. Working on this project has been a second chance to do just that! Not only the WWII guys, but we meet and listen to a variety of young and old warriors from across all military branches and conflicts and from all walks of life who come to visit the museum. To not capture their spirit and stories would be a tragedy.

Peter Knepton: *I have been around airplanes all my life. My father had an almost 50-year career working for Grumman Aerospace in New York, and then at Gulfstream, here in Savannah. I jumped at the opportunity to also work for Gulfstream and worked there as a mechanical engineer for 33 years. My career made me appreciate the technology that goes into designing and manufacturing any aircraft, be it a 40-million-dollar Gulfstream IV or a World War II B-17G. I got interested in the Eighth Air Force from a good friend, Bill Warner, who was a flight engineer on a B-17 in the 100th Bomb Group during WWII. I joined the Eighth Air Force Historical Society even before the National Museum of the Mighty Eighth Air Force was opened in 1996. I was a volunteer in the early days of the museum, helping run the two movie theaters. So I was honored to return in January 2013, to work with the restoration team. I have been able to use my professional skills in researching old Boeing drawings that we use to reproduce parts, and I have helped out as a photographer, with administrative duties, and I have even helped the restoration crew on the floor several times.*

The best thing about working with this group is not only working with a dedicated team, but meeting and talking to the veterans. Hearing stories that they never told their family because it was too painful to remember, and seeing how emotional the veterans become, knowing our crew appreciates the great sacrifices that they made for all of us, is very rewarding. I think that is why I volunteer here: hoping that the next generations will remember the sacrifices of the WWII Eighth Air Force veterans and knowing that many gave their lives so we can remain free.

Bill Liening: *I started with the* City of Savannah *restoration at the very beginning. I had a personal interest—my dad was a B-17 crewman in WWII—and I had been a career flight crew member in the US Navy.*

My qualifications in aviation started when I entered the Navy to become an aircraft mechanic. My goal was to become a flight crew member. I am very proud of the fact that

I became a (P-3) flight engineer on an aircraft that had four engines with propellers on the front and had a bomb bay in the center of the airplane, just like a B-17. If you look at the profile of a P-3 in flight, I think it resembles a B-17.

Jerry McLaughlin, our project manager, put it very well during an Eighth Air Force Association Reunion when he told the gathering of Mighty Eighth veterans that the volunteers on this aircraft were their children and grandchildren. We were the youngsters sitting up past our bedtime listening to the stories our fathers told with their friends. Many of us entered the military, or an aviation career, because of those stories. We aren't restoring this aircraft to gain a reputation or to make money for the museum. We apply the talents we have to this aircraft in order to say "Thank you!" to the men like my dad who flew on them in WWII.

Bob MacDonald: *I remember as a young boy growing up in Colorado Springs during WWII that entire formations of B-17s would fly over our home. It's a very moving experience, so many years later, to be working to restore one of those airplanes. It wasn't until I was grown up that I learned about the sacrifices that the men in those airplanes made. It's very powerful to be able to honor those men.*

Guy McDonald: *As a United States Air Force veteran, a student of military history, an aviation enthusiast, and a radio geek, what better project could I ever hope to be involved in! My service as an aircrew member took place four decades after WWII, yet I still feel a connection to the men who flew in the Flying Fortresses. It's a privilege to play a small part in restoring the* City of Savannah.

Jack Nilsen: *I must give credit to my wife for pointing me in the direction of the museum. I was employed at Savannah Air Center, responsible for their quality control function and providing liaison with the FAA as the accountable manager. This was a stressful job, and I needed some sort of diversion when I was away from work. Her suggestion to join a flying club or maybe the Civil Air Patrol*

went unheeded. Then she brought up the museum. One day I stopped to have lunch at the museum restaurant to check the place out. I got into a conversation with a volunteer who had been involved with the B-47 and was told they were getting a B-17. Since I had always been interested in WWII aircraft, he suggested I apply as a volunteer for the project. I had only been in a B-17 once before, during a visit to the museum in Chino, California, where the Piccadilly Lilly *was on display. It had suffered the ravages of time since its movie career and was a sad sight, but certainly filled my square of getting to see the inside of one. When I saw the* City of Savannah *for the first time, I was glad to see its condition was better than I had envisioned. Dirty, yes, but structurally sound. I could see the long road ahead to get to the point where the project would start to show some progress, but I had been that route in the restoration of cars. The process of restoration is a long one. The project not only provided the therapy, if you will, that I was looking for, but an opportunity to apply old skills I had used as an airframe and power plant mechanic many years before. I have always found it fulfilling to see something that I have created at the end of the day, and the* City of Savannah *has certainly served that purpose. That's why I'm here.*

Jim Odom: *My dad was in the Mighty Eighth during WWII. He was in the 401st Bomb Group in Deenethorpe, England. He died when I was 21. I didn't get a chance to ask him all the questions I have now. He was in the ordinance group, a master sergeant loading bombs and bullets on B-17s. My mother once told me that he had mental struggles when he came back. I think it may have been watching all of those planes leave after they loaded them, and not all of them came home. Maybe it was the ones that did come back, but were all shot up with injured or dead crewmen inside that had an effect on him? The ground crews felt somewhat safer, but they had to deal with their own problems. He was a great father and taught me a lot. Now all I have are his papers and other mementos from the Mighty Eighth and the flag that was draped over his coffin. I am named after him.*

When the Mighty Eighth Museum was established, my wife and I went to see it and thoroughly enjoyed our visit. It was such a thrill to see the diorama of dad's airfield at Deenethorpe under glass in the Combat Gallery! I was hooked on the museum right there. When I heard that the B-17 restoration team was being formed and needed people with aviation skills, I figured I would volunteer to help out. It has been fun. I really enjoy working with these guys who are passionate about the airplane and wanting to do it right. The work has given me a great sense of pride as we have been able to work through some tough challenges. Some of these challenges have been stressful as we work so hard to get things just right. I think we worry sometimes more than we should. All that I do at the museum is in memory of my father, and I am so very thankful that they allow me to be on the restoration team.

David Pinegar: Do you know how hard it is to save your paper route money when you're 14 years old to take flying lessons, or when mom finds your log-book and wants to beat the snot out of you for doing such a dangerous thing like taking flying lessons? This love of aviation has carried through some 40 years: hundreds of model airplanes, thousands of flight hours logged. Today I work in the aviation industry in Savannah and enjoy every minute of it. Go figure!

When I found out a Boeing B-17 was coming to our area, there was no doubt in my mind that I would be involved. The company that I work for, LMI Aerospace, has a strong community relations policy, so I also planned to get them involved. When the B-17 arrived in January of 2009, LMI had just started new programs with the Boeing 767 and 787. What better way to show our involvement with the community than to help with the restoration of the City of Savannah, a Boeing product.

We started our involvement with the project by recovering all the control surfaces with new fabric that is sewn into place. Over a period of 18 months I was able to teach about 30 LMI employees the art of rib stitching, which I had learned from building flying model airplanes. LMI donated over 33 square yards of material to do the job, enough to cover an entire Piper Cub.

I had never been interested in WWII aircraft, or their stories, until I got involved with the City of Savannah. Hearing the hundreds of stories from people that visit the Mighty Eighth Museum to see the

B-17: *pilots, radio operators, gunners, and mechanics—they are all represented. It was easy to get hooked!*

Rocky Rodriguez: *I have always been a serious fan of WWII aircraft. After a 37-year career in the United States Air Force, the news of a B-17 restoration in Savannah brought me to the Mighty Eighth as a very early applicant to participate in the project. An avid fan of World War II movies and documentaries, I was always impressed at what the airmen had to do to complete their missions. I was so impressed with Gregory Peck as the commander of the fictional 918th Bomb Group in* Twelve O'Clock High *that I joined the USAF. The skills I brought from my Air Force career as an aircraft electrician allowed me to really make a contribution to the* City of Savannah *project. This was a great experience.*

Darrell Schwartz: *Since I was a child I have loved anything to do with aviation. At a young age my uncle, who flew a Piper Cub, would land in our clover field to pick me up for a ride. I am also fascinated with World War II history. I have so much respect for all of those who fought and served and feel an obligation to keep this history alive to pass on to future generations. I love listening to the veterans' stories at the museum, such as the pilot whose wife said that he had bombed her home in Germany. While I was in the mountains of Peru, I met a lady from Atlanta who heard that I was a volunteer at the Mighty Eighth. She was so grateful for what we are doing that she sent me her husband's book,* Luck of the Draw, *by Frank D. Murphy, with a personal note of appreciation. Mrs. Murphy told me that her husband was influential in obtaining this plane for the Mighty Eighth. It is tremendously rewarding working with such a great group of volunteers.*

Bill Schwickrath: *I am a member of the baby boomer generation born right after the war. I grew up in the South and was fascinated with the history of both world wars. As a young boy in the 1950s, I would listen to veterans tell stories of serving in the wars. It instilled a healthy respect in me for the sacrifices these men made on our behalf.*

I have always been mechanically inclined. I rebuilt old cars such as Model Ts and Model As and built a lot of model airplanes. When Mort Glick told me that he was volunteering at the Mighty Eighth to restore the B-17, I got interested. I volunteered for the Saturday work crew in early 2013 and the experience has been wonderful. Working on a 70-year-old airplane that was beloved by all that flew it is a great experience that makes you proud of the work that is being done by all the volunteers. But the most important aspect of volunteering on the B-17 restoration effort is that I get to listen, once again, to veterans, now in their 90s, tell stories of serving in the war. Work comes to a standstill when a veteran visits the museum and starts talking about flying on B-17s. The sacrifices these heroes of America made on our behalf were enormous and to think they will soon be gone is a loss for us all. We have limited memories when it comes to past wars. Today, little is mentioned about the hardships and sacrifices our veterans made in WWI, because those veterans are no longer with us. I do not want that to happen to the heroes of our generation. That is why I am here. I want to contribute to the preservation of our history so future generations understand the sacrifices that our heroes, the members of the Greatest Generation, made on behalf of future generations of Americans.

Milt Stombler: As I was only four years old at the end of WWII, I don't remember anything more than some of the music and ration stamps. The beginning of my love affair with B-17s began many years later when I saw photos of B-17s that made it home despite incredible combat damage.

My serious interest in aviation in general began almost 50 years ago when I got my pilot's license. I was a co-owner of a Mooney (the trainer of the Israeli Air Force at the time). This was my first opportunity to get "down and dirty" maintaining an airplane. Shortly after I retired to South Carolina, I heard an announcement that the National Museum of the Mighty Eighth Air Force needed volunteers to restore a B-17. I joined the renovation team and it has become an important part of my life.

An experimental physicist by training (AKA "lab rat"), I expected to bring some skills to the project. Instead, I found myself to be the least talented among a group of retired military aircraft mechanics, *airplane builders, woodworkers and just "good old boys" who can fix anything. Working with this diverse team has been a wonderful learning experience and a true joy.*

In addition, I have met a number of museum visitors who were WWII B-17 crew members. Hearing their stories filled my heart with awe. My feelings for B-17s are now dwarfed by my admiration of the crew members that flew them in combat. When I am inside the City of Savannah, *I think of the hardships and terror that those crews endured. I am now working for those veterans, and hope more of them can get to see the love and sweat our team has lavished on "THEIR" airplane.*

Scott Stovall: *I joined the United States Air Force in 1964 to become a pilot. After I did my time, I got out and was a pilot for Delta Airlines for almost 33 years. I moved to Savannah in 1997 and started volunteering at the National Museum of the Mighty Eighth Air Force as a tour guide.*

I had flown with some pilots who were WWII Eighth Air Force veterans, but I knew very little about their story. After all these years I have come to have a great respect for what they did and how they persevered. It has been a great privilege to be associated with the people restoring the B-17. What a great tribute to the ordinary men who did extraordinary things with what they had in order to win WWII.

Dave Talleur : *In 1944 I was a five-year-old kid. I grew up in a small country village north of New York City, and spent the days lying on my back in the grass with my friends watching the overflight of all sorts of aircraft. Every day and every sighting was an adventure. Those planes were on their way to bases in England, or patrolling the U.S. coastline in search of enemy ships. The sound of any airplane would set all hearts racing, and all eyes would be turned to the sky. The challenge was to be able to be first to spot and identify the plane. During that period toward the end of WWII, many small children were able to identify the B-17, B-24, P-47, P-51, P-38 airplanes, and many others, and it was a matter of pride to always get them right.*

The Flyboys, in our young minds, were not only heroes, but to us even gods. We had no idea of the dangers they were flying toward, and would be much older before we'd be able to understand and appreciate their deeds. Although certainly not gods, all were heroes. Too many of those young men would not come home again.

My love of the planes of that era, appreciation of the sacrifices by the men that faced the horrors of war, and a commitment for love of country and freedom, only grew in me as the years went by. After a hitch in the USAF and a long career in commercial aviation, I found a way to continue that dedication and interest through the restoration of the City of Savannah. *It has been a great privilege and honor to be involved in this work, and to help provide a monument that honors those men and educates the next generation in such an important piece of our history. My hours spent with the* City of Savannah *allowed me to work with some of the most dedicated and talented people I have ever known. I also had the privilege of meeting a number of veterans, especially WWII survivors and their families, and listening, humbly, to their stories and remembrances.*

Ted Voorhees: *Being a Johnny-come-lately to the restoration crew (September 2014), I regret missing out on the major part of the restoration prior to 2014. With two daughters living in the Georgia and South Carolina areas, every trip down for a visit provided me the opportunity to visit the museum, to enjoy the exhibits and stand in awe at the progress being made on the B-17. In July 2014, we moved to Bluffton, South Carolina, and after a month of unpacking, I managed to find time to stop at the museum and offer my services. Finally, I was going to be a part of a program that would allow me to touch a WWII plane that previously, I could only dream about.*

My interest in airplanes started in the late thirties. My dad would take Mom and me for a Sunday ride that invariably ended at a grass strip airfield. To say I became hooked on flying and airplanes at the various airfields would be an understatement. I saw all the flying movies that came to town, including the movie Test Pilot, *about the YB-17 with Clark Gable. I made model airplanes, listened to* Hop Harrigan *and* Captain Midnight, *etc. On December 7, 1941, Dad and I were listening to the radio when the program was interrupted to announce that the Japanese had bombed Pearl Harbor. At*

10 years old, I didn't understand what was about to happen to life as I knew it—gas rationing, ration stamps, and war bonds. After the war I joined the Air Scouts, where I had the opportunity to fly in a Link Trainer (wow). Also, the itch to learn to fly grew even stronger. Unfortunately, that itch would not be satisfied until 20 years later (raising a family). I also joined the Civil Air Patrol where I had my first flight in a big plane, a C-47 at CAP Summer Camp at Mitchell Field on Long Island. Fast-forward to 1965, when I began taking flying lessons. Now I knew what it felt like to be at the controls of a plane. Upon getting my license in 1970, I bought an Ercoupe. Having worked on car engines, I decided to rebuild the engine with the help of a friend and flew that airplane for many happy hours. With this background, I felt I could be of some help in the restoration project. Also, having served nine years in the National Guard, I felt I should pay tribute to my brave young brothers who fought and died for our freedom.

Scott Whitcher: *My first interest in aircraft was a passion for building model airplanes in my youth. I also studied drawings of enemy planes during the Korean War in the highly unlikely chance that I would make a sighting of one of them in North Carolina. After I graduated from high school I moved to Maryland, where I began to attend air shows within driving distance of my home. This resulted in a large collection of photographs of WWII aircraft that were displayed at those shows.*

My involvement with the City of Savannah began soon after its arrival at the museum. I had seen news reports of the plane's anticipated arrival and made inquiries as to how to volunteer to help in the restoration. While I had little or no expertise in aircraft restoration, I was ready to help where needed. It was a big surprise to many of us how much wood was used inside the aluminum skin of a B-17. I was glad that my carpentry skills were much in demand. My involvement has run from the initial work of taking the airplane apart, interior and exterior cleaning, to the disassembly and cataloging of the cockpit, and finally to becoming a member of the woodworking team. One of my main contributions has been the manufacture of the wooden ammo boxes required for each .50 cal. gun position. I have also been involved with several administrative tasks related to the restoration.

I feel that working on the City of Savannah *is a mission of love, to honor all those who maintained and flew in these planes during WWII, those who returned from their missions, and those who did not. Whenever I am working on the airplane and I notice a WWII veteran is visiting, it is a very emotional moment for both of us. More than once a veteran has come with his family and this was the first time he has talked about what he did during the war. I feel I am very fortunate to be able to be involved with this restoration project.*

Ray Willingham: *As a boy I loved all things mechanical: motorcycles, cars, and airplanes in that order. As a teenager in the late 60s with few options to the draft looming over my head, I thought how I could become a great pilot or crew member in the Air Force, or an ideal tunnel rat in the infantry. However, I had several problems; I don't particularly like heights or confined spaces! Having grown up feeling comfortable around open water, I picked an alternative route. I enlisted in the Navy while I still had some say about the matter. They trained me to be an aviation electrician. I worked on both small and large aircraft on land and at sea. During those years I gained a healthy respect for aircraft design and the crews that flew those aircraft. The latter was acquired from actual experience as I occasionally flew as a crew member. I now understand the courage and commitment required to perform the duties of the men who flew the B-17s.*

Fast-forward several years to when I was working as a professional geologist. I found myself being lowered down a 30-inch-diameter, 50-foot-deep hole in the ground, wondering where I went wrong (see above). Sometime later I was mapping at high elevation on some mountain in a country I didn't want to be in, again wondering where I went wrong (see above).

Those days are behind me now. Having retired several years ago, I began a small canvas design and repair business, basically to support my many varied hobbies, which include restoration of motorcycles, cars, and boats, generally in that order. When I was asked by a City of Savannah *team member to use my sewing skills to help out with canvas restoration on an actual WWII B-17, I jumped at the opportunity. Admittedly, with the exception of seats, I had no idea that any canvas parts or pieces were used inside the airplane. It made sense to* use canvas as it is lighter in weight and less costly than aluminum. So now I can add aircraft restoration to my résumé!

Working on the City of Savannah *is a mission to honor all those who flew in those planes during WWII, those who returned from their missions, and those who did not return.*

I feel I am very fortunate to be able to be involved with this project. Moreover, I value my friendship with my fellow volunteers who are a group of dedicated, committed people who share a desire to honor those who came before us.

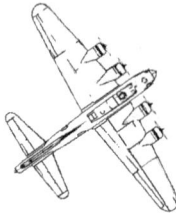

REFLECTIONS

"Gratitude unlocks the fullness of life."

Melody Beattie

As we brought this book project to its conclusion there were many concerns going through my mind regarding logistics, finance, and technical matters. So many issues that for a brief time I had forgotten about the cultural center of the organization that we had created with the *City of Savannah* project: IT'S ABOUT THE PEOPLE. I had to take a step back and say, "OK, I can deal with the all the administrative hurdles—what about the people?"

The first individuals that I had to consider in my thoughts were those for whom all this work was being done—the Eighth Air Force Veterans of WWII. The National Museum of the Mighty Eighth Air Force has three of those veterans currently serving on the museum's board of trustees. All three men saw combat over Western Europe during 1944–1945; Bud Porter as a gunner, Hap Chandler as a navigator, and Paul Grassey as a pilot. During the course of the restoration I have gotten to know each of the men as friends. Reminded of the many conversations I have shared with the three veterans, I asked each one to share their thoughts regarding the arrival of our B-17 at the museum in January of 2009, and what this restoration project has meant to them. Here is what they said:

Hap Chandler: The first time I saw the B-17 that we now call the City of Savannah *in the Combat Gallery of the Museum my mind jumped back almost 64 years, to December 11, 1944. On that day my unit, the 491st Bomb Group, was leading the entire Eighth Air Force in a bombing raid to Hanover, Germany. Our crew was designated the Deputy Lead for the high squadron of our group. We were at the very front of the entire 8th Air Force bomber stream.*

I was flying as one of two navigators in our crew. I sat in the nose turret as the "pilotage" navigator: my job was to compare the ground before the aircraft with maps and pictures of the course we were flying. We were on a perfect course and flew into the target exactly as planned. After dropping our bombs, we turned and joined

Hap Chandler, 1944. (Hap Chandler)   *Hap Chandler, 2015.* (Author photo)

up with the other lead groups at the designated rally point, on a 180-degree reverse course of the bomber stream that was following us. There were over 1200 four-engine bombers, B-17s and B-24s, in the formation, as well as an almost equal number of P-51 fighters. We flew for almost 45 minutes until we came to the end of those continuing formations in the bomber stream. Very few people in the history of the world have had such an experience.

As I stood next to the B-17 in the Combat Gallery at the Mighty Eighth, I thought of how I had peered from the nose turret of my B-24 and watched that awesome American military might flying across the German border so many years ago, and I thought how appropriate it was that this B-17 was now proudly exhibited in the National Museum of the Mighty Eighth Air Force. I silently wished the people who would restore the airplane the very best of luck in their effort. The City of Savannah, *I knew, would become a symbol of our country's gratitude to all of the young men who were in those airplanes that I watched in the bomber stream on December 11, 1944. Those who came home, and those who did not.*

Paul Grassey: (Pilot, 446th Bomb Group) *When I think about the* City of Savannah, *our B-17 at the Mighty Eighth, the first thought that comes to mind for me is to thank Walt Brown, our CEO when the B-17 arrived. He loved the Eighth Air Force and he wanted a B-17 at the museum very badly. I'm glad he lived to see that airplane arrive.*

Paul Grassey, 1944. (Paul Grassey)   Paul Grassey, 2009. (CoS Archives)

The first time I saw a Flying Fortress was in 1937 at the Cleveland Air Races. The amazing new Boeing bomber did a flyover at Cleveland Airport where the Thompson Trophy races were being held. It was quite a sight, coming in low over the runway with the unusual "blister" waist gun positions on both sides of the fuselage. I had never seen an airplane that large before. To me it truly was a "Flying Fortress." (Incidentally, I also watched Jimmy Doolittle, who would be my commanding officer of the Eighth Air Force, win the Thompson Trophy at the same event.)

I joined the Army Air Forces in 1943 when I graduated from high school. I wanted to be a bomber pilot, thinking about flying one of those B-17s. I did get to be a bomber pilot, but was assigned to fly B-24s. When I got out of training I was assigned to a crew and we picked up a brand new M model B-24 at Mitchell Field, Long Island. We flew that airplane, the Lady Luck, *over the Atlantic to England, then on 13 combat missions over Europe. The war ended in May of 1945 and we flew her home. The last time I saw* Lady Luck *was on the tarmac at Bradley Field in Connecticut. I can't complain: that B-24 took great care of us and brought my entire crew home in one piece.*

After I retired, my wife, Nancy, and I moved to Savannah and I began volunteering at the National Museum of the Mighty Eighth Air Force. As an alumnus of the wartime Mighty Eighth, I was much appreciated by both the staff and visitors. I was asked to serve on the board of trustees in 2008. I was the rookie on the board when it was announced that the museum would be obtaining a B-17 from the Smithsonian Institution in Washington. Apparently, there had been years of wrangling to obtain the airplane and the senior board members were very excited that the bomber was on its way to Pooler.

Shortly after the B-17's arrival, as the resident WWII bomber pilot, I was asked by a local TV reporter by the name of Mike Manhatton to do an interview in the cockpit of the B-17. Of course I said I would be proud to do the interview; then I discovered that the 70-year time span since I had last climbed into the cockpit of a bomber built in the 1940s had created quite a physical challenge. The restoration guys, who are all my friends, saw the problem and set up a ladder and several extra sets of hands to get me from the floor of the gallery into the left side pilot's seat. As Mike directed the placing of the cameras and the lighting I had to smile—my B-24 buddies from the war would yell very bad words at me if they saw me in a B-17. The feeling between the B-17 and the B-24 boys was like the Red Sox and the Yankees—there was no fixing it. Mike finally got the lights and cameras where he wanted them and interviewed me for what seemed like hours. I loved it. I was talking for all the young guys like me who had climbed into those B-17s and B-24s so many years ago. I was very proud to be representing all the air and ground crews who had served in the Eighth Air Force during WWII. We were given the best tools possible to do the job and we got it done.

Bud Porter: (Ball turret gunner, 95th Bomb Group) *I have been involved with the National Museum of the Mighty Eighth Air Force since before the building was put up, so I have memories of some great moments in the museum's history. My favorite memories are of the arrival of the B-17, followed by the trade that brought us a partial ball turret that we used as a display for several years, and finally, the purchase of the full ball turret that was made operational by the volunteers.*

We waited years to get a B-17 into the Combat Gallery. The day it arrived I made sure I was there to witness the event. That airplane was brought to the Mighty Eighth to honor all of the kids like me who flew over Europe 70 years ago and never came home. I think about them every day, every day! As a survivor I honor them by remembering who they were, and what they did, because I know, I was there.

Left: *Bud Porter in England, 1944. His "office" is behind him.* (Bud Porter)
Right: *Bud Porter, 2011.* (CoS Archives)

When I saw the silver airplane coming down the road to the museum, I was so proud to be a member of the organization that was going to restore her. Today I have a big space in my heart for that wonderful B-17 that has been named the City of Savannah. *My hat goes off to the volunteers who worked on the airplane. Many of them have become my friends over the years. It is astounding how the airplane looks today compared to how it looked when they rolled it in the door in 2009. The restoration job is more than I imagined that they could accomplish. The volunteers often ask me questions about what it was like to fly in a B-17 during the war, and particularly in the ball turret. I enjoy answering their questions about my time in the Eighth Air Force and particularly in that turret that they so diligently worked to restore. When the "half" ball turret, which was only a partial display version of a real turret, arrived at the museum I was thrilled that I could show visitors where my station was when flying missions. When the full ball turret was purchased for the museum by a generous donor, I met the two volunteers who picked it up in California and drove it all the way across country as they arrived at the museum. I have to admit I was disappointed when I first saw the full turret. It had the right shape, but inside there was not a single thing that looked familiar to me. It was just junk. Several months later, my disappointment totally disappeared when I looked at the final restoration just before it was going to be installed in the airplane. The interior of the turret looked exactly as I remembered it. Our restoration team is made up of some very talented people! The idea that the turret will actually operate for the public to see my home in the sky on my combat missions means a great deal to me. Whenever I walk into the Combat Gallery and look at the* City of Savannah, *my time in England with the Eighth Air Force comes back like it was only yesterday. It is hard to express my feelings for that airplane—I guess you could say that I feel like I am visiting an old friend. It's very emotional for me.*

In the previous chapter, entitled "Why I am Here," many of the volunteers stated why they had joined our project to restore the *City of Savannah*. During the period between January of 2009 and January of 2015 more than 150 individuals were officially on the books as volunteers on the *City of Savannah* project. Some put in thousands of hours. I had the honor of being the project manager of the restoration project during those six years. There is something to be said about leading a group where you have minimal, if any, technical knowledge of the operation, but are well aware of the mission requirements. I came to the project with that kind of management experience, and I believe it worked for us.

The basic tenants for success, as per Bob Mikesh, were in place: The airplane was inside a controlled environment, the museum provided us with the ability to raise money, we had a stable and structured management team, and the local community was wealthy with aviation expertise. Most important of all: the restoration attracted talented and devoted people with wide areas of expertise. These volunteers were both interested in aviation and had a strong understanding of the museum's mission to honor the WWII veterans of the Eighth Air Force. I would have to agonize over who, among the eligible candidates, needed to be included on a list of those who contributed most significantly to the project's success. I will not even attempt to put such a list together. What I must do is mention the several volunteers to whom I have a personal debt because they provided the very important advice and encouragement that I needed to manage the project for six years: Deputy Project Manager Dave Talleur, a USAF veteran who moved on to a full career as a pilot and corporate aviation manager; Jim Grismer, my friend of 45 years, confidante, logistician extraordinaire, and passionate patriot; Dr. Harry Friedman, as good a mentor as you could ask for; and Tommy Garcia, a man noted for his technical knowledge who should also be recognized for his skills in dealing with personalities. These are the people who got me through the project.

I asked each of these special people to make some final comments:

Dave Talleur: *When I joined the* City of Savannah *B-17 restoration crew in 2009 I had no idea how very attached I would become to the entire project. It became more than just participating in the preservation of a piece of history. Working with the very unique group of talented, dedicated professionals was a special experience. Added to the comradeship of the volunteers was the most unique opportunity of meeting and talking with visitors to our museum. Amongst the visitors, the most special experience was meeting the men who had served with the Mighty Eighth during WWII. I feel very strongly that we need to strive and complete all of the details of the final restoration and ensure that our B-17 attains "mission ready" status. I am confident that she will be returned to that state with her bombs loaded, her turrets operational, and the proper technology mounted within her airframe to provide a view of her fantastic interior restoration to the public. All of us who worked on this project are sure that the* City of Savannah *will accomplish her assigned mission at the Mighty Eighth, just as the men who flew the B-17s over the skies of Europe accomplished their mission 70 years ago.*

Jim Grismer: *I started with the project on day one. Shortly after the dedication of the* City of Savannah, *I came across a remarkable photo taken of the airplane by a professional photographer using carefully prepared lighting. The impact of the photo was startling to me. The airplane looked truly glorious. I had an immediate rush of pride that overwhelmed me. By God, I had participated in that lady's reincarnation! I was also holding less positive emotions. My take on the twilight of our restoration of the* City of Savannah *can be summed up as follows: in the final stages of the restoration of our beloved B-17, the tasks required for completion have been reduced to those that can only be implemented by our most-skilled volunteers. This inevitable fact in any technical project resulted in several long-time volunteers wandering away from us because there really is no more work for them. Morale for those remaining began to dwindle. We were clearly watching the "light at the end of the tunnel" come towards us. I have always felt an incredible bond with the men and women who have worked with us over the years. While several colleagues had sons working on* the project, I am the only volunteer with a daughter (Jane) involved. I have given considerable thought to how we can keep this unique and devoted team together as the City of Savannah *project is completed. The answer is obvious: SOMEBODY find us another airplane!*

Tommy Garcia: *When I first started with warbirds, my greatest thrill was to see that airplane fly. As time went on I began to feel that restoring a static display to exact status could be even more rewarding because the labor and effort would go into detail rather than flight capability. I had hoped to find a B-17 static display restoration project that was located in a controlled interior environment. The National Museum of the Mighty Eighth Air Force provided such an opportunity to me. That the Mighty Eighth restoration team welcomed me into their ranks is an honor. I am extremely grateful to have been a part of this project.*

The City of Savannah *is the first static B-17 display in the United States to meet the criteria for my dream restoration. The detail of the work on the airplane, from nose to tail, and the plans for demonstrating the working parts and interior of the airplane to the public are first rate and will, in fact, qualify the* City of Savannah *B-17 exhibit—in my opinion —as the most outstanding B-17 static display in the world!*

Harry Friedman: *As a visitor to the National Museum of the Mighty Eighth Air Force Museum stands and looks upon the* City of Savannah, *the importance of this B-17's presence as a memorial to the air and ground crews who served in the Eighth during WWII is blatantly apparent. The tears of the veterans who see this wonderful restoration are a testament to the exhibit's importance. What is less evident is the heart and dedication of the volunteers and staff of the museum who brought the airplane to where it is today. So, to me, this airplane represents several groups: those who fought and died in the sky over Europe; those who worked in extremely difficult conditions on the ground to keep the airplanes flying; and 70 years later, with equal resolve, their children, who worked to assure that the memory of the sacrifices made by their fathers would be remembered. My involvement with this restoration will always be a great source of pride to me, and a symbol of something that I did that really counted.*

SOME FINAL COMMENTS
FROM THE AUTHOR

I feel compelled to tell a story to begin my closing comments. It is a story that means a great deal to me, particularly because of the support it receives from aviation professionals who are part of our restoration.

January 17, 2015, was a very busy day for our restoration team. As previously detailed in Chapter 6, we spent that day mounting our turrets for the upcoming dedication. By mid-afternoon the *City of Savannah's* profile fully replicated the original B-17G silhouette as it appeared in the picture that was taken with a chaplain blessing the airplane and its crew on December 4, 1944. I found it interesting to watch the individual volunteers that afternoon, as it seemed that everyone was walking a full circle around the airplane in order to observe its profile and what had been accomplished during this very full day. Each visitor had two or three personal guides as they asked questions about the B-17, and the volunteers were more than happy to provide the answers. I stood alone in front of the nose of the *City of Savannah* and looked down the length of the airplane. I thought about the events of the past six years, and the words that Tommy Garcia had shared with me one night in the shop came back to me. "Jerry," Tommy said, "You won't believe this until it happens, but, some day this airplane will talk to you, and when that happens, it will become part of your soul." He was right. I didn't believe him—at that time. But then, as I stood alone and looked at the B-17, I felt that it *was* talking to me—I was the only person in the building at that moment who had been there when she was brought through the Gallery door, and now, as all her turrets were mounted, and her skin gleamed as it had on the day she left the factory, I felt that she was saying, *"Thank you for giving me life once again! I will make you proud!"* I know that most who read this will not believe what I experienced, but I know, and Tommy Garcia knows—the airplane spoke to me! It was an honor I will never forget, and Tommy was also right that the *City of Savannah* is now part of my soul.

I have been associated with many fine organizations, public, private, and volunteer, during my life. The *City of Savannah* project is quite unique from other organizations in that none of us went looking for this particular project, the project found us. Many start-up projects falter for lack of direction. Not so the *City of Savannah*—we have always had a very specific mission, defined within a larger mission: to restore the airplane as part of the museum's ultimate mission of honoring the veterans of the Eighth Air Force. The mission of our restoration team has never, ever, been disputed as to its importance or direction.

When you read or listen to the words of our volunteers you repeatedly hear the same messages: *We are honoring the veterans of the Eighth Air Force. I am a veteran. My career was in aviation. I have been interested in aviation since childhood. I am honoring a family member who served in WWII.* All of the volunteers knew why they were participating. Having been in the center of literally all of the events for the six years covered in our story, I heard the comments and the reasons our volunteers stated for being part of the project, but even more I watched a culture evolve within the group, a culture centered on creativity, perseverance, diligence, cooperation, and pride. Most of all, the group developed a distinct and unbreakable bond. We had a common cause that enveloped all of the reasons we were engaged in the project. *We had a mission!* Over and over I would listen to those with a technical knowledge that I could not begin to comprehend, discuss seemingly insurmountable challenges, but I knew they would always—always—come up with a solution, and they always did! "We can't do it" are words that were never uttered by anyone in this group. Our turrets were built nearly from scratch—and in the case of the tail turret, *totally* from scratch, with the exception of one brace, taken from the "Alaska turret" to ensure that we can say that our turret has a true history. Other restorations tell visitors that they do not demonstrate their turrets or other working parts because they might eventually malfunction. We confidently say, "We built 'em, if they break, we'll fix 'em." Tommy Garcia said it best when he described our restoration as being an "operational" static display, the only such B-17 exhibit in the world! The pride that you see in the faces of those volunteers who put this working display together to honor the veterans of the

Eighth Air Force is truly something special. *We believe that the* City of Savannah *is arguably the finest B-17 static display in the world.*

As stated above, our project was a mission within a mission. The entire reason that the National Museum of the Mighty Eighth Air Force exists is to honor the sacrifice and bravery of the individual members of that organization. Our job was to provide a symbol of their efforts. I think we did our job. We have honored the fathers and the grandfathers of our generation, the men who flew and supported those Eighth Air Force airplanes in WWII, and I'm proud to have been a part of that effort.

On behalf of all of those who took part in our restoration,

May God bless the **City** *of* **Savannah**
and may she shine brightly for generations to come
in her final home at the National Museum
of the Mighty Eighth Air Force.

JM

ABOUT THE AUTHOR

Jerry McLaughlin brought together his broad experiences as a history teacher, project manager and author to write **B-17 Flying Fortress Restoration.**

A native of the Borough of Queens in New York City, Jerry was raised in Lynbrook, New York and graduated from Long Island University with a degree in United States History and Education in 1973. He served in the United States Army from 1969-1971. After a thirty-year career with the Federal government, he retired from the Central Intelligence Agency in 2003 as a member of the Agency's Senior Intelligence Service.

Jerry began his volunteer service with the National Museum of the Mighty Eighth Air Force as an archivist in 2005, and along with two colleagues received the Shuler Award for Museum Service in 2007 for their efforts in reorganizing the museum's archives. He was selected as the Project Manager for the *City of Savannah* restoration at the project's inception in January 2009, and held that position until the dedication of the airplane in January of 2015.

Jerry's first book, **D-Day+60 Years**, was published in 2004. He and his wife, Denise, reside on Skidaway Island outside of Savannah, Georgia, with a recently rescued Wheaten Terrier who now goes by the name of Annie.

Connect with Jerry at: smallhistory@aol.com or through www.B17restoration.com

CPSIA information can be obtained
at www.ICGtesting.com
Printed in the USA
LVHW022228240521
688350LV00020B/1895

9 781940 013251